NEWS

What are the conflicting interests at work behind choosing what gets covered in the news, and how? Addressing these issues with examples across a range of media including print, radio, television and the internet, Jackie Harrison explains the different theoretical approaches that have been used to study news, as well as providing an accessible introduction to how news is produced and regulated, what counts as news and how it is selected and presented. Written in a clear and lively style, *News* is the ideal introductory book for students of media, communication and journalism. Topics covered include:

- introduction to the concept of news
- growth and development of news
- technology, concentration and competition
- balancing freedom and responsibility
- regulatory control of the news
- making the news.

Jackie Harrison is Professor of Public Communication in the Department of Journalism Studies at the University of Sheffield. She has written widely on television violence, European audio-visual policy, the culture of news production and the changing digital television environment.

ROUTLEDGE INTRODUCTIONS TO MEDIA AND COMMUNICATIONS

Edited by Paul Cobley *London Metropolitan University*

This new series provides concise introductions to key areas in contemporary communications. Each book in the series addresses a genre or a form of communication, analysing the nature of the genre or the form as well as reviewing its production and consumption, outlining the main theories and approaches that have been used to study it, and discussing contemporary textual examples of the form. The series offers both an outline of how each genre or form has developed historically, and how it is changing and adapting to the contemporary media landscape, exploring issues such as convergence and globalization.

Videogames
James Newman

Brands
Marcel Danesi

Advertising
Ian MacRury

Magazines
Anna Gough-Yates

Youth Media
Bill Osgerby

News
Jackie Harrison

Cyberspace
Mike Ledgerwood

NEWS

Jackie Harrison

Routledge
Taylor & Francis Group

LONDON AND NEW YORK

First published 2006 by Routledge
2 Park Square, Milton Park, Abingdon, Oxon OX14 4RN

Simultaneously published in the USA and Canada
by Taylor & Francis Inc.
270 Madison Ave, New York, NY 10016

Routledge is an imprint of the Taylor & Francis Group

© 2006 Jackie Harrison

Typeset in Perpetua and Univers by
Florence Production Ltd, Stoodleigh, Devon
Printed and bound in Great Britain by
TJ International Ltd, Padstow, Cornwall

British Library Cataloguing in Publication Data
A catalogue record for this book is available from the
British Library

Library of Congress Cataloging in Publication Data
Harrison, Jackie, 1961–
    News / by Jackie Harrison.
        p. cm. – (Routledge introductions to media and
        communications)
    Includes bibliographical references and index.
    1. Journalism. 2. Broadcast journalism. I. Title.
        II. Series.
    PN4731.H335 2005
    070.4–dc22   2005020196

ISBN 0–415–31949–8 (hbk)
ISBN 0–415–31950–1 (pbk)

In loving memory of my cousin
Frances Heaton

CONTENTS

SERIES EDITOR'S PREFACE

There can be no doubt that communications pervade contemporary social life. The audio-visual media, print and other communication technologies play major parts in modern human existence, mediating diverse interactions between people. Moreover, they are numerous, heterogeneous and multi-faceted.

Equally, there can be no doubt that communications are dynamic and ever-changing, constantly reacting to economic and popular forces. Communicative genres and modes that we take for granted because they are seemingly omnipresent – news, advertising, film, radio, television, fashion, the book – have undergone alarming sea changes in recent years. They have also been supplemented and reinvigorated by new media, new textualities, new relations of production and new audiences.

The *study* of communications, then, cannot afford to stand still. Although communication study as a discipline is relatively recent in its origin, it has continued to develop in recognizable ways, embracing new perspectives, transforming old ones and responding to – and sometimes influencing – changes in the media landscape.

This series of books is designed to present developments in contemporary media. It focuses on the analysis of textualities, offering an up-to-date assessment of current communications practice. The emphasis of the books is on the *kind* of communications which constitute the modern media and the theoretical tools which are needed to understand them. Such tools may include semiotics (including social semiotics and semiology), discourse theory, poststructuralism, postcolonialism, queer theory, gender analysis, political economy, liberal pluralism, positivism (including quantitative approaches), qualitative methodologies (including the 'new ethnography'), reception theory and ideological analysis. The breadth of current communications media, then, is reflected in the array of methodological resources needed to investigate them.

Yet the task of analysis is not carried out as an hermetic experiment. Each volume in the series places its topic within a contextual matrix of production and consumption. Each allows readers to garner an understanding of what that communication is like without tempting them to forget who produced it, for what purpose, and with what result. The books seek to present research on the mechanisms of textuality but also attempt to reveal the precise situation in which such mechanisms exist. Readers coming to these books will therefore gain a valuable insight into the present standing of specific communications media. Just as importantly, though, they will become acquainted with analytic methods which address, explore and interrogate the very bases of that standing.

ACKNOWLEDGEMENTS

To my colleagues: Jonathan Foster, John Richardson, Lorna Woods; and Sadie Clifford – thank you for your advice and time. To my editor Paul Cobley, it was more than time and advice I received. I am deeply grateful for your constant encouragement, and wise (and pointed) comments on the various chapters you had to deal with. Thank you. To particularly helpful others: Richard Deverell; Martin Hamer; Gavin Hewitt; Karen Sanders; John Steele; Rodrigo Uribe; Bridgette Wessels and Stephen Whittle, my gratitude.

My love as always to my parents, Joan and Ron Mason, who continue to contribute that intangible and unnameable element which allows me to carry on when I feel like doing something else. Finally to Neil, where nothing needs to be said.

INTRODUCTION

News is more easily pursued than defined, a characteristic it shares with
such other enthralling abstractions as love and truth.

(Roshco [1975] 1999: 32)

THE CONCEPT OF NEWS: ASSUMPTIONS AND ANALYSIS

This book is an attempt to write the 'story' of news: what I believe to
be its constituent features, its various manifestations and, of course, its
significance. If I were writing the philosophy of news, the points I make
in this Introduction, which is the matrix through which I conduct my
interrogation of news, would be the book itself. However, given that I
begin with what I believe news is, the rest of the book is hopefully a
coherent account which follows that definition faithfully and, more
importantly, reveals the story of news as it is today: in short its character, nature, history, purpose and value. To begin with, the familiar
word 'news' belies its highly contested meaning. For generations writers
and theorists have questioned what makes news, what is news and what
function news does or should play in society. We all need and rely upon
news; we have to invest trust in those who tell it to us. News reflects
our need to know about contemporary events as they occur. We return
from holiday and immediately check what has happened while we have
been away. There may be a sense of relief if the events that have occurred
and which directly affect us, are trivial, or merely constitute exciting

gossip. Events which do not directly affect us may be of interest or seem important because they are significant in their own right (water is found on Mars), or we may empathize and perhaps send aid to those involved in the story (major natural disasters such as earthquakes, cyclones or tsunamis). Some stories can have a different type of impact upon us, becoming part of our collective memory (the destruction of the Twin Towers in New York on 11 September 2001; the death of Princess Diana on 31 August 1997). Some stories may merely entertain us for a short time (the dash for freedom made by two pigs on their way to the slaughterhouse; the rescue of a duck trapped in ice, or a ghost seen at Hampton Court). While this book recognizes that news can be selected and expressed in a variety of ways by a range of different news tellers, the focus of this analysis of news is concerned, first, with the constituent features of news itself and, second, with their impact on practice, namely what those reporting the news actually do and why.

This book explores the nature of news by analysing its deep characteristics or intellectual and practical architecture (outlined in Table 1). This analysis and its conceptual language is the way I exercise my discussion of the news. To be precise, news can be understood through its orientation towards the truth and contemporary events. In short, there is an expectation that the reporting of contemporary events which comprise the news is based on an orientation towards truthfulness, which in itself demands 'a respect for the truth' (Williams 2002: 11). News journalism is therefore not necessarily concerned with establishing 'The Truth', since this would require tellers of an event to know everything about it and to remove any element of subjectivity from their story. None the less, it is possible to accept truth as an aspiration, one which recognizes the value of truth through a disposition towards truthfulness. And while we might admit that the truth is impossible to attain in anything other than a forensic or scientific setting, although even here it is not guaranteed, I remain convinced that the aspiration to truth (along with an interest in contemporary events) is an essential feature of the news.

Those who select and tell the news have a different perception about their relationship to truth from those who consume the news and those critics (academic or otherwise) who analyse the news. Too often critics of the news fail to recognize this, preferring to criticize the exercise of journalism itself, because it 'has always been a philosophy conducted with one eye on the balance sheet' (Conboy 2004: 19). In this book the constituent features of news (what news is) and the environment within which news is produced and consumed will be discussed. As Table 1 shows, the deep characteristics of the news refer to the different levels at which it may be analysed; namely its philosophical orientation, its

Table 1 The deep characteristics of news and news journalism

NEWS

An orientation towards truth through truthful accounts of contemporary events

NEWS JOURNALISM

Disposition towards truthfulness	Interest in and accounts of contemporary events

CORE VALUES OF NEWS AND NEWS JOURNALISM

Accuracy	Sincerity	Location Space/Place (here)	Contemporaneousness Time (now)

ROLE OF NEWS JOURNALISM IN SOCIETY

Freedom of expression	Individual and collective responsibility of the journalist and the journalism profession	Plurality and diversity of access and representation	Fast and reliable information

NEWS JOURNALISM PRACTICE

Impartial, balanced, accurate and fair news	Law Regulations Codes of practice	Journalistic determination of interest/ importance, leading to different types of reporting and responses to new audiences for news. Varying editorial policies	Obsession with nowness and live reports. Illusion of non-mediated news

dispositions and interests, its core values, its role in society and the impact these characteristics have on practice. By using the following approach we can explore both what news is, consider what news should be and also identify factors which shape the character of the news which is mediated to the audience.

As Table 1 shows, the news has an orientation towards truth through a truthful account of contemporary events. News journalism is the usual and practical outcome of this. The disposition towards truthfulness has the core values of accuracy and sincerity, while the interest in accounting for contemporary events has the core values of the here (space/place) and now (time). These four core values combine to define the news in terms of its practical manifestation and social and cultural features. And yet the relationship between these four core values is not harmonious. It is tense where, for example, the requirement for understanding contemporary events immediately is offset by the requirement to be accurate, or where the core values are particularly, or in combination, subject to vectors of change such as techno-logical development, the internationalization of news flows, increased commercialization and competition within the news industry, fragmentation of audiences, deregulatory media policies and so on. Overall it is these vectors of change that have had an impact on the way in which news is selected, packaged and consumed and, as we shall see, have provided the greatest challenge to the truthful accounts of contemporary events.

For the purposes of my account of news I use throughout the book the insight that Williams (2002) provides, which is that a disposition towards truth and truthfulness contains the qualities of accuracy and sincerity. I believe that the news has this disposition and that these virtues represent the core and professional values of reporting contemporary events as news.

To deal with accuracy first: it is not the purpose of the news to promote or persuade; this is usually the job of rhetoric and propaganda; nor is it the job of news to engage in fiction or deceit. If information is presented in this manner then, strictly speaking, it is not news, although it may still be called 'news' by news organizations and journalists. Where contemporary events are little known or understood but deemed significant, the news report should reflect that fact, as should all subsequent reasonable inferences that constitute the report. These inferences must be articulated as 'judgemental' or 'best guesses' and not as factual accounts. While facts and judgements can coexist in a news report, proper news reporting articulates each according to its status, and in this way achieves accuracy. As we will see in our consideration of events leading to the Hutton Report in January 2004, problems of accuracy, fairness and impartiality in reporting arise when reporters' own judgements are presented as facts. Indeed, the most important of the BBC's basic editorial values were defined as 'truth and accuracy' by the BBC in an internal review (The Neil Report 2004),[1] conducted in May/June 2004, following the Hutton Inquiry (see Appendix 1). Accuracy as a core value of news consists of more than reporting facts and figures in an accurate way, but requires that accurate judgements are made by those reporting the news. The ability to provide an accurate and truthful news story is also dependent upon access to information and freedom to report. To this end many democratic societies have allowed or even established particular freedom of expression rights for the news media.

We will see in our story of the news that a requirement for accuracy was established as a historical precedent which had an impact on the practice of news reporting, since it entailed the development of a particular set of skills and techniques to 'tell' the news. In order for a teller of a story to achieve accuracy, he or she also has to decide the appropriate amount of 'investigative investment' (Williams 2002: 87) that is needed to find out as much as possible about a particular event, in order to deliver as truthful an account as possible. Today, accuracy has continued to be a core value of news and, in the case of broadcasting, also carries with it particular regulatory demands placed upon news broadcasters, articulated primarily as a requirement for their news to be impartial, balanced and fair. Throughout the book we will see how the important core quality of accuracy is both challenged and upheld by the historical, economic, social and political context within which news journalism operates. The development of trust between the news (mediated by the news organizations and news journalists) and the audience is dependent upon the extent to which the news is perceived to have the quality of accuracy.

Concerns about truthfulness also bring us to Williams' second virtue: sincerity, which entails 'a disposition to make sure that one's assertion expresses what one actually believes' (ibid.: 96). If a journalist (and/or the news organization) is trusted, then it is possible that the viewers, listeners or readers will also believe some or all of what is said. Problematically, while a journalist may not actually lie, an act which Williams (ibid.: 96) describes as 'an assertion, the content of which the speaker believes to be false, which is made with the intention to deceive the hearer with regard to content', a story may be misleading if the journalist does not, or cannot, express all elements of the story, or explicate any doubt and uncertainty he or she has. Actually reporting the doubtful nature of a story in all its complexity means that it would take longer to tell and may have little impact upon or significance for the audience. Journalists use strategies to make the story 'stand up', by providing accurate facts and figures and other descriptive information, and by finding sources who will make strong truth claims for and against the story. In this way the journalist can claim *sincerely* that a story is accurate, balanced and meets the requirements of impartial reporting. For very simple and straightforward stories, this technique is an effective way of presenting information quickly in an authentic and accessible way. The problem arises when stories are more complex, in particular when they relate to long-running issues such as war or conflict. While the audience is given the chance to decide which truth claim or side they take, this technique cannot accurately report complexity, doubt or shades of grey. The failure to provide the audience with a full and accurate account of issues and events can have consequences, as Philo and Berry (2004) observed during their study of television news coverage of the Palestine–Israel conflict. They found that 'for many viewers, their level of interest in news related very directly to their level of understanding of what they were watching' (ibid.: 257). Thus a story could be reported sincerely but inaccurately.

In order for news to achieve the core values of accuracy and sincerity, all the facts and information should be reported in a manner which provides as clear a picture of events as is possible. While this may result in a very long-winded and complicated tale, posing problems for broadcast news in particular, it remains an aspiration fixed in the ideal (and perfect) expression of news journalism. As a practical expression and style of news journalism it is obviously much more suited to investigative journalism, documentary and current affairs (Harrison 2000) than forms of news journalism associated with a particular emphasis upon the value of immediacy and the details of access (limited, partial or otherwise). Yet one of the defences of the growth of news which does not tell the whole story is that today there is plenty of information available to audiences via different sources if they choose to access it.

Sincere journalism has a disposition towards being truthful (and its associated core value of being accurate) an ideal best expressed through the cliché of 'telling the whole story'. However, different news organizations which have varying news agendas will tell the same story in different ways and provide different degrees of background information. 'Telling the whole story' may well be limited to the nature of the medium, the news policy of the news organization, rules of impartiality, lack of information, lack of resources or time to pursue the story, lack of space to tell the story fully and accurately, and so on. Equally, failing to 'tell the whole story' may be about being unable to place an event into an historical context, or being unable thoroughly to report the complexity of an issue. In either case the sincere journalist will be frustrated, as will be the viewer or reader who desires an accurate account. For example, the problems that journalists face when trying to tell a complex story, such as the Israeli–Palestinian conflict, were summarized concisely by *Channel Four News* journalist Lindsey Hilsum :

> There are two problems . . . how far back do you go is one and the other is with a conflict like this, nearly every single fact is disputed . . . I have to, as a journalist, make a judgement . . . I know it's a question of interpretation so I have to say what both sides think and I think sometimes that stops us from giving the background we should be giving.
>
> (comments taken from a longer quote in
> Philo and Berry 2004: 245)

Problematically, a sincere aim to be accurate and therefore truthful can also be frustrated by a variety of factors beyond the newsroom and the news medium, such as the insincerity of sources, news management by vested interests, a political culture which attempts to 'spin' stories and so on.

As Onora O'Neill (2002: 63) points out, there is a fundamental problem as to 'how we can tell which claims and counterclaims, reports and supposed facts are trustworthy when so much information swirls round us' in an era of recirculated news stories, public relations, media management and global gossip on the internet. The extent to which gossip, rumour, spin or different truth claims are resisted or challenged by those reporting the news has an effect on the type of news which is selected (what is seen to be important or relevant) and the way it is reported (which elements or aspects of a story are emphasized and why), and the extent to which it is researched and verified. As Williams (2002: 125) emphasizes, one important element of the 'virtue of accuracy . . . lies in the skills and attitudes that resist the pleasure principle, in all its forms, from a gross need to believe the agreeable, to mere laziness in checking one's investigations'. Lies are the antithesis of news, but adding drama, exaggeration or sensationalization to make a story more exciting, or concentration on one particular event (often resulting in news media frenzies) that can over-emphasize a risk, or imply that nothing else of importance is happening in the world, is insincere.

Recognizing that freedom of expression requires the exercise of responsible reporting, and that the news is subject throughout the world to a range of regulatory environments (from the legal to the voluntary code of practice, from censorship to press freedom inscribed in a written constitution), news providers are subject to both particular, more or less

harsh regimes or constraints, as well as a more or less imposed requirement to be truthful when reporting contemporary events. Needless to
say, the tension between the former and the latter varies, just as the
levels of trust which the audience has in relation to the truthfulness
of the news provided by different organizations vary between different
news providers (Hargreaves and Thomas 2002).[2]

In the British context, broadcast news is under unprecedented
scrutiny by the new regulator OFCOM (Office of Communications) in
its review of Public Service Broadcasting (PSB). PSB refers to a system
of broadcasting which aims to serve the public interest and fulfil a democratic role[3]. It entails the undertaking of a range of tasks or duties which
inform, entertain and educate citizens, to foster among them a sense of
social cohesion, responsibility and belonging[4]. Central to these duties is
the universal provision of impartial news and current affairs information
alongside a diverse range of other 'quality'[5] programming. As OFCOM
prepared to undertake its new duties on 29 December 2003, it indicated
concern about the contribution PSB can and should make to the news
environment, and has observed that 'there are parts of today's schedules
which do not give us the shining glow of good citizenship. News
and current affairs is (sic) an obvious example of where there is a tough
challenge' (Clarke 2004a: 14). OFCOM's three-phase review takes
into consideration news provided by Independent Television News (ITN)
as well as the BBC and will feed into the Charter renewal process which
will occur up until 2006. OFCOM issued its first stage report on 21 April
2004[6] in which it signalled a rethink of the remit and core purpose
of the BBC and its news provision, and its second stage report
(30 September 2004)[7] advocated the establishment of a Public Service
Publisher to supplement the BBC's PSB provision. Its third report
(8 February 2005)[8] revisited recommendations of the first two reports
and highlighted the need for competition and plurality in PSB provision.
At the same time The Hutton Report (see Appendix 1) continues to
influence the nature of news in Britain[9]. The Report perceived a neglect
of the core news value of accuracy and a lack of impartiality (amounting
to insincerity) in practice, and questioned the relationship between the
BBC and the government and its system of internal editorial control.[10]
This is close to saying that what occurred was that the need for and value
of truthfulness, when reporting a particular contemporary event, was
temporarily and inexcusably lost from sight.

To repeat: Table 1 shows that the news has a philosophical and intellectual architecture manifest in its disposition towards two essential
properties: truthfulness and the understanding of contemporary events.
I wish to turn my attention now to the second essential property of news,

namely the reporting of contemporary events. In seeking to understand the constituent features of contemporary events, we need to consider the core values of time and place/space (the here and now) which, as Table 1 shows, may be used to think about the way in which news journalists engage with and explain the world through their assessment of how interesting and important an event is, and the different types and styles of news reporting and language that are used. The core values of space/place and time are important when we consider the historical development of telling the news in oral cultures through to the complex multi-media world of the twenty-first century.

The story of news is one which has faced and overcome temporal and spatial constraints, allowing individuals to communicate across extended stretches of both time and space (Thompson 1995, and see Chapter 2). In early oral cultures news could only travel as far and as fast as the person carrying it. News from outside a particular vicinity or location was generally brought by a stranger/traveller figure who would invariably be greeted by a series of questions about what was happening beyond the immediate and known. The stranger/traveller figure would then inform the audience with an account of events from 'elsewhere' which occurred in the recent and relevant past. It was only by leaving their immediate vicinity or by acquiring occasional news from the stranger/traveller that those living in a specific setting and oral culture could learn of the outside world. Their experience of news was restricted to its 'simultaneity'; that is, news defined by its proximity or locality (Thompson 1995: 32) or relevance (contemporaneousness) Overall, oral cultures' news mainly comprised hearing about events occurring within the immediate locality and within a contemporary timescale; it was reported by word of mouth and was mediated by the dispositions and circumstances of the teller. Truth and gossip co-mingled, although we can reasonably assume that in relation to news the value placed on accuracy and sincerity was as high then as it is now. The news teller was unlike the Homeric storytellers who would poeticize a mythic and golden past.

The development of technologies such as the telegraph and the telephone changed the relationship which news had with time and place/space, resulting in an 'uncoupling of space and time' (ibid.: 32). The 'uncoupling' occurred because the experience of simultaneity could be divorced from locality. Once news could be transmitted to different localities it became possible to experience events as simultaneous, even when they were 'detached from the spatial condition of locality' (ibid.: 32). Eventually individuals in many different localities could all experience the same event simultaneously (although it would be after the event had actually occurred). As we will see, the development of printing and then printed newspapers, alongside postal, transport and communication networks such as the telegraph and telephone, allowed news to be disseminated on a wide scale, transcending the constraints of geography and allowing news to become local, national and global in orientation. News could also be selected, told and presented in different ways. News values no longer needed to be bounded by locality, custom or the disposition of one news teller, but by a range of other considerations – costs and revenue, audiences and the pursuit of influence or power. The act of printing also meant that the news became fixed and for a time news had become durable; it could be read and reread. It was now 'a matter of record'.

The development of broadcasting allowed the transmission of live pictures and sounds over long distances and further overcame the constraints of time and space. News assumed an immediacy and capacity for reporting events which rendered the 'here and now' as a standard for global reporting – any event, any time, anywhere. Today, twenty-four hour television news and the internet have the power to convey the live and immediate, while seeming to render the constraints of 'here' or place/space irrelevant. And while these developments raise questions about whether the accuracy and reliability of news are compromised by the speed of dissemination and the live nature of broadcasting, the development of different types of mediation of the news has necessitated the development of new forms of writing. These have long 'distinguished [themselves] from other related literary forms . . . centred on the transitory and the contemporary and [have] foregrounded the political and public aspects of writing like no other' (Conboy 2004: 19). Mediation has also required that news must be told in a way which 'gains the maximum effect . . . within allowed disciplines of space and time' and so must be 'clear, unambiguous and to the point' (Hodgson 1989: 5). The changing ways in which news has been mediated have meant that news content, production and consumption have developed and changed over time.

As we tend to equate a great deal of what we call news with the work of journalists (of which reporters, correspondents, editors, feature writers, subeditors and so on are types) it is important to note here that care must be taken when using words such as 'journalism' or 'journalists', because not everything they produce can strictly be called 'news'. Bourdieu (1996: 70) observes that the 'journalistic field' which developed in the nineteenth century was composed around the 'opposition between newspapers offering "news", preferably "sensational" or better yet, capable of creating a sensation, and newspapers featuring analysis and commentary'. Halberstam (1992: 11) demarcates 'news' and 'non-news' very narrowly, claiming that 'the greatest part of most newspapers or "news" on TV and radio is not news'. He sees news as nominalistic, covering single events and not states of affairs, aiming at the current rather than the past or future events and producing a report of an event, but not the experience of an event. Overall, Halberstam's view belies the complexity of news presentation, such as its long-established ability to be expressed in a variety of styles. For example, a hard news style used by both the print and electronic media presents the facts in the first line and is impersonal in approach (Boyd 2001), and yet in broadcasting, features are included within a news programme as the 'softer' news element, requiring a different approach to telling the story. The 'feature style' is used to lead 'the audience into the story rather than presenting them with the facts in the first line' (Boyd 2001: 73). Features in the press are generally regarded as 'non-news editorial content' (Hodgson 1989: 31) and include in-depth investigation specials, readers' letters and horoscopes, articles on gardening, cookery, fashion, motoring, holidays, showbusiness, sports gossip and so on (Harcup 2004). Often background features are pegged to a news event and used to give more explanation or context to the news and to allow journalists to develop a point of view. Unlike news where new facts and figures are gathered to tell the 'story as it is found' (ibid.: 29), feature writers assemble facts and figures (some new and some old) and use them to provide an argument or explanation about an event. From the point of view of a journalist, a feature is 'a piece of explanatory, deductive, writing form from which bias is inseparable', and which contains comment and analysis, whereas 'news writing . . . is an objective first-time disclosure of facts' (ibid.: 32). As we will see in Chapter 5, journalists' belief in their ability to be 'objective' in their news reporting is problematic. David Randall (2000) questions the value of a clear-cut delineation between news and features, arguing that both approaches to writing could benefit from lessons learned from each other. For him, the separation of the two forms of writing produces 'narrow thinking' and a lack of adventure and flexibility, which result from applying a strict formula for writing news, whereas features could probably benefit from 'less indulgent writing' and 'sharper research' (ibid.: 193–4).

Several types of journalism exist, some of which produce news and some of which do not, in the strictest sense of being the first-time disclosure of facts. News may be categorized in several ways: tabloid; quality or prestige; specialist; local civic; gossip; alternative; investigative; advocacy journalism and journalism of record (McQuail 2000: 340).

Fred Inglis (2002) cites Martha Gelhorn's article about the surrender of German troops in 1945 as an example of great journalism. He writes that it is:

> Journalism which does exactly what journalism should, is truthful, faithful to the facts, bearing witness of human actuality to those who could not actually be there, and then matching the story with adequate feelings and moral judgement. Doing so, it becomes art.
>
> (ibid.: 3)

At the other end of the spectrum is journalism which has been described as:

> loaded with political or ethnic significance liable to unleash strong, often negative feelings, such as racism, chauvinism, the fear-hatred of the foreigner or xenophobia. The simple report, the very fact of reporting, of putting on record as a reporter, always implies a social construction of reality that can mobilize (or demobilize) individuals or groups.
>
> (Bourdieu 1996: 21)

David Randall (2000) puts it more simply: journalism is either good or bad, and even the best journalism is produced within a set of constraints and limits imposed upon those gathering, selecting, reporting and presenting news. Some of those constraints change over time. Those involved in the news business today are experiencing the effects of powerful forces such as rapid technological development, increasing competition for a fragmenting news audience and the development of a global news market. Concerns have been raised in many quarters about the negative effects these changes have on news journalism, ranging from fears of 'dumbing down' and trivialization, to loss of journalistic independence and further diminishing of public trust in the news media; all of which can have a negative impact on the news's orientation towards the truth.

To summarize, I define the news throughout this book according to the following five precepts:

1 News has an orientation towards truth through a truthful account of contemporary events, and news journalism therefore has a disposition towards two essential properties: truthfulness and the understanding of contemporary events. The former has the core values and analytic qualities of accuracy and sincerity, the latter the core values and analytic qualities of the here (space/place)

and now (time). From these values and qualities we can identify elements of journalistic practice which are central to the nature of news: the tradition of impartiality; self-regulation, regulation and codes of practice; engagement with the here and now through journalistic discernment of what is relevant, interesting and important; different types of journalistic explanation of events and an obsession with immediacy.

2   There is 'not one news journalism' (Harcup 2004: 5) but many: tabloid; PSB; serious; radical; civic; current affairs; documentary and even personal. These types emerge primarily as a result of the engagement which the news journalist or news organization has with the news itself. Thus the extent to which news organizations or news journalists are impartial (the degree of accuracy, investigation and fairness employed in selecting and telling news), adhere to codes of practice, engage with the world (the nature, breadth and depth of news selection), are attached to live reporting (where raw footage increasingly replaces an 'end-product'), or only use reliable and well-sourced information collectively, defines the type of journalism deployed. The development of many types of news and news journalisms simply mirrors the fast-changing, digital, interactive, news-saturated environment in which we live and the competitive nature of news organizations.

3   News is what is judged to be newsworthy by journalists, who exercise their news sense within the constraints of the news organizations within which they operate. The news selected must interest their own particular audience or readers, giving rise to the view, common among many print journalists, that 'the broad shape and nature of the press is ultimately determined by no one but its readers' (Whale 1980: 85). The expansion of customized news forms and the growing levels of interactivity indicate an increasingly pronounced regard for the needs of audiences, in news selection and consumption across a range of news media. However, there are indications that news audiences are now accessing a range of 'news' sources, beyond those traditionally provided by the mainstream media, perhaps challenging news professionals' definition of news.

4   Journalism and its products (in particular news reporting) are seen to be important because they make positive or negative contributions to our understanding of society and its political processes. Recognition of this function and the value of truthful and accurate news reporting underpins the protection of freedom of expression, the exercise of law, PSB and the regulation and self-regulation of the commercial news media. The extent to which these

requirements are imposed upon news organizations is consistently being questioned and re-evaluated in a rapidly changing multi-media news environment.

5 News serves both a public purpose (underpinned by normative expectations placed upon it by society and in part reinforced by professional values) and, in most cases, also has commercial value. The nature of the relationship, or balance, between its public purpose and commercial purpose is a crucial constituent feature of news and requires a constant balancing of these different priorities in news media policy.

STRUCTURE OF THE BOOK

There are three conventional and formal dimensions to understanding news: news production, news articulation or content and news consumption. Throughout this book the views of journalists, audience survey data, public opinion data, articles written in the press, as well as academic literature, will be used to identify different views about news. News is a complex social, economic and cultural institution. Because of this we must understand the historical, technological, economic, social and political conditions of its selection, production, output and consumption: in short, its evolution and significance. The locale and focus for my analysis will primarily be print and broadcast news with attention paid to the internet where relevant. The internet is not (at least not yet) a unique platform for news production or content; it is primarily a distribution network which facilitates news consumption. Generally, internet news is part of the offerings of a traditional print or broadcasters' news service. There is some news journalism which is unique to the internet (see Chapter 7) but the dominant forms of news remain within the setting and culture of print and broadcast news journalism. With regard to illustrations and examples used throughout the book the majority are usually, though by no means exclusively, British rather than American, though the points made are universal.

Broadly speaking, the structure of this book follows Table 1. Chapter 1 explores a range of views about news and some of the main theoretical approaches used to study it. Common-sense views held about the news by television viewers and newspaper readers (a response that viewers and readers have learned through cumulative exposure to the conventions of the medium), practitioner views (a response that journalists have learned — or are learning — via socialization and training), and a wide variety of academic perspectives of power, ownership and control in the media are considered.

Chapter 2 outlines the historical and technological development of early print and broadcast news, and explores some of the reasons for the development of particular habits, skills, forms and codes of practice used by news journalists in Europe and America. It considers some of the historical precedents which are still adopted by news journalists today, which reflect the core values of news, such as the reporting of contemporary events through an engagement with the 'here' and 'now', and the establishment of the quality of truthfulness established through a requirement for accuracy and sincerity and a desire to provide news which may be judged to be accurate, impartial, balanced and fair.

Chapter 3 concentrates on developments that have occurred during the past twenty-five to thirty years, which have exacerbated some of the tensions inherent in the orientation of the news both to truthfulness and its interest in contemporary events. The chapter discusses the growth of new news media in the context of rapid technological change, concentration of ownership, the growth of global news organizations and the consequent increased commercialization and competition which have affected the packaging and selling of news and arguably the nature of news reported. This chapter also considers 'new' forms of news (twenty-four hour television news and news on the internet) which prioritize immediacy in reporting.

Chapter 4 explores the way in which the news media in particular are regarded as the most important channels for disseminating information to the extent that they are seen as 'agents of democracy' (Allan 1999: 3). This chapter considers the ways in which society holds a set of normative expectations about the role of news media and a need to protect the news's disposition towards truthfulness. These normative expectations include a concern to protect freedom of expression and a recognition that the exercise of free speech is carried out in a responsible manner. Thus the policy impetus in some democracies to curb broadcasters' freedom to express whatever they please and to enforce quality or responsible news journalism is also explored.

Chapter 5 examines how news is produced in the newsroom and the constraints and pressures under which journalists work, particularly the impact of external influences, interference by owners, the nature of the editorial system (referring to examples from the Hutton Inquiry and Report), financial constraints, time constraints, and the effects of digitization on journalistic routines and practice. The chapter will draw upon, and refer the reader to, the key approaches to understanding how the character of news is shaped through journalistic practice.

Chapter 6 concentrates on the challenges facing television news providers which are leading to the production of different types of news in the twenty-first century. The discovery that television news is now less effective at reaching younger viewers, ethnic communities and those from social groups III (M), IV and V,[11] as well as being linked in part with a decline in interest and trust in politics, has resulted in a flurry of surveys and adjustments in the broadcasting sector. Consequently, the nature of contemporary television news content (news values) and the presentational styles used need to be analysed and compared with recent analyses of news audiences. Also considered are the growth in number of news media outlets, the changing patterns of news consumption and the increased competition for audiences, which have raised concerns about the extent to which these developments are causing news to 'dumb down', with audiences left less well informed about their localities, politics and international affairs. This argument is juxtaposed with those which provide a more positive assessment of current television news, where emphasis is placed upon audience choice, the ability to explore the news in greater depth and breadth, even to the extent of being able to seek out news from sources beyond those provided by traditional news organizations.

The concluding Chapter 7 returns us to the problem of defining what news *is,* its possible future and *what it should be.*

2

VIEWS ABOUT NEWS
Common sense, practitioner and academic

INTRODUCTION

Opinions about what is news vary in accordance with who is discussing it. Kevin Williams (2003: 16) identifies three levels at which discussion about news occurs: the common-sense level, the practitioner level and the academic level. Although both common-sense and academic views often provide a critique of news and the profession which writes and mediates it, the two are quite different. Critical common-sense views are not grounded in empirical evidence or theory, although it appears that some early pessimistic critical academic theories did serve to underpin people's articulations about a 'golden era' of news and to justify the assertions that standards are slipping, or that the quality of news is in decline.

Academic research is undertaken via a variety of disciplines, which, as we will see, base their concern in problematizing and theorizing the content, production and consumption of the news. Practitioner views often reject academic and common-sense criticism of their work, in particular arguing strongly against any accusation of bias in their output, or refuting any overt control of their practice. Most journalists prefer to concentrate on their duty to provide objective news (as far as it is humanly possible to do so), their ability to be first with the story and the lived reality and serendipitous nature of news reporting, which leaves no time for the 'construction' or 'shaping' of news. Some journalists write considered articles about the nature of their profession or the meaning of journalism.[1] Although many of the antagonisms between the academy and the profession are being eroded, as journalists increasingly involve themselves in further and higher education institutions, journalism education remains based on the belief that reporting is a skill to be learned through experience and practice, that learning by doing is the only way to 'know' and report the news.

COMMON-SENSE VIEWS ABOUT NEWS

At the common-sense level, we are all of us at one time or other members of a news-consuming audience and, as such, have some under-standing of the news media. We will read, watch or listen to the news and may even engage in public debate about it. Sometimes nostalgia is expressed for a bygone golden age of journalism (which may never have existed), and sometimes we recognize and appreciate that the changing nature of the news media environment reflects the complex nature of contemporary news provision and increased consumer choice. The Secretary of State for Culture, Media and Sport in Britain recently observed that 'in a multichannel world of smart video recorders, audi-ences will go elsewhere if they detect any hint they are being patronised' (Clarke 2004a: 14). A questionnaire survey of 1,355 people by MORI in April 2003 identified 'distinct breeds' of British news gatherers in the audience who can be specifically targeted (see Chapter 6).[2]

A popular way of obtaining insight into common-sense opinions about news has been through the use of focus groups, surveys and question-naires targeted at audience members. As the share of the audience for news decreases in a multi-media environment, news organizations have become increasingly concerned about retaining audiences and under-standing what engages and interests them. The findings have then been used, to differing extents, by news organizations to help them repackage their news presentation as well as to influence the types of news stories which may be covered. Focus groups[3] have been used by print and broad-cast news organizations since the 1990s to help them to tune into what the audience wants from their particular news product and in order to gain more viewers, listeners or readers. Focus group research has proved to be a very popular qualitative method used to gauge audience or reader opinion about news products. Prioritizing what the audience appears to want rather than pursuing a journalist-led news agenda can lead to criticism about falling standards and a change in the character of news. In this vein the BBC was recently criticized for coverage which is more 'Madonna than Mugabe' (Clarke 2004a: 14) or, alternatively, more 'Madonna than Macedonia' (Wells 2001). The Blair government (and OFCOM) have expectations about the quality and standards of BBC news and PSB generally, but consider that the audience must be offered the opportunity to express its opinions. Consequently both the BBC[4] and OFCOM have conducted public opinion surveys in the lead-up to the renewal of the BBC's Charter to broadcast, with OFCOM aiming to place 'viewers and programmes . . . at the heart of the review which will inform the future shape of British television'.[5]

While the use of focus groups or surveys may be seen to be helpful in garnering the common-sense view of news as it is seen by the public, their use as an arbiter of journalistic standards can be problematic. The adoption by different news organizations of so-called 'feminized' news agendas, or 'lifestyle'-oriented news, or 'more accessible or relevant' news stories, has led to accusations of dumbing down from some academics (Franklin 1997) and journalists (Bell 2002). Criticism of mass culture has come from intellectuals of both the Left and the Right and is not a new phenomenon. Critics of popular culture have long lamented the decline in standards of one sort or another (for insights into this lament see, especially, Hoggart 1958). The classicist and poet Matthew Arnold (1822–83) is generally viewed as one of the founding fathers of the thesis which viewed popular culture as vulgar and inferior to 'real' culture, which he famously defined as 'the best of what has been thought and said in the world' (Storey 1993: 21). The literary and social conservative critic F.R. Leavis (1895–1978) was highly influential in the 1930s with his pessimistic view of the decline and homogenization of cultural standards and the idea that they could only be maintained by an elite minority (Lough 2002). The poet T.S. Eliot held the same view (see below). On the non-conservative side, the critical theory of the Frankfurt School[6] with its unorthodox sense of Marxism (the Frankfurt School is sometimes referred to as neo-Marxist or Marxist influenced)[7] also expressed the belief that mass popular culture would undermine creative thinking and reduce cultural standards. The founding fathers of the school, Theodor Adorno and Max Horkheimer (1973), and Herbert Marcuse (1972), were particularly concerned with the baleful effects of mass cultural expressions and imposed orthodoxies, as later in their different fields were both Walter Benjamin (1970) and Jurgen Habermas (1989).

Supporting the above concerns is the belief that allowing mass prejudices to manifest themselves as dominant cultural values produces limited intellectual and cultural expressions. Expressed more moderately this is akin to saying that allowing viewer preferences to influence decisions about broadcast content changes the basis on which content standards are evaluated. Rather than working to a set of so-called objective standards (imposed upon the viewing public by a public service broadcaster made up of elite professionals, 'the great and the good' in society), standards based on viewer preferences will be judged by ordinary people's tastes. Such tastes may be transitory, partial and ephemeral; they are certainly no guarantee of objective standards by which to measure value. Even if a programme is successful in terms of its popularity, this does not necessarily take into account the quality or value of the programme. As Richard Hoggart (1995: 155) argued: 'no programme is ever justified by the answer: "But they enjoyed it". So does a cat playing with a dying sparrow.' These sentiments have an echo in earlier concerns. T.S. Eliot, giving evidence to the Pilkington Committee on the future of broadcasting in 1962, said that 'those who aim to give the public what the public wants begin by underestimating the public taste; they end by debauching it'.[8] Both Hoggart and Eliot seem to anticipate the two underlying assumptions of the dumbing down debate. First, the negative view that audience preferences may lead to lowest common denominator content; second, increasing competition in the news media environment, which has led to harder-fought battles for ratings and readers, has led to inferior news provision. These arguments, however, are not as clear-cut as they may at first seem. As Harcup (2004: 88) notes, the dumbing down concept is 'far too simplistic to do justice to the complexity of today's journalism – or journalisms'. I would also add that at times the charge of dumbing down is too often wistful or nostalgic and in both cases wrong, as we shall see in the Chapter 2, where I argue that the history of news does not support the charge.

PRACTITIONERS' VIEWS ABOUT NEWS

Practitioner views reflect the range of skills, training regimes, practices, norms and values within which news journalists work and which are used to explain and justify their activities and to define news. Some practitioners' perceptions about their work in selecting, editing and presenting news are antagonistic about the way in which academics analyse news, seeing academic analysis as an unwarranted attack on practitioners' professional integrity and autonomy. In this regard, Harcup's (2004) book juxtaposes many of these divergent views in a helpful way, as an overview from a journalist/academic able to measure some of the academic theories against the lived reality of journalistic practice.

Some long-lived and over-worked practitioner definitions have become professional clichés which seem to express the essence of journalism and help to define news. Many students of journalism will be familiar with the statement while that, 'dog bites man' is not news, 'man bites dog' is; or that news is anything that makes the reader say 'Gee Whiz' (Bogart, quoted in Mott 1950: 376, 126). These clichés encapsulate the idea that news must be unusual or out of the ordinary; it has to be unexpected and make people talk. For example, on 23 January 2004, *Sky News* reported a story about a 75-year-old man who had suffered a grazed knee after having been knocked down by a milk-float 'driven' by a dog which had somehow got into the front seat and sat on the accelerator pedal. Bogart would no doubt agree with the following proposition: 'milkman drives into dog' is not news; 'dog drives into milkman' is news.

Willmott Lewis similarly captured the need to grab the audience's attention when he remarked:

> I think it well to remember that, when writing for the newspapers, we are writing for an elderly lady in Hastings who has two cats of which she is passionately fond. Unless our stuff can successfully compete for her interest with those cats, it is no good.
>
> (Quoted in Sherrin 2003: 165)

News journalism is often referred to as the first draft of history, where 'much of what appears in our columns is of lasting interest and in some cases like wine improves with age' (Kemp 1982: 15). While this is sometimes used to indicate the importance of news, it also relates to another feature of news: its obsession with contemporary events, such that 'news, as a form of knowledge, is not primarily concerned either with the past or with the future but rather with the present. . . . Once published and its significance recognized, what was news becomes history' (Park 1940: 670). As Park thus observes, news has a 'transient and ephemeral quality' (ibid.) and all news journalists recognize this characteristic as a vital element of their professional practice: namely that news must be contemporary, or at least move an existing story on.

As we have seen, the orientation of the news to report contemporary events means that news covers events as they unfold, or in the immediate aftermath of their occurrence, at a time when facts or the factual case are likely to be least known or certain. Often, though, news coverage will be used to subsequently provide some kind of historical documentation which may be used to retell the story in future accounts. The idea of a 'news legacy' is, however, not the same as providing a detailed historical account or even a first draft of history. Often news stories offer only a snapshot of an event captured at a particular time.

The inability of news to pursue stories which do not seem significant at the time results in a patchy and partial history which is marred by inconsistencies in the overall narrative. Of course, this is not to say that news accounts are inevitably either inaccurate or insincere, merely incomplete when judged as history. As Bernard Williams (2002) points out, bad things generally happen suddenly, constituting an event, whereas good things generally develop more slowly. Unless the outcome or process of development is perceived to be newsworthy, long-term developments are generally not reported.

Important historical events may also be ignored. A particular event which was not at the time deemed to be newsworthy (President Lincoln's visit to the Ford Theatre to see the play *Our American Cousin*) achieved news value due only to an unforeseen event (his assassination by John Wilkes Booth who shot him at point-blank range in the back of the head) (Williams 2002). It is often the case that the news media are not there to report or capture the event as it happens; the best they can hope to do is to cover the aftermath, piecing together the event from a variety of witnesses and participants. A good journalist must choose between different accounts of the same event (engaging in a battle of rhetorics) in order to come up with an account which aims to be as truthful and accurate as possible. The aspiration to provide a truthful account, or first draft of history, is full of pitfalls however, because ultimately the picture which is portrayed involves weighing and interpreting the evidence and using it to piece together a story.

The dilemma for journalists claiming to use contemporary events to produce something which is historically significant may be considered in relation to the methods used by two ancient Greeks who are sometimes credited with being the first journalists, historians or correspondents (Halberstam 1992). The first, Athenian General Thucydides (460–400 BC) attempted to provide a reliable account of the Peloponnesian War (431 – 404 BC between Athens and Sparta). Thucydides gathered all the available evidence he could from witnesses to events. On the basis of the evidence, Thucydides then decided what he believed was a true account of events and wrote accordingly. 'I thought it proper to record the facts of the war, not from chance information nor from my own impression, but in accordance with the most accurate investigation possible of each particular, not only in the situations of which I heard from others, but also in those at which I was present myself' (Hammond 1967: 429). Conversely, Herodotus (484–425 BC) enquired after everything and gathered all he heard, and reported it whether he believed the accounts to be truthful or not. His interest was the story; the account and the patterns of explanations revealed that he was not, as Thucydides is often described, 'scientific'. Everything was of interest to Herodotus and he arranged his accounts in the form of tales which contrived to produce an imposed unity and historical pattern which was both dramatic and most 'suitable to be read aloud' (ibid.: 337). And while we might say that Thucydides was more truthful in the particularity of his contemporary account of the Peloponnesian War, it is Herodotus who is referred to as the 'father of history'[9] for what ultimately is his wonderful storytelling.

Today, news reporters are not encouraged to tell wonderful stories. They are constrained from doing so via their professional practices, which consist of a variety of regulations, codes of practice, training and development of techniques to promote accuracy and fairness in reporting. Academic critics of news content continue to argue that journalists use gathered evidence in a particular way which misrepresents specific groups in society. This may be because of the practice of irresponsible journalism (for example, the use of source material without checking its reliability and provenance, such as The Daily Mirror's use of pictures of the abuse of prisoners by British soldiers in an Iraq prison which were later revealed to be fake, or the use of internet gossip sites by some newspapers as a source of news); or journalism which 'unwittingly' misrepresents groups due to the influence of hidden ideological pressures and values within which journalists work (see, for example, research undertaken by the Glasgow University Media Group 1976, 1980, 1982). In response to these academic critics practitioners have claimed that news is the first draft of history, a claim which is based solely upon the belief in their professional ability to provide both a truthful and objective contemporary account, which over time becomes an equally reliable historical account. In fact this claim rests on a simple view of the historian and ignorance of historiography or, to put it another way, writing history is more than being journalistically reliable. In addition, as we shall now see, even the claim to reliability as the cornerstone of journalistic professionalism is disputed.

ACADEMIC VIEWS ABOUT NEWS

The study of news has attracted scholars from many academic disciplines, and opinions about the contribution news makes to society vary. News is studied from a variety of perspectives. Scholars in the fields of sociology, history, politics, economics, anthropology, law, psychology and management have all viewed news as an area worthy of study. Many academic studies have tended to question what *makes* news, rather than what news *is* (Halberstam 1992). Attempts to define news often 'tend to dissolve into lists of newsmaking events' (Roshco 1975)[10] which explain the criteria of newsworthiness via the properties inherent in any selected event (see Galtung and Ruge 1965; Harcup and O'Neil 2001). As we will see in Chapter 5, many explanations of what *makes* news generally offer only a partial or one-dimensional explanation of news value and do not tell us what news *is*.

The development of language has acted as a formal and informal structuring system through which we understand and organize the world we live in, and news language in this regard is significant. Bell (1991: 1) believes that the media have a vital role to play in our understanding of the world, as individuals living in Western countries 'probably hear more language from the media than they do directly from the lips of their fellow humans in conversation'. Today, the everyday lives of many people are saturated by media language and images, most commonly via television, which is 'now the supreme news medium . . . the only [one] presently capable of reaching across the whole of British society' (Hargreaves and Thomas 2002: 5), although of course we can also get our news from radio, the press, mobile phones and the internet. News, made up of words, pictures, graphics and moving images, has a high status as a particular subsystem within language and holds an important position in everyday life and culture (Hartley 1988). News language also has a particular 'signifying power (the power to represent things in particular ways)' (Fairclough 1995: 2). For example, the use of specific words can be particularly significant because they are not value neutral. As Bourdieu (1996: 20) observes: 'words can do a lot of damage: Islam, Islamic, Islamicist – is the headscarf Islamic or Islamicist?'[11] The study of language in the news has been widely researched and it is not the purpose of this book to cover the same ground (but see, for example, Hartley and Montgomery 1985; Van Dijk 1988; Bell 1991; Fowler 1991; Scannell 1991; Fairclough 1995; Cameron 1996; Bell and Garrett 1998; Scollon 1998; Ungerer 2000; Nylund 2003; Richardson 2004).

Negatively, Minogue (1997: 7) focuses his attention on the profession of journalism, seeing it as 'an engine for turning everything into a cliché'. News feeds our ability to gossip, chat and socialize as well as encouraging our ability to be voyeuristic. News organizations can easily pander to this dimension of our human fallibility, feeding that particular appetite with dramatic stories and images. On a positive note Halberstam (1992) emphasizes the importance of news as a central element of human communication, whereby knowing what is in the news keeps us all connected to the world around us. For him news is an important part of our lives, as it is 'the focus of much of our anger, hopes, curiosity and ruminations' (ibid: 19), thus providing us all with a common social dialogue. As we will see in Chapter 4, there are even higher hopes for news, namely that the information which it provides can create informed citizens who interact with each other in a discursive forum which informs, entertains and perhaps even educates us.

Some important theoretical approaches used to study news

In practice, studies about news have generally been placed within a range of different theoretical frameworks. These frameworks are often derived from the intellectual tradition and particular discipline from which the writer or student of news comes. The 'field' of news study has been linked to particular elements of news: its production, content and consumption; and to particular themes and issues: the reporting of crime, race, gender, politics and so on. These elements and themes are often grounded in particular theoretical perspectives supported by methodological approaches which may be used to find answers to specific questions. Sometimes a methodological approach, such as the non-systematic collection of a variety of data via content analysis, interviews, surveys or observation of journalists at work, is undertaken due to a desire to explore a particular theoretical proposition or to prove a particular argument (Briggs and Cobley 1998). Yet again, data may be gathered in a systematic way to undertake a more general 'fishing expedition', where a researcher collects data to see what story it empirically reveals or tells (see Deacon et al. 1999). From the 1930s, American research, led predominantly by Paul Lazarsfeld, focused upon data collection which was used 'scientifically' to measure the content of the mass media. Assumptions about their effects were then extrapolated from the data on the content. In later years such work found commercial application as information could be collected about audiences which could be used by media owners and advertisers. As Briggs and Cobley (1998: 5) observe, it is worth noting that 'the study of [news] media is bound up with interests, biases, influences, arguments, motives and instrumental applications'. Such interests, biases, influences, arguments, motives and instrumental applications may be discerned in many academic approaches to the study of news. Each will amount to a different analysis of what news *is,* and they are worth bearing in mind when attempting to provide one's own formulation of news. The most important of these may be summarized accordingly.

Marxist political economy and critical political economy

The Marxist political economy perspective[12] (hereafter 'political economy') searches for answers about the question of dominant power structures and reduction of diversity in the news media, by addressing and analysing their structure of ownership and control. Early political economy approaches often explained the relationship between capitalist ownership and news media content in instrumentalist terms, whereby the former resulted in content which was shaped by the values of the ruling class (Tumber 1999). More recently, researchers have considered 'the impersonal laws (economic determinants) of the marketplace' (Cottle 2003: 9), focusing on the way that owners gain commercial control over sectors of the news media industry through mergers and acquisitions, vertical and horizontal integration, monopolistic and competitive activity. The actions of news corporations, in their need to gain profits, meet shareholders' and investors' demands, and maximize audience ratings to sell to advertisers, are used to explain organizational activity, workplace practice and the output of the news media.

However, theorizing about the news media (and the media in general) from this perspective has generally been focused on collecting data which inform particular theoretical speculations. In order to understand the causal link between the economic determinants of the media and the content of the media, researchers from this perspective need to analyse the professional ideologies and work practices of media professionals *within* the news organization. Although, as we discuss later, journalists work in an environment which places constraints on their practice, there are also some elements of resistance and autonomy evident in their day-to-day activities, indicating a degree of professional agency (Stevenson 2002) and communicative intentionality on the part of journalists. The political economy perspective has undertaken little systematic empirical investigation on the complex links between the ownership of media companies, corporate strategies, management forms, and the production and content of the news (Eldridge 1993). The rebranded *critical* political economy has recently turned to 'structuring processes informing audience involvement and cultural consumption' (Cottle 2003: 12), but still largely neglects the production process.

Tracing links between owners' interest, news production and content has become more complex in nature. Old-fashioned newspaper barons, such as Northcliffe, Rothermere and Beaverbrook in Britain, Randolph Hearst in America and Springer in West Germany, have largely been replaced by corporate managers who are often involved across a wide range of media, with diversified interests and priorities (Hargreaves 2003). The recent growth of transnational corporations (TNCs) on an unprecedented scale means that a great deal of news journalism is now produced by companies for which the news may not be the primary activity. Silvio Berlusconi of Italy, who combines being Prime Minister with ownership of commercial television channels, and Rupert Murdoch, who seeks to create the best political and economic conditions for his various media ventures (which range beyond news into entertainment programming and publishing) are in some respects different from their predecessors due to the scale and nature of their operations.

Journalists' responses to theoretical concerns voiced by academics vary within different organizational contexts. Usually, though, they regard their own professionalism and autonomy as proof against academic theories which speak of any overt economic or ideological domination of news and its content (Harrison 2000). Although, as the journalist Michael Wolff observes, the link between individual activity and proprietorial control may not always be obvious to the observer or the journalist in the newsroom:

> Any mega media conglomerate is really, as anyone who has worked in one knows, a confederation of more or less non-co-operative parts. It is quite possible that only in periods of acquisition, sale or big share-price losses, do the people who work for a mogul actually personalize their part in this grand scheme and do their literal follow-the-mogul duty. Otherwise mogul employees are mostly able to passive–aggressively defy, if not ignore, their mogul master.
>
> (Wolff 2004)[13]

Of course, this is not to say that journalists do not work within proprietorial constraints, even if on a day-to-day basis they are not aware of overt intervention.

There are many examples where proprietors have exerted their influence via direct editorial intervention, and of course economic and financial considerations are constantly in the purview of managers, owners and shareholders. Robert Maxwell regarded *The Daily Mirror* as his personal 'megaphone' (Curran and Seaton 1997: 48). McChesney (2000: 275) cites an example of two journalists who were sacked after refusing to alter their story in line with the News Corporation's instructions, whereas Conrad Black would determine the news agenda by offering polemics against what he saw as 'hatred for Israel' (Greenslade 2003a: 645). Sometimes the proprietor may be less hands-on, but none the less will set the attitude and direction of their newspaper, appointing editors who are generally in agreement with the owner and know the limits and boundaries they must observe (Sanders 2003). Consequently, a proprietor may own numerous papers but they will all take the same line on certain issues, such as their attitude to the 2003 war in Iraq, their support or antagonism towards membership of the European Union;[14] they may also exercise general support for particular political values, or support for particular prime ministers,[15] while still pursuing different news agendas and storylines. They may also adopt different presentation styles or modes of addressing the news consumer.

Sometimes it is difficult to identify precise uses and abuses of power, or to say exactly how this directly affects journalistic practice or news content. None the less, policymakers have been concerned about the problem of excessive use of power and market domination by some media owners, and measures are adopted to prevent excessive concentration of ownership in many countries.[16] Policies aimed at ensuring that a diversity of ownership exists are enacted in the belief that this may lead to a diversity of editorial approaches, or at least prevent companies from creating bottle-necks or misusing their market power. However, as Hargreaves (2003: 161) points out, plurality of ownership may not guarantee a diversity of editorial perspectives, as the news media are 'great imitators of each other'. This is particularly the case in very competitive markets where the news media seek to attract audiences or readers away from rivals by making their news more appealing, and by using established tried-and-tested formulae rather than risking experimentation and diversification. In this regard, public service broadcasters play an increasingly important role in providing a news service which is distinct from the commercial sector. Paradoxically, concerns about the decline in news media diversity and quality of news resulting from concentration of ownership are occurring at a time when the amount of news provided is increasing exponentially across a range of different outlets, such as mobile telephones, computers, digital television, digital radio and free newspapers.

Culturalist approaches

The culturalist approach is not homogeneous; it is diverse and one strand is often critical of another. Nevertheless, I think it reasonable to begin with Raymond Williams. In the 1960s, Williams made an important contribution to our understanding of culture in general and television in particular. Williams used content analysis and other empirical methods to examine popular culture, in an attempt to see 'culture' not simply as a text which was somehow separate from its social context, but to recognize the institutions of cultural production themselves as worthy of study (Lough 2002). Williams (1974) moved away from the traditional Marxist model which linked culture and ideology to the economic base of society, towards a neo-Marxist theory which involved analysing other elements of society — in particular the role of institutions, social processes and cultural and expressive forms. He argued that popular culture(s) had great value in their own right, and like other cultural or expressive forms, were products of complex social processes, institutions and aesthetics. He used insights offered by structuralism, explaining the world as socially constructed from signs, hidden meanings, codes and symbols, and came to understand television as a technical and cultural form which has its own particular aesthetic complexity, but which remains rooted in a particular shared ideological and social base.

Like other dominant ideology perspectives, the culturalist approach suggests that the news media produce a value-laden product, which may seem 'neutral', but in fact represents many establishment or other dominant views. Stuart Hall's work at the Centre for Contemporary Cultural Studies at the University of Birmingham in the 1970s was highly influential in this regard. It incorporated neo-Marxist, structuralist and semiotic theories, where the media are understood as settings for a never-ending series of contests between conflicting social forces, competing views of the world and messages. They were not mere conduits for purveying a single ruling ideology. Drawing upon the political sociology of Antonio Gramsci, Hall (1980) emphasized the possibility of oppositional decodings (alternative readings)[17] of journalistic messages by audiences, providing an important insight about the way in which ideological messages can be resisted by audiences and about the struggles 'played out within the moment of the text' (Cottle 2003: 11). From Hall onwards we can understand the cultural approach as achieving three things. First, like the political economic perspective, it locates the source of 'bias' and influence on news in an environment external to the news organization. Second, it recognizes that this environment is replete with different and competing views and expressive forms wanting to be read, listened to or viewed. Third, it moves away from understanding news consumption solely in terms of class or socio-economic determinants and has introduced ethnicity, gender and age as factors to be considered. Indeed, recent cultural approaches argue that positioning individuals and trying to understand their news or media choices or habits solely in relation to a particular class or set of socio-economic determinants is patronizing, since it assumes that people read and view what they do for no other reason than their social or material location.

Although it seems obvious that differences other than our social and material location contribute to explaining our relationship to the news, they have been seen to be very important, as a brief look at mass society theory demonstrates.

Two propositions support the explanatory power of mass society theory. The first is that knowledge is situationally determined, meaning that what an individual knows is based on his or her location in an elitist social structure (Mannheim 1936). In other words, a modern society is class and materially based, and elites dominate. The second is that public opinion is a powerful form of social control, a point first made by Ferdinand Tönnies in his distinction between *Gemeinschaft* (traditional society where people were bound together through personal and communal ties) and *Gesellschaft* (modern society where interpersonal relations are impersonal, and individuals are rootless and isolated), a distinction sometimes referred to as 'community' and 'association'. In the case of the former, social control was achieved through concord, folkways, mores and religion, in the case of the latter, it was achieved through convention, legislation and public opinion (Martindale 1961: 84). The power of a political elite to control the mass media for the purpose of generating propaganda, designed to influence and manipulate public opinion, was first seen in Nazi Germany and in Stalin's Soviet Union. These and other totalitarian regimes of the 1930s led to concerns about the ability of the media to exert power and control in other political systems. In particular, the power of elites in democratic societies to access and use the media was seen to be problematic, and in the same light was the ability of America, as a dominant producer of cultural products, to export material to Britain (today France leads Europe in objecting to the influence of an emerging American hegemony). The influx of Hollywood movies into Europe in the 1950s led cultural critics to express their concern about the effects of mass-produced, cheap and sensational material on British culture (Hoggart 1958). Leading Marxist-influenced scholars of the Frankfurt School, such as Adorno and Horkheimer (1973) and Herbert Marcuse (1972), argued that this material represented an insidious influence on free thinking, creating 'false' desires through consumerism (Baran and Davies 1995). These views, not shared by Raymond Williams or Stuart Hall, may be summarized as regarding the audience pessimistically, seeing it as lacking the ability to interrogate media messages or to engage in a 'politics of opposition' (Cottle 2003: 11).

Although the culturalist perspective has offered important insights about the way audiences consume cultural products, a weakness of this perspective is that it has little to contribute to the analysis of the production process in the newsroom. Instead, an 'interpretive' and 'qualitative' (McQuail 1992: 13) approach to the study of the production process is used, which often ignores the micro-sociocultural context in which it occurs. The culturalist approach prefers to concentrate on the consumption of texts. Assumptions about the production process are made through the interpretation of the texts and the ideological messages found therein. The field of cultural studies today tends to centre on popular culture on screen and television, and has little to say about media policy, or the contemporary threats to plurality, diversity or PSB through policy decisions and industrial activity (Ferguson and Golding 1997). Cultural studies is none the less the 'dominant paradigm for analysis of the media', although as noted above, competing areas emerge from within it with great regularity: most recently post-feminism, postmodernism and post-colonialism (Lough 2002: 256). However, as Lough points out, 'in recent years the antagonism between [the political economy school of thought and cultural studies] seems to have been thawing as both realize that neither has the monopoly on useful analysis' (ibid.: 219).

News as an organizational product

In contrast to a political economy approach which Schudson (1989: 12) perceives as a 'rather blunt instrument for examining a subtle system'[18] the study of the social organization of newswork seeks to understand the actual practices involved in producing news. This is an area which Cottle (2003: 4) refers to as a 'relatively unexplored and under-theorised "middle-ground" of organizational structures and workplace practices'. Organizational approaches tend to see the views expressed by the political economists and culturalists as being rather conspiratorial (McNair 1996). Rather than focusing on the external factors which have a causal effect upon the content of the news or the audience, organizational approaches concentrate on the production of the news. Production processes are seen to be features of journalistic organization which ultimately affect output or news content. Schudson (2000: 188) summarizes the key concerns of those who study news organizations as being, first, the controls and constraints imposed upon journalists by organizations, which override any views or values of individuals working within the organization, and second, the 'inevitability of "social construction" of reality in any social system'.

Some researchers take the view from this perspective that news-work is influenced by a dominant ideology. Molotch and Lester (1974), and Tuchman (1978), who takes a symbolic interactionist or social constructionist view of journalism and society, see news as the social production of 'reality' and consequently argue that news does not actually reflect reality, but is determined by those who hold power in society. Early research concentrated on the way news was selected in the newsroom, pointing initially to the individual copy taster as the gate-keeper in the selection process (White 1950). This explanation was later expanded to include the whole news organization in the process of gatekeeping (Shoemaker 1991). Studies which examined the manner in which journalists worked considered the ways in which they used the professional norm of impartial reporting and routines to structure their news day and avoid criticism (Tuchman 1978). These insights, coupled with views about how and why journalists conformed to news policies (Breed 1955), have underpinned a series of ethnographic or observational studies undertaken in newsrooms (Epstein 1973; Altheide 1976; Schlesinger 1978; Tuchman 1978; Gans 1979; Fishman 1980; Soloski 1989).

Although the use of routines and impartiality norms is helpful to news organizations, since they reduce the probability of maverick journalism, or the danger of libellous reporting, conflict between journalists and the organization within which they work has also been identified as a routine part of journalistic life (Soloski 1989). Researchers have gener-ally perceived this conflict to be between the values of the journalistic profession and the organization, with individual journalists seen to have little influence on the final news product.[19] However, any conflict which arises has generally seemed to be under control. Epstein (1973) argued that journalists modify or control their own views (via the professional belief in the importance of dispassionate reporting) and that other factors also have an impact on news and journalists, such as economic and technical requirements and fear of reprisals (Breed 1955).

These studies indicated that a great deal of news organization has been based around routinized behaviour, professional ideology and a produc-tion context shaped by a variety of constraints and occasional conflict. Fishman (1980) concluded that the world in which the journalist gathers news is predominantly bureaucratically organized and based upon organ-izational prerequisites which served to structure the form the news would take. From this perspective, 'news is the result of an organized response to routine bureaucratic problems' (Rock 1973: 73) where the logistics of journalistic practice revolve around organizational factors such as shortage of time, cost constraints and forward planning, as well as the use of routines to structure news work.

Better understanding of the way in which newsmaking was organized indicated that news journalists routinely operate within news 'beats' (as in police beats) to obtain most of their stories: courts, political institutions, the police and large businesses. As news journalists obtain the bulk of their stories from such sources, journalism has been explained as a relationship between journalists and officials, where only particular types of sources (elites or powerful voices) are routinely granted access to the media (Cottle 2003: 15). The social organization of newswork, which prioritizes the use of routines, and the dependency on the professional and routinized norm of objectivity in news reporting which underpin news judgement (Soloski 1989), has reinforced the impression that journalists unconsciously produce news which is supported by values which favour elites in society. However, as we will see in Chapter 5, constraints placed upon journalists may be counterbalanced by journalistic professionalism which traditionally carries with it a degree of scepticism or distrust of individuals who try to force a particular point of view upon them. In principle journalistic agency suggests that action may be independent of constraints, so that journalists may also be able to reject attempts at manipulation by sources or the use of spin.

Problematically, as we will see, changes in the demographics of newsrooms, where older journalists are being replaced with younger or 'rookie' journalists, may undermine the levels of interrogation of sources traditionally associated with the profession. The loss of older, more experienced journalists in some news organizations, particularly at the local level (Ursell 2001, 2003), coupled with a growing number of senior journalists moving into public relations and providing sophisticated press releases which are written in a journalistic style (see Chapter 2 for a discussion of the 5 Ws and How, and the use of the inverted pyramid), is leading to an increased likelihood that the contents will be used rather than challenged by inexperienced journalists (Hargreaves 2003). At the local level in particular, companies are hiring experienced journalists to give them a higher profile and inexperienced journalists view their ability to turn press releases into a piece of copy as a sign of their growing skill. This means that at the local news level, some stories are promoted and shaped by journalists working for non-news organizations. Some researchers question who actually has the most power in the source–journalist relationship. On the one hand, Gans (1979) and Cohen (1963) argue that powerful sources generally have the most control over the story, whereas on the other hand, Hess (1984) has argued that journalists have the most power. Stevenson (2002: 226) advises that we consider the ability of journalists to 'actively intervene' in the news process, as this will reflect the degree of agency they hold, and the extent to which journalists either support or contest dominant ideological values in society.

Journalists therefore operate within a large number of constraints as well as having 'to negotiate demands or attempted use of power or influence' (McQuail 2000: 249). The diversification of news has meant that while traditional large-scale news operations can still be explained in terms of some of the earlier studies, some news programmes, it seems, cannot. Matthews' (2003) study of BBC's *Newsround* programme aimed at children shows how the relationship with the child-based audience has 'become the overriding factor shaping and delimiting the programme's environmental news agenda and presentation' (ibid.: 144). It is likely that other non-mainstream news programmes are increasingly determined by perceptions of the audience, a finding which contradicts early studies such as that by Schlesinger (1978: 106), which refers to the audience as the 'missing link' in the production process. The relationship between the news organization and its audience appears be changing due to further differentiation of news (Harrison 2000), and this is a theme we will return to in Chapter 6.

In contrast to the critical academic study of the news and media, the practitioner view is that the use of objectivity norms and other 'neutral' factors such as the constraints of time, or the practical necessity of layout and design, actually override the ideological intentions of journalists. This is a view that is dismissive of the idea that the bureaucratic organization of newswork produces its own ideology. Practising journalists consequently deride 'media studies', which mainly analyses the products and consumption of journalism and generally finds evidence of bias or stereotyping therein, as being overtly politically correct and misunderstanding the complexities within the practice of journalism (Williams 2003).

Cottle (2003: 17) calls for a conceptual shift from 'routine' to 'practice', by which he means that a sense of journalistic agency should be incorporated into any analysis of news production. He argues – and it is a position which I take into account – that journalists are more knowingly involved in their activities than some of the earlier studies imply. In short, although this book will consider the routinization of journalistic practice in Chapter 5, it will also include throughout a qualified sense of agency, whereby *some* journalists *sometimes* engage in a productive dialogue and interrogation with source material they encounter, and exercise reflective practice. Indeed, as Cottle observes, they are not, as Hall (1982: 82, cited in Cottle 2003: 17) suggests, 'simply "unwittingly, unconsciously" serving "as a support for the reproduction of a dominant ideological discursive field"'.

New media theory

Recently, interest has also turned to a new area of analysis which Williams (2003) refers to as new media theory, as scholars examine the changes which have occurred through the rapid growth of global communications and the development of new technologies. These technologies have allowed people to communicate almost instantaneously around the globe, breaking down the constraints of space/place. An optimistic approach is to argue that a new set of technological coordinates has emerged which have created an information society. Information society constitutes a break with the past, and is driven by information technologies and not by the interests of social class or capitalism (see Bell 1973). For Castells (1997) this has created a global society and a new information age. Two things need to be noted here: the role of technology and the forces of globalization.

First, the view that technology changes society or leads to an information society brings us uncomfortably close to a technological determinist position.[20] A technology-led theory of social change sees technology as the causal factor and often the single or main cause of transformations in society. Taken to an extreme, the entire form of society is seen as being determined by technology, which transforms institutions, social interaction and individuals. Technological determinism therefore focuses on cause-and-effect relationships (see Toffler 1970, 1980; McLuhan 1964); however, in practice it is really difficult to isolate or identify causes and effects in society. In particular we will see that technological change may both push and inhibit the way in which news is gathered, produced, presented and consumed, (Winston 1998: 2). Technological developments such as the printing press, the telegraph and later, analogue and digital transmission systems, which have occurred alongside innovations in news production, selection and presentation, will be considered later in this book. However, it is worth noting here that such developments have had to coexist with wider concerns such as the protection of the core qualities of news: namely the requirement for accuracy and a belief, by regulators, audiences and most journalists in the value of truthfulness. Consequently, the news cannot be seen simply to be a product of technological change, although news producers have undoubtedly harnessed certain technological developments to both produce and disseminate news.

Second, as Dahlgren (1995: 8) indicates, media scholars sometimes employ a 'discourse of globalization' through which they try to understand the tendency towards the growing influence of global news media organizations on international flows of news. There are, however, problems with the idea of globalization as an explanation for the changes occurring in society on a global scale. As a descriptive term, 'globalization' may be used to categorize a range of paradoxical and contradictory changes occurring in the world (Giddens 1999). However, as Rosenberg (2000: 2) points out, while we cannot deny that 'worldwide social relations' exist to an extent which is unprecedented, problems arise when a theory of globalization is invoked to explain these phenomena. As he points out, we finish up in a circular argument where 'globalization as an outcome cannot be explained simply by invoking globalization as a process tending towards that outcome' (ibid.). While the use of the term as a descriptor helps to understand the social processes which have occurred leading to an intensification of global social relations, its use as a theory transforms globalization into an 'explanation for the changing character of the modern world' (ibid.: 3) and is more problematic.

This book uses the term 'globalization' as a description of some of the developments which have occurred, in particular the growth of news media organizations that can disseminate information on a global scale. Two broad issues arise here. First, there is the extent to which large news media organizations (these can be news agencies such as Reuters or news organizations which have international reach such as CNN or the BBC) dominate or shape national news agendas. Second, the growth and development of the internet has meant that news (whether accurate or inaccurate) has instant global reach. Problematically, much of the empirical research undertaken to evaluate the globalization of mediated information concentrates on the amount of media products which enter particular countries, and assumptions about any cultural 'effects' are extrapolated on this basis. Further research needs to be undertaken to understand the degree of cultural resistance to news stories reported and disseminated by organizations or individuals operating outside the control of the recipient nation-state. What does seem clear is that there are differing levels of opposition to the domination of news agendas in different localities which may hamper the development of cultural globalization (Thussu 1998). Furthermore, it is highly problematic to identify what constitutes a particular national or local cultural identity in the first place, so to quantify any particular challenges to it from external influences is complex and time-consuming, since the nature and range of changes, developments and resistances occurring in global communications are complex and varied.

Belief in both the power of globalization and the 'determining effect of technology', however, underpins media policy (Clegg et al. 2003: 39) at the European level, and in Britain. The common strand is the contention that the world is becoming more connected through technological advances and that a revolution is occurring, one which transforms society for the better. Central to this view is the idea that greater connectivity among individuals, companies and nations is forming what is often referred to as cyberspace, and the development of virtual communities and new forums and formats for electronic publishing, communication and commerce. These developments have been seen to comprise an information society, where in theory everyone can create, access, use and share information and knowledge, allowing citizens to achieve their full potential. In the news context these developments have in theory led to new possibilities for audience engagement with the news. The information available in a so-called information society necessarily covers a wide range of themes and topics which contribute to the education and knowledge of citizens, and a number of institutions, including news organizations, contribute to the educational and knowledge base of society. The news (at its best) may therefore be said to contribute a particular type of information to an information society, namely an accurate account of some (not all) contemporary events, through which citizens can become informed about a range of current affairs.

Critics of the optimistic view of technological change point to the domination of information flows by certain voices, and the information gap between the rich and poor nations, as well as information poverty which can exist within national boundaries (Schiller 1996; Norris 2000). From this perspective, there has not been an information revolution. Society has merely become increasingly 'informatized' whereby there is an increase in information in modern society, but this does not constitute a new society, or necessarily a break with the past (Webster 1995: 29). Several researchers have expressed concerns that 'new opportunities for old exploitation' are occurring (Curran and Seaton 2003: 302; Haddon 2000). As the flows of information around the world are hampered by material inequality, which means there is not equal exchange of ideas and information in the global news media environment (Schiller 1989, 1996; Golding 1994), an information gap occurs. There may seem to be more information available, but it is merely being selected, prepared and presented via the old economic and social conditions which have always controlled information flows (Barnett 1997), a process that may reinforce existing social inequalities.

Concerns are also being raised about the impact of competition and commercialization on the news product. Just as technological change becomes intertwined with the growth and development of global news media, so do other vectors of change: commercialization, competition, concentration and commodification. Again, causes and consequences are difficult to identify systematically, although there is broad agreement that something significant is happening. We will see that a divergent range of views are in evidence, with some contending that news is turning into bland 'newszak' (Franklin 1997: 4) through the greater use of entertainment values and 'homogenous "snippets"' (ibid.: 5); entertaining rather than educating (Frost 2002). This is often seen to have deleterious social and political effects. The constant criticism and scrutiny of the coverage of politicians' private lives in a salacious manner, for example, is seen to reduce trust and interest in politics (Fallows 1996).[21] This is a concern also shared by some practitioners: in 2002, the BBC, conscious of its responsibilities as a public service broadcaster and keen to re-engage younger viewers who might have been put off by news' trivialization of politics, undertook a review of its coverage using surveys and focus groups (Kevill 2002a). Whether or not it succeeded is open to question. It may not be the message which is the problem; for the young it could be the medium.

The reported growing interest of young people, who use the informality of internet weblogs or chat rooms in order to discuss and debate political issues which are in the news, perhaps provides an indication of the potential for the development, rather than diminishment, of the political news genre:

> You only have to Google your way through a random selection of weblog-gers – average age well south of 35 – to realize that the younger end of the web is obsessed with the goings-on in Westminster and Washington.
>
> (Carr 2003)[22]

CONCLUSION

Of the above three ways of looking at news – commonsensically, practically and academically – each, for our purposes, has value and limitations. Of value is the way a common-sense approach to news recognizes our immersion in news, the way we attribute it to an explanatory purpose and use it to understand contemporary events. Practitioners' views reveal an unembarrassed attachment to a healthy scepticism about any understanding of news or news production and news journalism which undermines what they regard as their professional (or vocational) worth and autonomy (i.e. the way that news reporting is 'really done'), while academic theories reflect upon the deeper nature and value of news in all of its aspects. The limitations to each approach may be summarized accordingly: common-sense and practitioners' views tend towards a minimalist conception of news, which focuses on what is practised, while academic theories tend towards an abstract conception of news which focuses on the analytic significance of these practices. This is a deliberate caricature in order to make a point, but traditionally we are offered a choice: either in order to understand news we should remain concerned with the way we use news and the way it is produced, or we should step back from this and reflectively reveal the true nature of these activities. Both approaches need to be combined (as I have tried to show in Table 1), since it is clear that there are a number of developments taking place which challenge some of the traditional ways of understanding news.

These challenges centre on: the plethora of new news channels available and the new multi-channel news ecology which now exists; new news formats, different types and styles of news journalism and audience fragmentation and discernment. As to the significance of these challenges there is no consensus. Thus, for example, Norris (2000) has argued that the popularization of news has produced diverse news products which may well benefit audiences, Langer (1998) sees non-traditional news as an opportunity to challenge the dominant views expressed by the establishment, Fiske (1992) has observed that new forms of news may even offer an alternative reality to the established order, potentially bringing greater freedom to individuals, while Barnett (1997) sees the development of new forms of (news) communication as exacerbating social exclusion and reinforcing the existing 'old' media problems discussed above.

However, in order for us to assess these developments we must now turn our attention to and examine the historical origins of the philosophical orientation to news, which I have adopted and which I believe explains news and news journalism today. We will see how technological and political change allowed news producers to overcome the restrictions of place/space and time as news moved from an oral cultural setting to a literate and printing cultural setting.

3

FROM BALLADS TO BROADCASTING

The historical growth and development of news

INTRODUCTION

We can further and more comprehensively understand what the news *is* (as well as what *makes* news) by looking at what news journalists actually do, *when* they started to do it and *why*. While a historical approach is not new (see Cranfield 1962; Harris 1977; Boyce *et al*.1978; McNair 1996; Curran and Seaton 1997; Allan 1999; Rudin and Ibbotson 2002), it still remains valid if we are to have a full account of what news is. By adopting a historical approach I wish to identify how the development of particular habits, precedents, practices, traditions and rituals of journalism enables us to further understand the core values of news and news journalism, and its relationship to accuracy, sincerity, space (here) and time (now).

PRINTING NEWS

For some analysts an historical account of news begins with the origins of humanity and the development of language (Hartley 1988). Human communication of news and information has existed for as long as human beings have lived together, a necessary part of the human battle for survival, as well as for the establishment of some sense of social identity, order and belonging. Interestingly, today there are signs that 'news by word of mouth, may be playing a larger and larger role as more traditional news genres decline' (Hargreaves and Thomas 2002: 5). However, with various technological developments came changes to the ways in which human language has been recorded and distributed, thereby providing communicators and recipients with a greater range of options beyond interpersonal communication.

In preliterate cultures, stories and apocryphal tales would be passed by word of mouth to the next generation, with the likely consequence that anecdotes and memories were gradually modified over time, or as Carpenter (1946: 5) suggests, they were 'retold to suit their narrator and audience' and often referred to conditions which were recognizable and recent. Crisell (1997: 3) reminds us that this early form of communication was 'live' because the senders and receivers had to be within hearing distance or visible. As Allan (1999) notes, the development of writing or the use of pictures helped record keeping, assisting control of the distorting effect of time on the oral reporting of historical events (although it is still possible that different generations could have interpreted signs and pictures differently from their ancestors). The written word eventually became transportable through space when it was carved into stone or wood, and with the development of papyrus, clay, parchment and later paper, which was first used in Britain in the twelfth century.

However, media historians tend to agree and point to the development of the printing press as being the evolutionary event that changed the nature of communication throughout Europe (Thompson 1995), establishing the roots of modern mass communication (Williams 1998). Although movable type was also invented by the Chinese (Allan 1999), and Hargreaves (2003) reminds us that China had official information sheets in the tenth century, it is Johann Gutenberg who is credited with being the inventor of the printing press in Germany in 1457 to 1458. He adapted a wine press using moulded letters to produce multiple copies of the same work (Allan 1999). The first printing press was set up in England by William Caxton in 1476.[1] Printing was not developed primarily for the purposes of news dissemination; indeed, the Gutenberg printing press was used initially to print small Latin textbooks and then the Gutenberg Bible. None the less, the advent of printing is very relevant to our story of the news. McLuhan's (1964: 9) claim that 'the medium is the message' meant that for him it is 'the medium that shapes and controls the scale and form of human association and action', and in this light the Gutenberg printing press had particular significance. McLuhan believed that content is obliterated or subservient to the channel through which it is delivered, implying that what is said is of less importance than the means by which – or how – it is said. This technologically determinist position sees culture and change as determined by the powers and limits of each generation's communication technology.

In this vein McLuhan (1962) argued that a change of consciousness was brought about by the advent of the printed word. The ability to reproduce texts accurately and swiftly led to greater homogeneity and the distribution of single points of view, which could be consumed by many people.

Although many do not agree with McLuhan's view about the extent to which a particular medium affects content, it is undoubtedly the case that news, along with a broad range of other types of communication, is and has always been embedded in the communication technology through which it is disseminated. The relationship that news has had with technology has therefore had particular consequences for its character. Printing allowed identical stories to be reproduced many times and to be disseminated among a greater number of readers; simultaneity of reading the news was uncoupled from the spatial condition of common locality (Thompson 1994), and the dissociation of 'here' and 'now' is very relevant to the way in which the news developed and was consumed. Printed material gradually replaced the handwritten manuscripts, news-sheets and texts already in existence, and the number of books, newspapers, magazines in circulation grew in number. As news and information became increasingly available, the number of people consuming the printed word increased and its value as a commodity was recognized (Thompson 1995). All who were able to read, or to listen to a reading, had access to identical versions. Different views arise about the nature of news content which emerged from these developments. For McLuhan (1964: 18) the result was an inevitable homogenization of content and a blurring of distinctions between the types of messages disseminated, with the consequence that 'the "content" of a medium is like the juicy piece of meat carried by the burglar to distract the watchdog of the mind'. In contrast, Thompson (1994: 33) argues that the significance of the printing press was actually vested in its content which affected 'the social organization of symbolic power'. The significance of printing for Thompson was that it was able to produce and disseminate symbolic forms (in particular the ideas and messages of power holders) throughout society on a previously unprecedented scale. Writing and printing also allowed a distance between the sender and receiver to be established, precipitating the change in communication from being 'live' to being 'lifeless' (Crisell 1997: 3).

Here it is worth considering the differences in the way that news is stored and passed on in oral cultures and in literate and printing cultures. Ong (1982) argues that in an oral culture knowledge is not owned, but performed; furthermore, knowledge or information is stored in the language and memory of the people who pass it on. The telling of the story involving an evaluation of whether an event is actually newsworthy, significant or important was necessarily related to the pre-existing network of knowledge which existed, and was bounded by its limitations and the time within which it was told. As Thompson (1995) observes, a communicative transaction is more durable when it is written down than when it is spoken, so in oral societies it was almost certainly the case that news stories would differ as slightly different accounts were told over time to different people, giving rise to changing versions of any event. In close-knit communities the sincerity of the teller of the news could be assessed and judged and the extent to which the news was a truthful account of events evaluated through cross-checks with other people or eyewitnesses. In this way an important level of trust could be established between the teller and receiver of the news. Distant or remote events could not be known of as they actually happened due to the practical difficulties in transcending the limitations of geography and spatial boundaries. Stories or news from distant places could only be told some time after the event and gathered only by someone who had been outside the immediate locality. This probably entailed relying on the account of a stranger, who also may have been retelling a tale told to him, perhaps reducing the accuracy of the news. Indeed, there is evidence that the telling and retelling of stories in oral fiction led to variations of the same heroic epics, folk-tales and fairy-tales in different locations (Carpenter 1946).

In contrast, literate and printing cultures render the live person-to-person transmission of news largely redundant. Although accounts of live speech or actions are the currency of print news, they are captured in ink and provide one version of a contemporary event which only has a residue of the liveness of the occurrence. As we have already seen, McLuhan (1962) lamented a loss of diversity of live accounts of events once stories became fixed and standardized in print. In a similar vein, Anderson (1983) argued that the production of multiple copies of the same contemporary event meant that the language and way of telling a story was fixed and standardized into a dominant vernacular. Once printed works were circulated beyond the immediate locality in which the event occurred, numerous people could, on the same day, read the same account of a news event which occurred in a place and to people unknown to them. For Anderson, the dissemination of standardized accounts of events helped to fix the boundaries of what he referred to as imagined communities (ibid.). Literate and printing cultures may therefore be said to inaugurate the process of globalizing the transmission and consumption of news by making the live and local nature of a contemporary event less important to its telling. The range for covering events is extended as the time and distance away from that event is compressed. The contemporaneous nature of news is extended through a shift in technical capacity to record the newsworthy.

The extension of news coverage did not happen in a social or political vacuum. The consequences of this new capacity were apparent. Alongside the transformation of news by printing came a concomitant interest in these developments by the politically motivated. At first the news was disseminated by particular elites, and reflected either their world view or what they wished readers to receive. Quite simply the news was, for a time, rooted in the economics and technology of printing. As the first printing presses were generally private and commercial enterprises, the distribution of symbolic forms was commodified, distributed and organized to make a profit, ultimately facilitating the growth of a commercially based system of communication. It was the growth of this commercially based system of communication that made it increasingly difficult for traditional elites to continue to retain control of what was recorded and printed. Religious and political power could be more effectively challenged through the distribution of new views and ideas on an increasing scale. Printing began to move from just reinforcing authority and loyalty, informing citizens about taxes and laws (Sreberny-Mohammadi 1995), to also promoting heterodoxical views.

The development and growth of the printing press encouraged an expansion in print literacy and a reduction in the reliance on face-to-face or image-based communication used in medieval societies (Ong 1982). Throughout the late fifteenth and early to mid-sixteenth century those in positions of power or desirous of influence were increasingly expected to be print literate. Where news is concerned, however, power relations were never a simple matter. As more works were printed, readers were not in thrall to just one authority; they were also able to study a variety of views and opinions, and to use them to form their own ideas. Such study was the precursor to the development of the 'bourgeois public sphere' (Habermas 1989) in eighteenth-century Europe, where individuals assumed a right to discuss their own opinions in public (see Chapter 4), effectively challenging the Church and other authorities (Williams 1998).

PRINTING, REPORTING THE NEWS AND THE CONSTRAINTS OF SPACE AND TIME

Although the development of the printing press is generally seen as challenging the distribution of power and influence by extending the scope and audience for news, the origins of the actual 'newspaper' and the development of news reporting remain contested. Chalaby (1996: 303) argues that 'journalism is an Anglo-American invention', whereas Stephens (1988) argues that journalism was born in the weekly gazettes or journals produced in Venice in the second half of the sixteenth century. Others have traced the origin of journalism (but not newspapers) back to the daily reports of news events which were published by the Romans in manuscript form (Frank 1961). The *Acta Diurna* was in effect a daily gazette published in Rome by the authority of the government during the later times of the republic, and under the empire their publication ended with the relocation of the empire's seat of government and administration to Constantinople. They contained a variety of daily news events, including the activities of the Senate and courts (Franklin 1997). A variety of pamphlets and newsbooks were distributed in the early sixteenth century informing readers about battles and other important events; however, these were not necessarily evidence of news's grounding in a literate culture. Ballads and broadsheets were often *sung* in the streets, acting as the main source of news information for the illiterate lower classes. 'Walking newsmen' were common in major European cities in the sixteenth century and would give people news in exchange for payment, with St Paul's in London being a favourite spot for the disseminators of news in the first half of the seventeenth century (Hoyer 2003: 452). According to Altick (1957: 28, cited in Franklin 1997: 74), ballads were the 'precursors of a later era's sensational newspapers', with graphic tales of executions and disasters providing the main sources of news, sung aloud to audiences.

Not surprisingly, news in this form was not divorced from entertainment where a concern for accuracy was certainly less valued than delight in the theatrical. Indeed, Crisell (1997: 3) refers to this type of exchange of news and information as 'live theatre', noting that the news had a theatrical or dramatic characteristic. A comprehensive picture of the evolution of news is given by Smith (1979: 9–10), who argues that the publication of news developed through four phases in Europe during the seventeenth century. He identifies these phases as, first, the 'relacioun' or single story, often published some time after the event (not so much 'news', as 'olds'); second, a 'coranto'[2] brought together the single 'relaciouns' which were published on a weekly basis; third, a 'diurnall' brought together stories which happened over several consecutive days into a weekly overview, and finally, a 'mercury', where the writer addressed the reader in a personal voice alongside an 'intelligencer', which addressed the reader in a more formal 'journalistic' manner.

Overall, though, it remained the case that the extending range of news, altering the boundaries of space and time and increasing the spread of news, rendered news itself a 'problematic form of knowledge' (Atherton 1999: 48) not easily contained, managed or governed through either geopolitical boundaries or particular orthodoxies. More news meant a diversity of opinion and debate. Furthermore, this was compounded by the fact that printing news about contemporary events at regular intervals led to 'the creation of modern cultural conceptions of information in time' (Conboy 2004: 19). Regular improvements in printing publication dates, the establishment of deadlines, and increasingly effective distribution methods and channels fostered people's expectations as to when they would be able to read (and subsequently comment) about events. The increased availability of news generated 'critical resistance' (ibid.: 20) to particular orthodoxies, as information and knowledge once restricted to a privileged few became linked to the motives of its providers and to the ability of a more general and widespread audience to pay for and consume news. Put simply, publishers understood that producing news-sheets at regular periods of time led to the creation of a market for news. The point now was to maximize that market. With this came a familiar lament. The circulation of printed reports beyond diplomats and other elites 'threatened that privileged economy of communication', leading to 'resentful snobbery in criticisms of printed news from elite circles' (ibid.: 20). This form of criticism has become a recurring theme, and today it is usually accompanied by the mantra that the news is 'dumbing down'. The attack, then as now, focuses on the way the spread of news coverage represents a decline in cultural quality, promotes inaccuracies and is sensationalist (insincere). Indeed, the news was increasingly regarded as such in direct proportion to the numbers of readers, thereby producing the odd proposition that the news is increasingly untrue in accordance with its availability to greater numbers of people or, put another way, that the truthfulness and sincerity of news decreases in direct proportion to its increase in availability to greater numbers of people.

In seventeenth-century Britain news developed as a site of political conflict, where it has remained ever since. The Star Chamber (1632) banned the printing of foreign and domestic news (effectively banning all newspapers and pamphlets), followed by a *Decree Concerning Printing* in 1637 which restricted the number of newspapers to be published in London to twenty (McNair 1996). While the English Civil War (1642–48) saw thousands of news publications and pamphlets emerge with new and radical ideas containing diverse and vociferous challenges to political authority, the 1649 Treason Act made it a capital offence to print criticisms of Parliament (Williams 1998). The Star Chamber was abolished in 1641 and the Treason Act 1649 proved to be 'unworkable' (ibid.: 20). However, Oliver Cromwell reintroduced a strict licensing system for printers in 1655, and in 1662 Charles II introduced a Printing Act which granted a monopoly of news publishing to the *Surveyor of The Imprimery and Printing Presses* and limited the number of master printers to twenty. Both measures effectively reduced the number of books and pamphlets that were published and rendered newspapers 'virtually non-existent' (Cranfield 1962: 2). Gradually though, absolutism (in all its forms) was successfully challenged and replaced with Enlightenment views of economic, political and intellectual freedom. The restoration of the monarchy in England, with its new subservience to parliamentary authority, and later the abolition of censorship prior to publication in 1695, allowed British journalism to begin to develop. The early efforts at printing and press censorship had failed.

The 'news', such as it was during this period, varied in quality. *The London Gazette* began printing in 1665, but although it has been described as an authoritative 'official' newspaper, it contained little political news and certainly did not challenge or criticize the government. Samuel Pepys wryly observed that the paper was 'very pretty, full of newes, and no folly in it'.[3] Britain's first national daily newspaper is generally accepted to be *The Daily Courant* published in 1702 (Hargreaves 2003). While not an 'official' newspaper, endorsed by the authorities, it comprised mainly items taken from other 'official' publications and relied upon stories from Europe (Allan 1999). Interestingly, its British news was taken mainly from the 'official' *London Gazette* (Cranfield 1962: 10). However, despite attempts to maintain political control of news outlets the authorities were thwarted by the use of other media. Those readers in London who could afford it also bought newsletters which were written by professional newswriters who charged a premium price for their handwritten, intellectual and challenging accounts of political life.

Despite attempts to restrict the press and other news publications, the middle classes and bourgeoisie of England, Scotland, France and Germany established informal networks of communication and information exchange in coffee houses (the height of coffee house culture being *circa* 1680–1730), establishing what Habermas (1989) called the 'bourgeois public sphere' (see Chapter 4). During the first half of the eighteenth century, critical literary and political opinions were articulated in newsletters written by professional newswriters who went from coffee house to coffee house and from the Old Bailey to Whitehall, gathering and disseminating news. Crucially, these men also circulated their work to a few large provincial towns. These newsletters gave rise to a source of news which Habermas (1989: 60) argued was 'for the first time established as a generally critical organ of a public engaged in critical political debate: as the fourth estate'. The idea of the fourth estate is important in relation to the role of news in society. Thomas Carlyle (1901: 152) attributed the term to Edmund Burke's observation that 'there were Three Estates in Parliament; but, in the Reporters' Gallery yonder, there sat a Fourth Estate more important than they all'. Between the seventeenth and nineteenth centuries the three estates in Britain were the Church, aristocracy and the House of Commons. Today they are the executive, legislature and judiciary. But what both Burke and Carlyle meant was that the fourth estate is essentially a fourth power (albeit power premised on the freedom of expression) which acts as a counterbalance and check to the other three estates no matter how they are defined. For them a free fourth estate was essential to good government.

However, people living in the provinces in seventeenth-century Britain were only able to hear about the operation of the three estates via *The London Gazette*, personal letters from friends in London and, if lucky, a few handwritten newsletters. The 'vast mass of the population lived on a starvation diet so far as news of the outside world was concerned' (Cranfield 1962: 4). For those eager for news in the provinces and regions, the growth of the provincial press was slow and uneven. When the Printing Act of 1662 expired in 1695 it was possible to print and publish a newspaper without a licence. As newspapers grew in number the 'same' story was told in a variety of ways in different newspapers; thus while printing could be seen to produce homogeneity in the sense that the identical version of the story would be disseminated widely by one newspaper; diversity of accounts nevertheless emerged as different newspapers emphasized different elements of the story. This meant that it became increasingly difficult for the reader to establish an accurate or consistent account of events. Although more news was available, there was less chance for a reader to verify the facts than a listener had in oral cultures. The distance between reader and journalist and the increasing numbers of newspapers and journalists working to different editorial or organizational agendas meant that readers experienced an inability to check a story, or would read the same story but from different perspectives. Combined, they produced a scepticism towards newspapers that still persists. The advent of print and the expansion of newspapers meant that there could be less certainty about how truthful an account might be, or how sincere and accurate it was. In addressing this, coffee houses in London began to take a wider variety of newspapers from which readers could make up their own minds, aided by discussion and debate of different 'informed' viewpoints. Newspaper readers were learning how to read their newspapers by learning how to interpret journalistic accounts of news. A discerning readership began to form that maintained their scepticism as an interpretive filter through which to interrogate different accounts of contemporary events.

As competition increased between the different publications, some printers moved out of London into the larger provincial towns, and at the beginning of the eighteenth century the first provincial newspapers emerged,[4] although the growth of provincial newspapers was uneven. By 1792 fifty provincial newspapers existed in England, but there were only nine in Scotland and none in Wales (Williams 1998), as printers were attracted primarily to areas of prosperity (Cranfield 1962). News was a commodity, printed on a regular basis, in a 'cycle of periodicity' for profit (Conboy 2004: 23). Then, as today, the news media fed off each other, although in the eighteenth century the practice was more transparent and extensive. Weekly papers reprinted news articles from daily papers, and provincial newspapers took their news from a range of London newspapers and newsletters. The provincial printers did not try to provide original news or claim responsibility for what was printed, and the variable quality of the London newspapers meant that the printers 'found it safer, and certainly infinitely easier, to concentrate upon presenting as large a "collection" of items as possible' (Cranfield 1962: 30). This meant that in the provinces the onus was also placed on the reader to try to make sense of the variable accounts and different truth claims which were available (something which the expansion of news forms has made more necessary today). In this way the responsibility for the content remained with the London newspapers and newsletter writers and not the local printers, and audiences had to make up their own minds about the true nature of events. Local papers were therefore not local in content, but deemed provincial only by virtue of their being printed in a particular region.

The ability to send news to the regions using improved methods of transport and the postal service meant that the constraints of space and time were managed by printers who, with their practical concerns for 'getting the paper out', set precedents for news production which still exist today. News production in the regions was particularly limited by the constraints of technology. Printing technology of the eighteenth century had evolved little since the Caxton hand-press which meant that production was slow, since only two men could work at the press at once and technological restrictions affected the layout of the paper, its size as well as the number of copies printed and its distribution range.[5]

In the provinces, newspapers were generally only produced on a weekly basis due to the labour-intensive and slow nature of production; therefore the 'cycle of periodicity' (Conboy 2004: 23) was largely beyond the printers' control. London newspapers were brought to the provinces via three postal deliveries per week. Printers had to organize their newspaper layout to manage the flow of news from London, a problem which grew once postal deliveries were made daily. Printers had less and less time to organize the flow of news and to ensure that their newspaper contained all the latest news and information from the capital (Cranfield 1962: 32–34). A familiar feature of news production which developed was the management of time and space pressures alongside the desire to get last-minute news published (elements of practice which underpin news journalism today). The solution then was to reserve space in the newspaper for the last post (a sensible and pragmatic way of ensuring maximum contemporaneity). Even today, newspaper production planning and logistics builds in the capacity to adjust an edition swiftly to accommodate events which have just happened (see Chapter 5).

The shortage of space available for news and the need to produce news to fit into a restricted space had become problematic when the Stamp Act of 1712 levied, among other things, a tax on paper, which became known as a 'tax on knowledge'[6] (Allan 1997: 299; Williams 1998: 25). In order to get around taxes levied on page size, printers exploited a loophole in the Stamp Act, which had not given any official definitions of the size of the sheet to be taxed. Printers changed the size of their newspapers, reducing them from one and a half sheets to a half sheet of much larger paper which could be folded down the middle, marking the origins of the broadsheet (ibid.: 26). This produced a piece of paper which provided nearly as much space as that used before the Stamp Act, but reduced the tax payable on it.

The management of space was also crucial for the development of advertising in the press. Although many newspapers had not used advertising to great effect, they began in the early 1700s to realize its value as a means of funding and profit. Indeed, so too did the government, and the 1712 Stamp Act levied a duty of one shilling on every advertisement, regardless of its length (Cranfield 1962). To save space for news, but retain income from advertising, the print for advertisements was made smaller than that for news (ibid.). Advertising revenue survived a further Stamp Act in 1757, which doubled the stamp duty to two shillings per advert. Gradually newspaper page size grew and typesize became smaller. Towards the end of the eighteenth century, with taxation offset by advertising revenue, the number of pages increased and more news, information, gossip, opinion and advertising could be included in newspapers (Curran and Seaton 1997). As the demographics of readership changed, advertisements targeted more ordinary everyday aspects of life, rather than concentrating on property and luxury goods (Cranfield 1962). More and more readers could now be 'sold' to advertisers as potential customers, which meant that increasingly the production of local newspapers could grow and develop as viable business concerns. Local news no longer needed to be a derivative of national news exported to the regions from the capital, but had its own local characteristics and integrity. Local news could originate from and be sold within a particular region. Defined by geography and history, regional concerns began to help shape local news values, journalistic selection and explanation of contemporary events. The constraint of space had, in effect, moved from the size of the newspaper to the geographical area the newspaper served. In this way the regional news media become identifiable via their location which defined their relationship with readers and advertisers.

While news was able to become more local in focus and orientation, it was also able to travel further and faster than ever before. In short, it could be more international in scale. The invention of the electromagnetic telegraph in America by Samuel F. B. Morse in 1835[7] eventually allowed information to be sent via electric cables over land and, via sea bed cables, across oceans. The system was used by the news agency Associated Press, which had operators dedicated to news dispatches. For the first time news could be sent across land and sea faster than by any other means of transport available at the time. By the mid-nineteenth century news had entered a new era, one which reinvigorated the interest in ability to achieve an 'almost now' in the reporting of distant news events. Printing, alongside the telegraph and telephone, allowed the news to have extended availability, both on a local and a global scale. Innovations such as Koenig's steam press (1814) and the rotary press (1848) speeded up the printing process even further, allowing a larger number of copies to be produced, expanding the availability of news to greater numbers of people. As technology facilitated printing's ability to reproduce, the focus of the news was increasingly steered towards the commercial advantages to be gained in the pursuit of a large readership and the growth of the newspaper industry. News was also becoming more 'almost now' than ever before. The range of contemporary events which could be covered was extended as the time and distance from events became compressed.

The management of space and time was taking place in an enhanced fashion and rendering a new range of events 'reportable' and, as such, newsworthy. The development of printing created a new degree of 'space–time distanciation' (Thompson 1995: 21). The increasing separation of news events from news production coincided with the increasing separation of events from their location. Time was now managed via the adaptiveness of the production process and the frequency of publication, while space was managed according to a specific editorial and news remit (for example, local or global). Furthermore, it was printing that allowed information or news to be fixed and stored in manageable forms, thereby facilitating archives and the capacity to check events against other events for greater accuracy. In short, it was printing more than anything else that permitted the modern news system to emerge from the constraints of space and time.

THE EXPANSION OF NEWSPAPERS

During the eighteenth and early nineteenth centuries, newspapers continued to develop and diversify and to appeal to different readerships. *The Times*, which cost seven pence, was a 'serious' paper, restricting its readership to the educated elite, an image it retained until it was taken over by Rupert Murdoch in 1981. *The Times*, originally called *The Daily Universal Register*, was established in 1788. It focused on overseas news, dramatic occurrences in the British Empire, and pioneered the nationwide reporting of home news. Its output was very strongly editorialized, gaining it a reputation as '*The Thunderer*' (Williams 1957: 7).[8] The first tranche of the so-called radical press emerged in Britain in the late 1790s. Whereas the middle-class papers defended bourgeois interests and values, the radical press was particularly concerned with the rights of the lower classes. Neither types of papers reported news impartially. In particular the radical press saw itself as engaged in a political struggle. Consequently the news it selected and reported reflected its political bias. News stories would articulate class conflict (for example, reporting the actions of patrons in boroughs who controlled voting rights, or the unfair treatment of the working class by the aristocracy and the bourgeoisie). Indeed, the dissemination of news and information was seen by those fighting for radical reform to be of fundamental importance to their cause.

Suspicious of the types of education provided by the state, the radical reformers sought new ways to promote educational opportunities. The radical press, closely linked with the Chartist Movement (1836–1848), offered a news mix that included educational content such as notices of lectures, criticisms of schools and schoolmasters, and demands for social reform for the working classes. Funded in a variety of ways by the developing trade unions and other political activists, the radical press began to try to erode the working classes' acceptance of the existing social system by encouraging their political mobilization. Papers such as *The Twopenny Dispatch* took a campaigning stand and actively called for radical social change. At a cover price of only one or two pence, some of these papers achieved high sales.[9] For some, the expense of a radical newspaper was often shared, with one paper being read aloud to a semi-literate and illiterate audience. Readers and listeners who co-joined in this way increased the number of people who could be influenced by a news article.

The importance of print news in the struggle between first the ruling classes and the bourgeoisie and later between the working classes and the bourgeoisie was rooted in the nature of the medium itself. The printed word offered a very flexible and effective means to circulate views and information. Radical ideas could be easily disseminated across the country from town to town and newspapers could be read again and again, or read aloud to illiterate members of the community. Sedition became a common charge levelled against the radical press, and repeated attempts were made by the state to control news print through a variety of laws and taxes.[10] The laws of seditious libel evolved in colonial America. In 1671, Sir William Berkeley, Governor of Virginia, had echoed British sentiments about the control of news and information when he thanked God that 'we do not have free schools nor printing' (Mott 1949: 6, quoted in Cranfield 1962: 4). During the eighteenth century it was the case that 'a printer could be jailed for publishing the proceedings of the South Carolina legislature' (Page 2003: 14). However, as Hargreaves (2003) reminds us, writers such as Thomas Paine began to express their ideas in pamphlet form. Paine's case for American independence from British rule, entitled *Common Sense*, was published in 1776, fifteen years before the Bill of Rights (the first ten amendments to the Constitution) went into effect on 15 December 1791. Yet in contrast to the British press, the American press was directly linked to the right of free expression in statute. The American Constitution which was written in 1787 contained the First Amendment, which ensured that American journalists are able to select and report news stories free from constraints on their freedom of speech; in particular they are protected from governmental interference with their freedom of expression rights. The authors of the American political system believed that a free society could not exist without a free press (see Chapter 4).

The achievement of press freedom in Britain is often associated with changes in taxation, the repeal of the so-called 'taxes on knowledge' (Allan 1997: 299; Williams 1998: 25). The period 1853 to 1861 saw the abolition of advertisement duty in 1853, stamp duty in 1855 and paper duty in 1861. Yet Curran and Seaton (1997: 26) view the repeal of these taxes as a strategy of social control where 'the ruthless repression of the unstamped press in the mid-1830s had much the same impact as the campaign which set the press "free" 20 years later: the subordination of the press to the social order'. The press taxes were eventually repealed, not to encourage the radical press to flourish once again, but to allow the growth of the popular capitalist press. It was a press that promoted the values of capitalism and aimed at a wide readership, including the increasingly literate working class, through news and entertainment. Paradoxically it was also a press committed to its own freedom from official restraint. In fact it was as committed to press freedom as the radical press. Both believed in the principles of self-regulation. The impetus for the capitalist press to be free to promote its political agenda, prioritize the accumulation of profit and amass large readerships is distinct from the liberal pluralist view that the press should be free to act as a fourth estate and serve the public interest, but results in the same conclusion. Both agree that statutory regulatory controls would undermine their freedom.

NEWS, ENTERTAINMENT AND THE COMMERCIALIZATION OF THE PRESS

Today, the growth of cheap popular newspapers is criticized for both encouraging untruthfulness and speaking to the reader as someone who should be entertained rather than engaged. This criticism seems to regard the 'commercialization of news' as a recent development. In 1695 the expiry of the Printing Act caused a flurry of competition and the type of news which was published often pandered to the salacious appetites of the readership (Cranfield 1962). Although the eighteenth-century provincial newspaper may look different from today's regional news-paper, Cranfield (1962: 65) makes the point that the content has remained similar, since the 'tastes of its readers have scarcely altered at all. Then, as now, blood and sex reigned supreme in the pages of the popular press,' although the 'blood was preferably foreign blood, poured into fruitless battles against the might of English arms' (ibid.). Consequently, the provincial papers, which fed upon news from the London and overseas papers, were prepared to pander to public appetites for stories about low life, sex, blood, mass slaughter and the scandalous activities of elite families.[11]

The lack of coverage of local issues in favour of London-based news and information meant that those in the provinces were better placed to understand the impact of central government policies on their own industries and businesses. The diversity of tastes fed by the provincial press is shown by the development of three types of newspapers around 1720, which Cranfield (1962: 101) identifies as: those which contained news only, and only rarely printed letters or essays (for example, *The Derby Mercury* and *The Kentish Post*); those which contained a large proportion of literary content (for example, *The Northampton Mercury* and *The Leeds Mercury*), and those which were political newspapers (for example, *The York Courant* and *The Stamford Mercury*), which would not include lighter news or entertainment news. These were followed later by a fourth type of paper: the trade newspaper. However, by 1720 many papers began to provide more entertainment for their readers, a condition which has continued and in part has underpinned the nature and content of both the national and regional popular press.

As the cost of publishing soared and the running costs of news organizations rose, the need continually to increase readership was vital. New technology was purchased and more staff employed. Even though the repeal of advertising tax allowed popular press advertising to flourish, only very wealthy owners could afford to meet the high costs of newspaper production and to participate in competitive cover price cuts. Not surprisingly then, newspapers increasingly came to be owned by the so-called wealthy 'press barons', such as Alfred Harmsworth (who later became Lord Northcliffe) and his brother Harold (who later became Lord Rothermere). The former is generally viewed as the originator of popular mass-circulation journalism in Britain (Franklin 1997). Via his *Daily Mail* (1896) and *The Daily Mirror* in 1903, Northcliffe in particular proved to be extremely successful at providing new editorial content and a presentation style which appealed to a mass readership, maximizing advertising revenue, introducing new technologies, rethinking distribution (Page 2003) and adopting an alertness to new trends in journalism (Chisholm and Davie 1993). As such, he, perhaps more than anyone, helped to define popular news agendas.

In concert with the popular press in Britain, the penny press grew rapidly in America. In these papers the human interest story was central with political news marginalized, reduced to very small items, or reported in a way that would attract popular interest (Schudson 1978). Papers such as *The New York Herald* in 1864 'reported not only murders – while other papers were still publishing only court reports, [James Gordon Bennett the founder of the Herald] went to the scene of the crime and described the corpses' (Chisholm and Davie 1993: 100). In common with the British popular press, the American penny press 'spoke' directly to the people, arguably offering a new and 'different type of access to the public sphere, since they were able to declare a greater degree of political independence from government and party' (Allan 1997: 304). They also blurred the line between private and public life (ibid.; Schudson 1978; Schiller 1981) by concentrating on stories which were of domestic or personal concern. Large circulations were the goal, and competition for readers encouraged story presentation to become increasingly dramatic, with larger headlines and more space given to finance, sport, interviews and the description of personalities. According to Chisholm and Davie (1993: 102), this American or 'new journalism' was imported into Britain by C. Arthur Pearson, the founder of *The Daily Express* in direct competition to Northcliffe's *Daily Mail*. What now counted as news included accounts of events whose inclusion in a paper was designed to increase circulation. In short, entertaining the reader adopted the title of news,[12] a development that rather surprisingly was to raise rather than diminish standards of news journalism.

THE DEVELOPMENT OF PROFESSIONAL PRACTICES IN PRINT NEWS REPORTING

Just as the commercial press evolved, so too did news journalism. The focusing on items by the popular press which had relevance to the everyday lives of the readers meant that the professional practice of contacting sources of news such as the police, courts, local enterprises and religious institutions, and following the activities of the elite, became part of the routine of journalism. This practice has since been described as trawling the 'news net' (Tuchman 1978) or pursuing 'the news beat' (Fishman 1980), the mechanisms of which we will examine more closely in Chapter 5. The 'popular' approach to reporting the news sold a high number of newspapers through 'connecting' with the ordinary person and became established as part of the professional rationale of journalism.

News journalism was further defined by the development of impartial reporting in the nineteenth century (Chalaby 1996), particularly in America with the rise of the penny press (see also Allan 1997). In the early nineteenth century in Britain and America, journalists working for the so-called 'respectable press' (usually defined as the serious press) usually reported in a biased and partisan manner while favouring or supporting particular political parties. Correspondingly, the radical press used their accounts of events to further their social and political agenda. However, as Allan (1999) notes, the growth in attachment to reporting facts rather than editorial explanation developed alongside the increased tendency of editors to serve the popular interests of a particular section of the public. In England and America, impartial news reporting produced a specialized form of journalistic discourse or writing which sought to separate fact from opinion. It attempted to do so by employing a particular formula known as the inverted pyramid.

The 'inverted pyramid' is a framework used by journalists for organizing stories, and is one of the simplest and most common story-structuring devices in journalistic practice. As its name suggests, it is based upon an upside-down triangle where the narrow tip points downward and the broad base points upward. The broad part of the triangle represents the most newsworthy information in the news story, and the narrow tip represents the least newsworthy information in the news story. When journalists write stories using the inverted pyramid format they put the most newsworthy information at the beginning of the story and the least newsworthy information at the end, a technique which allows sub-editors or editors to cut a story without needing to rewrite it (Ward 1995). However, Pottker (2003) suggests that historically this writing style was and still is used by journalists to make their story more 'neutral' and therefore impartial. He argues that it teaches journalists to begin their story with a lead sentence that has to answer four or five 'W' questions, a formula which is still used and taught today. Harcup (2004: 2) refers to journalism as 'a form of communication based on asking and answering the questions: Who? What? Where? When? Why? And How?' The answers to those questions structure the way the story is written (the priorities of newsworthiness and news judgement) as well as ensuring that facts, figures and accurate description are included. By using this technique, journalists believe themselves to be more likely to produce an accurate and impartial account of events, and as a style guide for aiming at accuracy it clearly has great benefits.

The exact date, its origin and the precise reasons for the development of the inverted pyramid style (and therefore the explicit ambition to be impartial) are contested. Pottker (2003) summarizes four competing explanations. The first explanation adopted by some press historians (McNair 1996; Allan 1997, 1999; Noelle-Neumann et al. 1989, cited in Pottker 2003: 503) argues that technological change in the form of the introduction of the electronic telegraph in the 1840s produced situations in which the whole message did not always get through, and this prompted reporters to prioritize the most important news in the lead sentence while giving the less important news in the body of the message. The second explanation attributes the inverted pyramid to politicians attempting to steer public opinion through the release of official bulletins during the American Civil War which were reported verbatim by the press. Interestingly, Schudson (2002) argues the opposite. He sees the inverted pyramid style as a journalistic tool, which was actually used to contest and restructure the politicians' official bulletins according to what the journalist decided were the main points, rather than simply reporting them verbatim. The third explanation places the adoption of the inverted pyramid style of reporting after the 1880s with the development of mass literacy, which itself led to a change in public and journalistic expectations about the skills of journalists. Other writers such as Schiller (1981) prefer to link the growing desire to achieve journalistic impartiality to the increasing belief in rationalism and realism. Here it is argued that the growth of scientific knowledge challenged a romantic world which merely reflected and described human subjectivity; an intellectual milieu buttressed by rationalism, realism and science supported the view that it is possible to report a knowable and objective world impartially by adopting professional methods and techniques. Finally, the fourth explanation for the use of the inverted pyramid style of reporting relates to the competitive and economic advantages to be gained from a concise or 'hard' style of news reporting, particularly financial information which could be traded via the newly developing news agencies such as Reuters.

As well as competing with each other, all four explanations are judged to be historically unsound (Winseck 1999; Schudson 2002) because, as Pottker (2003) notes, the use of the inverted pyramid in newswriting (along with changes in layout, use of pictures and photographs and the sorting of news into subject categories) may well be motivated by the desire to find and develop better methods for selling news as a product, by making it more interesting and accessible to the reader. In this light, technological, political or cultural explanations appear secondary and, given the current news ecology (discussed in Chapter 3), Pottker's argument does seem convincing. It seems more likely that the development of a particular news style is to be found within the evolving world of journalistic practice rather than outside it. This is not to diminish the impact of technological, political or cultural forces at work on the news producer or news organization, but it is to say that style is an adaptive response that occurs in the context of the evolution of a profession. Indeed, where getting to 'know' readers or taking a 'reader-centred approach' is an imperative, then news reporting will attempt to engage the cultural and political world view of those readers as a matter of effectively communicating with them. Historically, such a reader-centred approach helped to increase the popularity of the press and contributed to the growth and expansion of newsprint. Occasionally the use of an impartial style backfires, as in the case of reporting unpalatable truths, 'failing to take our side' or being too detached. Impartiality in news reporting was, and continues to be, seen by most journalists and regulators as a 'good thing'. It is held that the reporting of facts without evaluative comment provides a fairer and more trustworthy account of contemporary events. However, as we shall see in Chapter 4, the professional goal of achieving impartiality in news reporting has raised concerns from academics about news journalists' belief in their ability to remove subjective judgements from news reports.

The principles of journalism which require the separation of news from comment and the organization of the news into the lead sentence containing the most important element, followed by the body of the story, is predominantly Anglo-American, and exhibits significant differences from the French Press (Chalaby 1996). The modern concept of news selection and production was developed by the Anglo-American press on the basis of a particular and agreed way of collecting and reporting information, and spread through other parts of Europe.[13] Chalaby argues that Anglo-American newspapers contained more and better information and news (they had more pages than French newspapers), were more accurate, were better organized in terms of news- and information-gathering (via a network of their own correspondents and the use of news agencies, such as the Associated Press in America and Reuters in England), and were able to access and print more up-to-date information. Anglo-American news was based on 'proper journalistic discursive practices, such as interviewing and reporting' (ibid.: 305) and was more international than French newspapers (ibid.). However, Gaunt (1990: 28) argues that the French press was (and still is) more of a 'journalism of expression than a journalism of observation', a bearing which still distinguishes it from the Anglo-American 'impartial' approach to news reporting. The French journalist in this framework of news is more of a 'commentator' than a 'reporter', producing 'reflective and critical analysis rather than active news gathering' (ibid.: 29).

Historically, news organizations have been somewhat double-edged in relation to their primary goals and purposes (Lee 1976), and this has had a consequence for the type of news which is selected and the way it is produced. Are newspapers primarily the arbiters of free expression (indeed, we have seen that the press has engaged in a political struggle against control of content through censorship), or are newspapers primarily a business or an industry (we have seen how the press underwent an economic struggle against taxes designed to restrict ownership and readership of the press, with a few emerging as profitable enterprises)? Such questions are not easy to answer, particularly when historians (e.g. Asquith 1978) argue that editorial freedom and the ability to have economic independence are both linked to the expansion of advertising from the mid-eighteenth century. Pottker (2003: 510) argues that it is important to recognize that 'mercantile interests and the [press] journalistic ethos are not diametrically opposed, but share (at least partly) the same aims', namely to reach as many readers as possible by the most effective and efficient means possible. As we have seen, Curran and Seaton (1997) argue that while advertising may be viewed as contributing to press independence, the operation of the press within a market system actually reduces press freedom in the sense that the press must work within a capitalist system meeting the demands of a competitive market.

To conclude, we can note that print news journalism from the eighteenth century onwards was increasingly underpinned by a necessary balancing of conflicting pressures, as well as a need to overcome a range of logistical problems. This is reflected in the mediated news itself. Control of the production of news has been achieved through pragmatic and expedient developments in presentation practices. These include changes in newspaper styles and shape; the range and type of news content made available to the public; acceptance of time and space constraints and the establishment of accepted ways of telling a news story. On top of all these was the adoption of accuracy, and the pursuit of accuracy and impartiality as tenets of professional practice when reporting news (which in the Anglo-American-influenced press sit alongside comment, features and partisan viewpoints).

A diversification of news styles has also been evident from the early eighteenth century. Newspapers have long provided different types of news for different readers, variously informing, educating and entertaining. They do so in order to maximize the number of their readers, a tactic shared with today's global corporations (see Chapter 3). At the same time the character of news was further shaped by the concentration of press ownership and the corresponding increase and diversity of press output. Thus we have seen the tendency of the news media to feed off each other, established in the eighteenth century, with competition for advertising revenue and audiences culminating in a diverse range of titles owned by fewer and fewer proprietors from the nineteenth century.

THE DEVELOPMENT OF BROADCAST NEWS

In the nineteenth century technological developments continued to transform the character of news presentation, and none more so than the camera. The development of photography reinforced the proprietors' and journalists' claim to greater accuracy and impartial reporting. The camera was initially taken by many to be an entirely neutral extension of human vision, like the microscope and the telescope (Jenks 1995), and as such an entirely neutral medium. Consequently news photography was seen as offering support for a particular news account. It was not seen as an extension of news reporting, rather an adjunct. Its contribution to accuracy and impartiality was recognized by the perceived limits of still photography itself, namely that photographs are 'fixed images of reality' which are 'lifeless' (Crisell 1997: 4) but which have the capacity to support a news account. In contrast the development of cinematography and then phonography did not fit well with the tradition of print news. They seemed capable of completely transforming news journalism. They offered first pictures and then sound, establishing what Crisell refers to as a quasi-live medium, introducing an unprecedented level of immediacy and drama into news reporting. Throughout the twentieth century, wireless[14] and television technology continued to raise the level of immediacy and drama to the point where they became defining characteristics of television news journalism.

Although the development of wireless and later television technology was a competitive international process, the broadcasting organizations which were eventually set up to transmit content using these new technologies were national organizations reflecting national concerns (Briggs 1961; Scannell and Cardiff 1991). Broadcast news was subsequently shaped through these national organizations and their particular culture (Harrison 2000). To understand the impact of these technologies on news it is worth briefly considering the British experience.

From the start wireless technology was viewed as a 'public utility,' part of the state communications system and therefore subject to state control. In Britain the Wireless Telegraphy Act 1904 was passed to give the Postmaster General the power to license the operation of wireless telegraphy stations. In 1922 the British Post Office received almost one hundred applications to broadcast, raising fears that the control of the airwaves could not be maintained. The problem was addressed through the formation of one large private organization, the British Broadcasting Company, from a consortium of private companies. However, concerns about the special nature of broadcasting and the influence it might have on the listener or viewer, namely the social and moral impact of broadcast content were reflected in the view that broadcasting could not simply be left to market forces. The British Broadcasting Corporation (BBC)[15] was a monopoly,[16] licence fee-funded organization, charged with a social responsibility, broadcasting free-to-air at the point of reception, universally available throughout the country, and in theory free of government control (Crisell 1997). The BBC's role was to uphold the 'highest standards of social and cultural life [and] its journalism would be put to the service of British democracy, informing audiences about public affairs' (McNair 1996: 68). As the idea of public service broadcasting evolved, so a public service news agenda was also evolving.

It was not until the Television Act 1954 that commercial television was introduced to Britain, becoming known as the Independent Television system (ITV). ITV could, unlike the BBC, but in common with the press, take advertising. Like the press it kept news and editorial material completely separate from advertising copy. The ITV system was from the start, and still is, governed by a regulator.[17] The news agenda that emerged from independent television was different from the BBC's. ITV was not remitted (from its inception) to follow the established BBC model (although it had some public service obligations), and its news provider, Independent Television News (ITN), was more influenced by the style of American news programmes.

The history of the establishment of the BBC and ITV allows us to define two broad phases or distinct periods of broadcast news in Britain: (1) 1926 to 1955; (2) 1955 to 1979. The third phase, 1979 to the present day, I shall deal with in Chapter 3.

Broadcast news 1926 to 1955

This period is often described as an era of 'monopoly' broadcast power during which the BBC alone innovated and then established its news formats, style and programmes. Although the 1927 Charter had given the BBC the right to establish a news service, owners of the press, well aware of the commercial value of the news, proved to be antagonistic competitors, fearing for their livelihood and lobbying successfully for statutory restrictions on the amount of news which could be broadcast. Furthermore, news agencies such as Reuters owned the copyright on the copy that was broadcast, resulting in sedate bulletins that could not be enhanced by the type of interviews or actuality which would be taken for granted in a radio bulletin today. The BBC did not secure from Reuters the freedom to edit and write its own bulletins until 1930, and consequently had to wait until then to try to turn what was ostensibly text-based information into a form that was suitable for the radio medium (Crisell 1997).

Writing for the listeners' ears rather than the readers' eyes proved to be a major challenge, as the 'Reuters material was still written in involved, cumbersome and flowery journalese' (Scannell and Cardiff 1991: 116). While the style of radio news was adapted into items written as briefly and simply as possible, the translation of complex concepts into radio news was sometimes beyond the journalists. In fact, the problem became so acute that on Good Friday 1930, the announcer declared 'there is no news tonight' (ibid.: 118). In 1934 the BBC's infant news service was removed from the Department of Talks and a separate News Section was formed (Crisell 1997), helping eventually to elevate the status of news within the BBC. The development of portable sound recorders meant that radio news journalists could go out of the building and record 'live' sounds and interviews to be played back later. The importance of live sounds was emphasized during the fire at Crystal Palace in 1936 when Richard Dimbleby telephoned a live report with shouts, fire bells and the sound of roaring flames as background noise (Briggs 1961), a technique which is taken for granted today. Broadcasting, through its ability to transmit live sounds and later pictures, was able to reinvent the relationship between the news and its audience. News once again attained the currency of liveness and immediacy common to oral cultures, which had been lost in the print medium and was able to transmit events live beyond the locality in which they occurred. This liveness added to the excitement of the news items, as well as making them seem more realistic and truthful. For the print medium this offered unprecedented competition and a threat to their previously unique position as news disseminators.

During the Second World War BBC radio became increasingly important and its reputation grew at home and overseas, with the BBC's radio news service having a remit 'to provide an extensive and credible news service' (Crisell 1997: 53–54). It was also used to transmit messages about the forthcoming D-Day invasion of 6 June 1944 to the Resistance Movement in France. Such strong reliance on the radio for news in Britain meant that by the end of the war BBC radio had become a vital part of British culture and was a very important national institution. Seen by some as an arbiter of good taste and standards, the BBC is generally believed to have held the public's trust and was perceived as the authority on many subjects. In contrast, television news failed to flourish and develop at this time, since BBC television itself remained underfunded and undervalued. At ten o'clock in the morning on 1 September 1939 the engineer in charge of transmitters received a message that they must be closed down by noon. There was no closing announcement made and BBC television went off-air until after the war. Despite the importance of BBC radio news during the war, by 1951 many in post-war Britain were critical of the BBC monopoly. Criticism was levelled at its elitist and paternalistic approach to broadcasting which was still based on the strict moral and religious values of its founding Director General John Reith.

The result of Reith's tenure had been a type of broadcast content which came to be seen as being increasingly old-fashioned, paternalistic and prudish (Briggs 1961). There was a general mood which favoured the introduction of commercial television and the promise of competition, although this was challenged by those who believed it would result in an inevitable decline in news standards. Frustration with the BBC's approach to broadcast content was increased due to technological developments which had opened up the possibilities for more services. Britain was beginning to enjoy a post-war boom with full employment and high productivity. As average earnings rose, people had more money for leisure pursuits and television became the chief agency of domestic recreation, and was linked increasingly to the idea of entertainment and relaxation. News programming was therefore simply one element of a broadcasting schedule which comprised entertainment, drama, variety programming and so on. Today, broadcast news has to coexist in a largely entertainment-oriented medium which has entailed, over the years, the gradual adoption of a more entertaining and engaging type of news programming.

Broadcast news 1955 to 1979

Colin Seymour-Ure (1991) describes the introduction of a second television network in 1955 as challenging the public service principle, because it broke the monopoly of the BBC and questioned the prestige of BBC radio, as well as the BBC's infant television service. The inception of the ITV sector was accompanied by the formation of a separate news provider, ITN. ITN was jointly owned by all the new independent television news channels and was nominated the sole news provider. The ITV companies poured money into ITN in exchange for news provision. The introduction of ITN as a competitor to the BBC in the mid-1950s eventually led to a period of innovation in BBC news programming (Cox 1995). Initially, though, the BBC was slow to understand the power of visual images, showing greater confidence with radio broadcasting. The BBC's catch-all department 'Television Talks' was illustrative of the preference for broadcasting the spoken word rather than pictures, meaning that its television news was presented in a manner more appropriate to radio (Hood 1975). Between 1946 and 1954, the BBC had not broadcast anything that would today be recognized as television news, simply a late evening broadcast of radio news read over a picture of Big Ben (Crisell 1997). In contrast, ITN used new unorthodox techniques to distinguish itself from the BBC, encouraging the personality of the newsreaders and correspondents to be developed. ITN's slogan was 'See it Happen on ITN' (Cox 1995: 65), and it used probing interviews and live broadcasting in a bid to bring the news to the audience in a more effective manner. In this way it challenged the rather deferential approach of the BBC to politicians and the establishment, and challenged restrictions on the coverage of controversial issues and elections (Rudin and Ibbotson 2002).

The effect of ITN on the way news was broadcast was significant. Indeed, Crisell (1997: 92) observes that 'independent television's greatest contribution to the history of broadcasting was to make TV news into something truly telegenic'. In June 1955 the BBC changed the title of its main news from *News and Newsreel* to *TV News Bulletin* and placed newsreaders before the cameras, although it took another fifteen months before the public were informed of their names (Cox 1995). The reluctance to update the BBC's television news output has been attributed to the BBC's head of news at the time. Tahu Hole was appalled by the 'tainting' of news by the personality of a newsreader (Crisell 1997: 92); until then, news had supposedly been neutral, detached and invisible. The appointment of Stuart Hood as head of news in 1958 heralded a new era in BBC news. Hood appointed a team of presenters who could compete with the now familiar ITN team. Major events such as the Cuban missile crisis of 1962 began to establish television as the news medium to which most people turned in times of crisis, as they became increasingly reliant on the pictures and sense of immediacy which only television news could offer.

While BBC television began to flourish in the 1960s in the era of the so-called 'benign duopoly' (BBC and ITV competitively, but peacefully, coexisting), BBC radio was under siege from pirate radio stations (radio companies operating without a licence to broadcast) such as Radio Caroline, which illegally broadcast pop music and critical and irreverent remarks about the Prime Minister from a ship in the North Sea. Although the BBC had faced down competition from pirate radio stations Luxembourg and Normandy in the 1930s, the BBC of the 1960s reacted to the competition more positively, using it as a catalyst to enter a new age of BBC radio broadcasting which took more notice of the wishes of the audience.[18]

Independent local radio (also called commercial radio) was launched in 1973 with its news provided by Independent Radio News (IRN)[19] which began broadcasting on the same day. Since its launch, IRN has continued to provide a twenty-four-hour service of national and international news. Originally the commercial radio stations paid for the news they received, but in 1987, the payments were replaced by six advertising spots which are 'owned' by IRN, which sells them to advertisers. News distribution was converted to satellite in 1989, making IRN far more efficient and profitable. The company was even able to return cash payments to the stations. IRN commissions most of its operations from outside the organization, paying ITN to provide news. IRN's success in the radio news marketplace shows how news can be successfully sold as a commodity, where international and national news can be packaged and repackaged to meet the demands of a news subscriber. IRN capitalizes on the commodification of its news to appeal to various radio markets, based on a radio station's ability to know its own audience accurately.

Following the development of commercial radio, a secondary broadcasting system was offered via the television medium in 1974. Teletext allowed the viewer to access continuously updated news and information presented in text with some graphics. The BBC offered CEEFAX, which literally meant 'see facts', and the ITV sector offered ORACLE (Optical Reception of Announcements by Coded Line Electronics). Teletext technology signalled an important development in the history of broadcast news, namely the ability of viewers to leave live broadcasting and access news at a time which suited them (see the Annan Report 1977). It also meant that news journalists had to learn new ways of presenting stories to the television audience in text form. For news providers text-based news on television presented a new challenge – how to present written news on what is primarily a moving image medium. This problem of restriction of space, or no room for pictures, has meant that new ways of writing news in a telegraphic and succinct style was developed. Today, those writing (or re-purposing) broadcast news for interactive text-based television, mobile phones and the internet have had to learn new ways of presenting the same story in different ways to meet the demands and constraints of the amount of space (usually determined by screen size and number of pages, viewer proximity to screen, and therefore words per screen and the ratio of text to image) available from the medium in which it is expressed. This is a situation which may well have been familiar to both eighteenth- and nineteenth-century print news journalists. While take-up and interest in text-based television news was initially very slow, by the end of the 1990s a mass audience was using it, with around 60 per cent of the population owning Teletext television sets (Gunter 2003). The ability of the audience to interact with television, particularly in relation to the growth of interactive digital television (iDTV) and the implications it raises for viewer engagement with the news, will be discussed more fully below.

CONCLUSION

This chapter has considered the historical development of the news media, namely print and broadcast news. It has also examined some of the reasons for the adoption of particular approaches to journalistic practice and news. As argued in the introduction to this chapter, only by looking at the historical antecedents of the news can we hope to understand the news in its orientation and manifestation: that is, its interest in truth and contemporary events as well as the form of its expression (thus far print, radio and television). In trying to understand the development of particular habits, precedents, practices, traditions and rituals of journalism we have seen that the relationship between the news media and technology is an old and established one. The management of space and time are long-standing and ongoing tasks. The pursuit of accuracy is an ideal which has seen a specific historical development, giving rise to stylistic forms and expressions to support this pursuit. Key determinants of the character of news, then, are fairly entrenched in the practices of producing news.

However, the past twenty-five years have witnessed massive changes in news production, transmission, content and consumption patterns. Global flows of news have, with more recent technological developments, facilitated the dissemination of greater amounts of news and information at a faster rate than ever before. The relationship between news and entertainment is currently uncertain. The rapidly changing nature of the contemporary media environment within which journalists work and audiences consume their products is challenging established views about news. The commodification of news and the pursuit of viewer ratings also impacts upon the nature of the news. In addition, as we have seen, while competition has long been a part of the news industry it has risen to new levels in recent years as the ownership of the news industry has become increasingly concentrated. It is these themes, familiar to us in their historical setting, that we now try to understand in their contemporary setting. The question is: What impact have recent developments had on the philosophical orientation of news?

4

THE MODERN NEWS ECOLOGY

Technology, regulation, concentration and competition

INTRODUCTION

I have used the phrase 'news ecology' not as a verbal ornament but because the word 'ecology' refers to the relationship of things as they interact with one another and their environment. In short, it shows the interdependence of forces at work that interact with one another to create today's news environment. Attempts to explain this environment which ignore the ecological relationship of technology, regulation, the concentration of ownership and the competition between news providers will not provide a proper understanding of the news. To take one example, technical innovation and capacity interact with the regulatory framework within which ownership and competition are conducted. As a result, issues such as censorship, the vertical integration of companies, cross-media ownership and market distortion combine criteria that are political, economic, legal and moral in a complex environment within which news production and reporting resides. This chapter examines this environment from 1979 to the present day, our third period noted in Chapter 2.

The past twenty-five to thirty years have 'been characterized by increasing globalization in economic, cultural and to a certain extent politico-legal spheres, by the revolutionary impact of . . . communications technologies and the reanimation of market-building capitalism after the collapse of communism' (Roche 2002: 103). While Webster (2004) notes that the period between 1945 and 1975 is distinguished by the prominence of nation-states, welfare provision, mass production, increasing mass consumption and the reliance on social class as a way of distinguishing people's different lifestyle choices, education and political affiliation. Since then these features no longer explain the environment in which journalism operates and news is produced and consumed.

From the late 1970s we have seen astonishing technological developments, legal and regulatory confusions and clarity, unprecedented levels of media company activity, growing competition between news suppliers and the development of a market-driven global news broadcasting environment. It is a period defined by the growth in news outlets and the amount, range and type of news available to the consumer. Audiences for news are now shared within and across different media platforms. All these changes have occurred alongside a process of deregulation, which has liberalized the news media market, allowing greater levels of media competition and concentration, and also encouraging a more market-led regulatory structure. Combined, these vectors of change have affected how mediated news is produced and consumed. One can be either pessimistic or optimistic about these developments.

For critical theorists the new news ecology has meant that the news resides in an environment dominated by market pressures and corporate exigencies to make profits. Consequently, they argue, the production context for news is shaped by predominantly economic motives rather than a desire to serve the public good. In such an environment the majority of the news media are said to address the audience as consumers rather than to speak to them as citizens. Audiences as consumers are not only sold products which are appealing and popular, but also audiences themselves 'can be considered as products of the media, harvested by the appeal of popular commodities and sold to advertisers by the thousand according to their purchasing power' (McQuail 2002: 10). Technological change and a more consumerist society generally have led to changes in audiences' preferences and consumption patterns. Critical theorists do acknowledge that broadcast news in particular has been protected from some of the market pressures which exist, ultimately, in the form of PSB obligations and regulation in the public interest (a theme taken up in detail in Chapter 4). Yet they also insist that despite these measures, the protected status of news is under pressure in the modern commercial media environment. Commercial news producers, according to Garnham (1990), now pursue strategies designed to target larger and larger audiences in order to maximize their advertising revenue. International media companies define their audiences and markets in global terms, and they diversify their news products, through repackaging, in order to sell them across a variety of different platforms and settings. This is especially true where cross-media ownership has occurred.

Overall, high levels of competition between news media organizations and the pursuit of profit-maximizing strategies have fuelled concerns that the news media are 'dumbing down' (Barnett 1998: 75). It is thought that they are marginalizing analytical news out of peak time schedules and encouraging the growth of tabloid values which change the focus of news selection away from the 'serious' (politics, public policy, social issues, economics, international affairs) to human interest news focused on showbusiness, celebrities, scandal and so on. At the same time a style of presentation has emerged which has made stories increasingly 'bright, light and trite' (Williams 2003: 230). To this end news providers have been accused of providing a less accurate or incomplete account of events than in previous, less competitive eras.

The 'critical' approach is not without its critics, most notably 'liberal pluralists' who see in the complexity of recent developments greater freedom, the end of censorship, greater personal engagement with the news and the creation of more open intellectual and political climates across the world. The dumbing-down critique has been criticized by those who argue that increased competition between news providers and the growth in news outlets have provided greater choice for consumers and that larger, wealthy corporations are better placed than smaller organizations to invest higher sums of money in their news operations, which are consequently more likely to provide quality news reporting (Collins and Murroni 1996). While there is little dispute that the media in general are becoming more competitive and concentrated than ever, there is much less agreement about the extent to which this actually results in real control of the production of the news in practice (Williams 2003). As for the idea that it is economic exigencies alone that provide the material base of the new news ecology, it is doubtful that it operates in quite so deterministic a way in producing 'news for profit' (see below). Nor is the idea of the hegemonic control of a few global media behemoths particularly convincing; it seems much more feasible, as I hope to show, that globalization and diversification go hand in hand.

Basically, liberal pluralists reject the argument that the concentration of news media ownership distorts the news production process as too economically determined (ibid.). The 'critical' approach, it is argued, tends to ignore the important role of PSB as a means to provide a different and distinct type of content.[1] From a liberal-pluralist perspective there is broad agreement that market forces have an impact on news content, though it is not the owners and managers who control the nature of that content but the consumers themselves. Furthermore, an instrumental approach which focuses on direct intervention in the news by owners may provide some interesting anecdotal statements about the character of news, but is not of much use when trying to understand all the characteristics of news provided by news organizations. The extent to which owners reflect a unified interest is questionable; different owners may have different interests, and it is unlikely that a single individual has the time or the ability to actually oversee the activities of a global media conglomerate (Negrine 1989). In short, the content the news is largely determined by the desires of the audience without whose interest the organization would fail. The liberal-pluralist view seems to accord with the view of many journalists where interesting the audience (usually by selecting something which would interest themselves) and giving the audience what they want, is routine. This is not to say that the quality of the news must inevitably decline. As Negrine (1989: 88) has observed, 'the medium still has to prove itself', or it is likely that it will lose both its customers and its advertisers.

I hope to combine both a liberal-pluralist approach and a critical approach which recognizes the role played by economic forces; the 'mode of production or political economy' (Murdock 1980: 54), in combination with constraints (both formal and informal) placed upon all those involved in the production process, from owners and managers to journalists and their customers.

THE NEWS AND RECENT TECHNOLOGICAL CHANGE

The development of communications technologies in the news sector is transforming workplace relations and encouraging labour mobility (Castells 2001). It is also enabling new media organizations to emerge with new types of work and new workplace activities (Dow and Parker 2001). Opportunities to develop new types of content, use new forms of delivery and to develop new workplace practices are consequently challenging traditional practices within established news media organizations (Marjoribanks 2000). Indeed, it is also argued that the distribution of news is more than anything else facilitated, if not actually driven, by advances in communications technology (Pavlik 1999, 2000).[2]

The press has seen the replacement of the hot metal technique of prepress production with computerized systems and the introduction of computing techniques to the production process: changes which have significantly altered established workplace practices (Marjoribanks 2000), the efficiency of news production and news distribution. The implementation of these changes and the subsequent resistance to them by the print unions[3] led in the 1980s to the loss of their traditional power, which had remained in their hands since the late seventeenth century. A central figure in this dispute was Rupert Murdoch who in 1985, following a period of unfruitful negotiations with the National Graphical Association (NGA) and The Society of Graphical and Allied Trades '82 (SOGAT 82), transferred his entire news operation from Bouverie Street and Grays Inn Road in central London to Wapping, a newly developed east London Docklands site. At Wapping Murdoch had secretly constructed a purpose-built printing plant which contained a new Atex computerized system. This system rendered many printing jobs redundant and allowed him to dismiss thousands of printworkers. These wholesale redundancies not only changed the balance of power within his news organization but also the way that news was produced (see McNair (1996); Marjoribanks (2000); Greenslade (2003a); Page (2003) for a more detailed discussion of Murdoch's strategy). A further printing plant established in Glasgow, along with the use of an Australian transportation company, allowed him to 'establish a union-proof distribution network for his titles' (McNair 1996: 147).[4] While the printworkers (or craftworkers) lost their jobs, journalists and other white-collar newsworkers found that their range of tasks expanded (as they learned to input news copy directly into computers) and their workplace environment was radically reorganized (Marjoribanks 2000). All of these changes had an impact on the production and type of news provided.

According to Delano (2000), the transition to computers from typewriters and the blue pencil meant that many older and more experienced newspaper sub-editors who disliked editing on screen accepted the redundancy packages on offer. Consequently, the age profile of newsrooms was changed, leaving fewer older and more experienced journalists to pass their wisdom on to new recruits. This, coupled with efficiency drives by owners and managers, led to multi-skilling and a younger workforce in broadcast newsrooms (Delano 2000) and, on occasion, it has also led to industrial dispute.[5] A consequence of the changing age profile in newsrooms was the possible neglect of previously important areas of news and the emergence of a gulf between older members of the audience and younger producers of news. A recent report[6] claimed that, when the famous English test fast bowler Brian Statham (1930 to 2000) died, virtually no one working at ITN was old enough to know who he was, or even to remember the time when cricket was a sport with mass appeal. Yet many of the television news audience are older viewers for whom Statham was one of the sporting idols of their youth.

During the past twenty years the development of new distribution technology has enabled the number of broadcasting platforms to grow, while the increasing availability of bandwidth has changed both the amount and type of news which may be broadcast. Until the late 1980s all broadcasting was terrestrial. When satellite television first arrived in Britain it was initially used to provide a programme feed to cable[7] companies, a development which allowed television news (and other programming) to be transmitted using satellite technology from different countries. Two news organizations in particular were to have a long-term effect on the television news industry: WorldNet and Cable Network News International (CNN). CNN International was aimed at an international audience, initially only broadcasting to a very small number of cable subscribers and hotels and producing a different type of programme from its American domestic variety. By 1989 satellite transmissions could be broadcast direct to home (DTH) via a satellite dish attached to the outside of a building with a decoder of signals inside the building (a set-top box). This initiated a new era of direct broadcasting by satellite (DBS) which, in countries like Britain with a poorly developed cable system, allowed householders to access a wider range of news programming.

Broadcasters such as British Satellite Broadcast (BSB) and Sky Television, which eventually became BSkyB and the BBC's World Service Television (WSTV)[8] were able to take advantage of satellite technology to enter the broadcast news market. Indeed, one could argue that news as a genre was as important to the establishment of satellite television in Europe as sport was later to become for the maintenance of satellite TV companies' profits. These developments in the early 1990s increased the number of players involved in twenty-four-hour transnational communication of news,[9] although different broadcasting companies made different levels of financial investment in their digital news channels.[10] Transition to digital transmission technology has been relatively slow and uneven throughout the world, although a variety of broadcasters have begun to adopt digital newsrooms as their potential has become clearer.[11] Digitalization has also allowed news provision to be expanded to new generations of mobile phones which now have screen services and web browsers built into them, with subscription news services provided.[12] Consequently, it is becoming increasingly difficult to consider broadcasting and print as self-contained areas, as news providers package and sell their products via the internet.

In the television sector, digital take-up[13] has accelerated and three types of digital television have developed in Britain: Digital Terrestrial TV (DTT), which has encountered various inauguration problems;[14] digital satellite television;[15] and digital cable television (see Appendix 2).[16] All offer twenty-four-hour news services, and a variety of interactive services are developing, facilitated by the continued development of broadband[17] and the upgrading of cable networks with two-way electronic systems. Three broad types of interactive services can currently be delivered through digital television, which have an effect on the way news is produced, presented and consumed. First are the stand-alone information services whereby the viewer can access news and information via a text-type service available through an interactive menu. Second, there is an enhanced programming service whereby a viewer can get information on items featured during the broadcast programme. Different pictures and text are transmitted simultaneously through a single channel so that viewers can select different combinations of these to be displayed on their screen using a remote control. For example, *Sky News Active* currently has eight mini-screens, each showing different types of news, headlines, brief news updates, weather, showbiz news and special items such as the Hutton Inquiry (which ran from 1 August 2003 to 28 January 2004). BBCi offers six mini-screens on its BBC News-24 channel: news, headlines, business, sport, weather and a topical subject in the news. Although the level of interactivity is minimal, the character of news delivered by these technologies is significantly different: viewers are offered greater choice and higher levels of detailed information. They are able to opt out of the linear broadcast programme and to pick and choose from a menu of text or alternative video screens. Third, transactional services allow the viewer to interact via e-mail or voting. Both BBCi and *Sky News* offer viewers the facility to send messages to the newsroom via e-mail or text, and *Sky News* invites viewers to press their red or green buttons on their remote control to register 'yes' or 'no' votes relating to topical news stories. Interactive digital television (iDTV) has the potential to expand and develop much further, with platform providers offering information services, video on demand, personal video recorders, home banking, gambling, games, dating and shopping.

Digital technology and the development of interactivity mean that new ways of publishing, distributing and accessing news information are being developed. First, whereas producers and publishers have traditionally controlled the content and delivery, digital technology allows viewers to have greater engagement with the news. They can vote on issues, make comments via e-mail or texting, which are read out almost immediately by news presenters, and they can follow the results of their voting or their messages being commented upon. In theory this development has the potential to transform our relationship with the electronic news media from an essentially passive one to an active one. However, the excitement about viewer engagement with broadcast news may be overstated. Viewers have long been able to offer comments and complaints by letter or telephone, just as newspapers have offered readers' letters pages and, more recently, responses by a readers' editor. The crucial difference occurring in the broadcast media is the immediacy of the response. In short, television news capitalizes on its ability to prioritize immediacy as a core element of its news provision. However, the agenda for discussion is still established by the news media organization, and participation by viewers is controlled and limited.

Despite these attempts to engage the viewer through interactivity, some users still see television as too low-tech or not interactive enough:

> For all of Question Time's cute experiments with text-message comments ('I thort mIcal hwrd was ded. Lol!') and red-button voting, TV does not do interactivity well – particularly when it comes to news and current affairs.
>
> (Carr 2003)[18]

None the less, news media organizations such as the BBC, BSkyB and ITN have innovated in their news provision, offering interactive services, distributing news across a range of channels and, in the process, have re-equipped their newsrooms with digital technology (see Chapter 5).

Technological change has enabled the broadcast news media to enhance their management of the constraints of space (via multi-screens and broadband capacity) and time (via rolling news, twenty-four-hour channels and videophones). These changes have allowed a greater flexibility that is in considerable contrast to that of news in the print medium. The prioritization of immediacy and its concomitant identification with the contemporary is seen not only in attempts to provide real-time engagement with the audience, but also in the character of news itself. As we will see in later chapters, modern-day broadcast news is now largely judged through its relationship to the live and immediate. Increasingly we see news journalists reporting from the precise site where events have occurred or are occurring. Live transmission adds to the drama and excitement of a news story. It can, on the face of it, seem to aid its veracity, but in fact there are problems with the broadcast news media's overwhelming attachment to providing instantaneous news coverage (see Chapters 5 and 6).

The internet

The development of text-based electronic news delivery began in the early 1970s with the use of CEEFAX and ORACLE and the Prestel[19] service which was launched in 1979. The growth in use of home computers opened up further opportunities for news delivery, and IBM and Sears developed a news network called Prodigy (Gunter 2003: 21). In America, in particular, the newspaper industry explored the potential of using electronic delivery systems to reach a home-based market. When Californian *San Jose Mercury News* went online in 1994, its personalized news service, accessed by keywords, established it as the 'cutting edge electronic news publisher' (ibid.: 22), offering a new type of news experience to the audience. In Britain the first newspaper to provide an online version was the *Guardian*. By the mid-1990s, British newspaper publishers realized that they needed an online presence if they were to keep up with the tastes and needs of the population, although many online sites had to scale down resources in response to the advertising recession which affected all media at the end of the 1990s and the beginning of the twenty-first century.

Instead of two different divisions, 'online' and 'off-line' newspapers have recently started to merge the two, or require that they both work in concert and not as separate entities. Increasingly, news organizations prefer to see the two products as complementary with each providing a different service, but reinforcing each other. The online version of the *Sun* helps to market the newspaper, and both it and the *Daily Mirror* have smaller editorial teams working to manage both the 'online' and 'off-line' newspaper. In contrast, the BBC's online news team is expanding. CEEFAX has now merged with BBCi with the aim of maximizing the use of the enormous news-gathering facilities at the BBC. The BBC argues that this is in order to provide news to an increasing number of outlets (Deverell 2004), an example of how even non-profit-oriented news organizations seek to diversify news provision to maximize their audience reach. BBC online is now one of the most popular sites in Europe. The growth of different platforms for receiving news has led the BBC to develop a system where the constituent parts of a news story can be disaggregated and then reaggregated for dissemination via different news outlets. It is now possible to almost completely uncouple the origination of the content from its manifestation (ibid.)[20].

The *Daily Mail* and the *Mail on Sunday*, which have consistently carried news stories about the dangers of the internet, did not launch a web version of the paper until December 2003, and, at the time of writing, the *Daily Express* and *Sunday Express* are currently the only major national papers without a web-based newspaper; the website simply shows a front-page copy of their newspaper which is advertised as being 'on sale at your newsagent now' and a list of headlines with some text provided.[21] Online news may be accessed in a variety of ways: completely free of charge (e.g. BBC online); largely free access via registration with subscription to certain areas of the website (for example, the *Independent* charges for access to comment pieces, archives, cryptic crosswords and articles by the Middle East correspondent Robert Fisk, while *The Times*, *Sun* and *Guardian* have launched subscription services on their websites which include crosswords, e-mail updates and digital versions of the paper). A full-subscription model also exists (the *Wall Street Journal* has operated a subscription model since 1996 and *The Financial Times* now charges for the majority of its content). These different approaches to funding the online news service perhaps reflect the degree of uncertainty among newspaper publishers about the willingness of the public to pay for an online product. Increasingly, news organizations are seeking to customize their online news further, providing text alerts delivered to mobile phones via short message service (SMS) and sending e-mail alerts or news summaries to users. The recent developments of mobile technologies, which will allow users to watch high-quality digital television images on their mobile phones opens up further possibilities foe news providers.[22]

There are clear differences in the character of news which can be provided by different media. Traditional journalism has been oriented towards clearly defined audiences which have usually been local, regional, national or, in the case of the BBC's World Service, international. Television news has capitalized increasingly on its ability to report contemporary events immediately, live from the scene, while print news, with its different and delayed publishing cycle, has adopted a variety of styles of news reporting and capitalized on its ability to produce depth, background and detail. Early online news provided by many newspapers was of poor aesthetic quality, since it usually comprised content which was simply moved wholesale from the print medium to the worldwide web. It generally failed to use any of the potential benefits to be gained from interactivity and hypertext, thus undermining the aesthetics of the newspaper since pictures and headlines were often separated from the text. This practice is now known in disparaging terms as 'shovelware' (Hall 2001), although today some newspapers make a virtue of putting an exact copy of their newspaper online to be accessed by people outside the range of print distribution.

Traditional news providers quickly recognized that in fact internet news can marry elements from both the broadcast and print world and provide a different type of news online. Pavlik (2001: 217) argues that this has resulted in a 'new form of news' which arises through contextualized journalism, and which uses multimedia, interactivity, hypertext and customization. Online news provides greater depth and breadth in reporting, and the availability of extensive content archives means that users can explore stories for themselves. News can be instantly updated, introducing a 'live' element to the website, and it can be accessed on a regional, national and global scale. Significantly, the most commonly accessed news sites are those which are provided by the traditional news media and are recognized as supplying truthful, trustworthy and accurate news (e.g. the BBC and *Guardian* websites), illustrating that the core news values of accuracy and sincerity have been successfully transferred, by some news organizations, into the internet world.

However, the nature of news available via the internet varies enormously. There are online news sites for which existing newspapers and broadcasters provide their own content, while some new news media organizations such as Ananova[23] are also online content producers. In contrast, aggregators such as Yahoo, AOL and Google index news from other sites. The internet also hosts gossip sites such as the Drudge Report,[24] which as we will see in Chapter 4 can break new news stories, but can also spread unsubstantiated rumours which may then become 'news' by virtue of being repeated by some of the mainstream news media. Gossip sites may report on the here and now in an interesting, entertaining or salacious fashion, but they lack the orientation towards truthfulness that news and news providers must have.

A further opportunity for gossip and discussion online occurs in the form of weblogs. The use of weblogs (or 'blogs') which are run by webloggers (or 'bloggers') have allowed authors to record their thoughts and views in personal diary-style sites and to provide links to other web pages which the blogger thinks are relevant. There are many different types of weblogs of varying quality and reliability. However, the difference here is in the character of the news and information which is provided. Unlike gossip sites which flourish on the use of unreliable evidence, bloggers are often eyewitnesses to events, able to offer a 'live' account of events (perhaps resonant of storytellers in oral cultures) albeit in printed form (although images from mobile phones are increasingly being used). Following the tsunamis that hit seven countries in December 2004, several newspapers and the BBC initially relied on bloggers from around the Indian Ocean for some of their early reports (Preston 2005: 3). Bloggers often have strong views and have sometimes sifted through other evidence (generally provided by the mainstream media) to offer a personal and subjective, but none the less informed, account of news events, which may then be debated or contested by other bloggers. As we will see in Chapter 4, the sharing of information via weblogs has been viewed by Papacharissi (2002) as having the potential for a cyber-democracy to flourish through a new type of virtual twenty-first-century public sphere. Others are less optimistic about the extent to which freedom of expression via the internet can escape corporate and establishment power and control (Curran and Seaton 2003).

Despite such misgivings, news journalists are increasingly engaging with both gossip sites and weblogs as a source of information, and encouraging their use. The BBC and the *Guardian* encourage users to contribute to their website through mobile weblogging (or 'moblogging'), whereby they can use images from a mobile phone or digital camera. Users can submit pictures to BBC online using multi-media messaging (MMS, which is SMS with pictures) or e-mail. Where appropriate, these pictures may be used to enhance breaking news stories, where those actually involved in the news event can provide their own visual perspective via pictures or text messages. Users are also being encouraged to explore stories further. Following the destruction of the World Trade Center on 11 September 2001, many message boards were created online by alternative and established news organizations, where people could use the enormous resources available on the internet to explore and discuss the story further and to provide eyewitness accounts. Personal journalism is now available as an alternative or supplement to the news provided by the mainstream news organizations, offering a plurality of views and sources of information.

The pursuit of immediate engagement with audience or readers' views is largely related to the news's orientation to be truthful and engage with the contemporary, to be up to the minute and able to respond to audience demands or needs quickly. Problematically, the orientation towards the contemporary can exist in tension with the news's orientation towards truthfulness. Many news journalists recognize this inherent contradiction themselves, even if they do not articulate it in this particular manner, seeing the internet both as a reliable and unreliable source of information; both tempting and dangerous. One of the most well-known and authentic blog sites was produced by Salam Pax during the war in Iraq in March/April 2003.[25] Pax became known as the Baghdad Blogger and his identity remained unknown until May 2003. His writing added a completely different flavour to the reporting of the war, providing insights into life for the ordinary citizens of Iraq:

> The worst is seeing and feeling the city come to a halt. Nothing. No buying, no selling, no people running after buses. We drove home quickly. At least inside it did not feel so sad. The ultimatum ends at 4 in the morning her (*sic*) in Baghdad, and the big question is will the attack be at the same night or not. Stories about the first gulf war are being told for the 100th time.
>
> (Pax 5.46 a.m., 20 March 2003)

The presence of weblogs on the internet raises interesting questions about whether they enrich debate and provide a wider variety of news and information, or whether they are inaccurate, peddle gossip and rumour and, in the case of the warblogs above, whether they clarify the facts or circulate propaganda. While the internet opens up the freedom for anyone to circulate 'news' and encourage debate,[26] as we will see in Chapter 4, others are more critical about its potential to enrich public knowledge.

The modern press, interactive television, mobile technology and the internet demonstrate the fact that (as discussed in the Introduction) there is not 'one news journalism' (Harcup 2004: 5) but many: tabloid; PSB; serious; radical; civic; current affairs; documentary and so on. These types emerge primarily as a result of the type of engagement which the news journalist or news organization has with its own understanding of news (orientation towards truthfulness), their attempts (or requirement) to be impartial (the degree of accuracy, investigation and fairness employed in selecting and telling news), adherence to codes of practice, extent of their engagement with the world (the nature, breadth and depth of news selection), extent to which their attachment to live reporting means that raw footage increasingly replaces an 'end-product', extent to which this is reliably informed information and, of course, their sincerity. The development of many types of news and news journalisms simply reflects the fast-changing, digital, interactive, news-saturated environment which we inhabit. It is an environment of global communication, deregulation of media and the promotion of the much-vaunted freedom of 'choice'.

NEWS AND THE CURRENT REGULATORY ENVIRONMENT

In order for a complex world to be reported on as accurately, sincerely and fully as possible, American and European policymakers and legislators have traditionally attempted to ensure that a range of news providers coexists to provide a diverse variety of news. To some extent this has worked. Research into the output of different news providers has shown differences in their news values and the stories which are selected (Harrison 2000; Hargreaves and Thomas 2002). Modern, Western-style democratic societies therefore seek to ensure that more than one version of events, as well as a variety of events, is reported. Traditionally this has been undertaken through policy intervention which has placed restrictions on the concentration of news media ownership: a measure based on the principle that a range of owners will result in a range of editorial values and views (DNH 1995: 16). In practice, regulation to ensure that a diversity of views is available has, for pragmatic reasons, focused on regulation of concentration of ownership rather than on measuring and tracking diversity of output. The latter, of course, is much less easy to define and enforce.

Despite these general views, the policies of successive governments in Britain and continental Europe (often through European Court of Justice decisions, but also through a deregulatory impetus adopted by member states[27]) have been deregulatory in focus and have liberalized ownership restrictions in the commercial print and broadcast news media sectors (McNair 1996). They have also placed emphasis on the importance of a strong media industry (Chalaby 2000), thereby encouraging mergers and acquisitions. The BBC has not been immune to the effects of deregulatory policies and the belief in the supremacy of market forces and the needs of 'the industry'. The rationale for funding from the licence fee has come under increasing scrutiny. Despite serious consideration being given to the privatization of the BBC and advertisement-based funding in 1986,[28] the BBC has continued to be seen to be the key institution which can ensure that a diverse range of news output continues to exist, in an increasingly concentrated and competitive commercial media environment. It is assumed that its PSB status will ensure that it offers something different from its commercial competitors. The current British government has been in the main sympathetic to the need to sustain and maintain PSB. Licence fee increases were awarded in 2000 and in April 2004.[29] However, OFCOM has, in its phase two and three reports, recommended to the government that a Public Service Publisher (PSP) be formed to redistribute £300 million of the BBC licence fee.

Deregulatory changes have raised concerns (Meier and Trappel 1998: 41) that the concentration of ownership means that the diversity of the news media will be reduced. More specifically, there are concerns that professional journalistic values will be replaced by the self-interested priorities of shareholders who seek only to make a profit[30] through the engagement of audiences with their product (Williams 1980; Herman and Chomsky 1988; Golding and Murdock 2000). Cultural critics such as Hoggart (2004: 47) remain critical of the increased concentration of ownership, because it exacerbates the addiction towards head-counting and ratings, and serves consumerism or 'the buying and shopping society' by a 'levelling' or 'thin reductionism of things and ideas' so that they become more palatable and enjoyable to consume. Golding and Murdock (2000: 75) see concentration as having an influence on the 'direction of cultural activity'. They argue that the concentration of news provision in the hands of a few global news providers contributes significantly to the 'commodification of cultural life' (ibid.: 75) and that this is currently masked by the illusion of choice. Others argue that the concentration of ownership is a negative phenomenon and will lead increasingly to homogeneity of news content (Williams 2003), especially if news and entertainment blur (McLuhan 1962, 1964). Hoggart (2004: 47) argues that the concentration of ownership produces products which are 'more easily-swallowed pap' pandering to the 'false democracy of populism': a view that echoes the criticism of popular culture (see Chapter 1) which is couched in terms of concerns about the decline of standards of one sort or another.

A study entitled *The State of the News Media 2004* undertaken by the Project for Excellence in Journalism (affiliated with Columbia University)[31] revealed that the character of the news in America is now shaped by eight main trends. First, most news organizations are chasing shrinking audiences resulting in problems for profit levels, which in return has resourcing implications in newsrooms. Second, investment is mainly focused on the dissemination of news around numerous affiliates or other news media interests, rather than in actually gathering the news. Third, twenty-four-hour news in particular has instigated a new era, where the market for news concentrates increasingly on getting and broadcasting the raw news footage and presenting it as the end-product. This has implications for the quality of some reports. Fourth, journalistic standards vary within the same news organization as news is gathered and repackaged for different audiences and platforms. Many news organizations have flagship programmes, but other elements of their output do not require the same journalistic standards (having implications for the core qualities of accuracy and truthfulness). Fifth, those traditional news organizations which are losing audiences and have not successfully increased audience contact via diversification of their product through other platforms, are increasingly returning lower revenues to shareholders and reducing costs in the newsroom. It is likely that the audience will eventually be put off by the poorer quality of the news provided by impoverished news organizations and turn to that provided by larger, well-resourced conglomerates.[32] Sixth, convergence seems to be offering positive benefits both to the audience, which has a wider range of options, and to the news organizations who can exploit the benefits of the new media to attract new audiences. In particular, the internet offers a news battleground where print and broadcast media, traditionally offering different styles and types of news from each other, can fight for the same online audience. Seventh, there is a question as to whether the internet will be a successful medium for news organizations, not because it is not a suitable medium for news, but because it may not produce the kinds of profits which will support systematic and good-quality news-gathering. Finally, the demand for high-profile sources who will sell a story has led to a new form of cheque-book journalism, as news outlets compete to get exclusive access to celebrity stories. While these trends are consequences of a free-market model for media regulation, which does not have the safeguard of PSB, many of the trends identified in the American study may now be seen to be relevant in an increasingly deregulated British context.

In both the American and the British context local and regional television news is now a front where questions of resources and quality of news are most under pressure. Two commercial 'experiments' in news provision illustrate this very well. First, as a recent comment piece in the *Columbia Journalism Review* (2003)[33] reported, local television news was continuing 'its steady retreat from serious journalism in favor (*sic*) of making money'. It referred the reader to an Atlanta-based company called NewsProNet, which produces 'generic news-you-can-use reports and investigations' (ibid.). These are news stories which remove 'references to place and other identifying features in its reports so that they can be dropped in anywhere in the country and passed off as a station's own locally produced segments' (ibid.). Second, the Sinclair Broadcast Group, Incorporated, based in Maryland, is reported to be test-marketing News Central which provides a 'one-hour mix of local and national news'. This is being piloted at its Michigan affiliate, WSMH-TV, with a view to expanding News Central to all sixty-two affiliates.[34] Most of the content is not original, but rather comes from other Sinclair affiliates or a CNN feed (ibid.). Both examples illustrate a willingness to operate a news service simply because providing 'news' reflects the fact that advertisers are more likely to purchase advertising space on stations with news than without (ibid.). Consequently, parent companies are looking at ways in which providing news will maximize advertising revenue but at the lowest cost. The search for a news template or formulae produced centrally and applied locally is such a way, and if applied across America (and subsequently exported) would represent a diminishment of news in favour of a news methodology that would render news journalism detached from the particularity or specific detail of contemporary events. Overall, the number of journalists employed locally across America has declined (ibid.), and there is now a fundamental lack of real diversity in news provided by broadcasters at the local level.[35]

In Britain the 2003 Communications Act illustrates the prevailing belief (manifest in their successful lobbying) that British media companies need to be able to compete in global markets. According to this view, for British media organizations to survive the predations of global companies they must grow through mergers and acquisitions in order to assure their place in world news markets. British policymakers have tried to balance two things: first, the needs of the media industry against the need to ensure freedom of expression via a plurality of views; second, to ensure that a public service element is retained through the control of programme standards, quality and content. The 2003 Communications Act has been criticized for liberalizing news media ownership restrictions[36] because it has allowed greater cross-media ownership between the broadcast and print sectors of the news media industry via lifting the so-called 20:20 restriction.[37] The Act has also liberalized the radio sector. The restrictions preventing anyone from owning more than one national analogue licence have been removed, along with the existing points system. A 'two plus the BBC' rule in the larger radio markets such as London and Birmingham now exists. This means that companies can now broadcast to 55 per cent (previously 15 per cent) of potential listeners in any one region, or 45 per cent if they own more than half of the local newspaper market.[38] However, the most controversial element of the Act was the proposal to relax foreign ownership rules on television stations, although public consultation on media ownership had explicitly signalled anxiety about any change in the restrictions on foreign ownership without reciprocal rule changes made by other countries. This measure will allow non-EU persons and organizations to own British broadcasters, but not vice versa. Concerns have been raised that this will encourage American or European communications conglomerates, such as the American AOL Time Warner, Viacom and Disney or the European Bertelsmann and Mediaset, to own British broadcasters.

The impact on news of these deregulatory policies has been seen and felt primarily in the changing pattern of news producer ownership in Britain and it is to that which I now turn.

NEWS AND THE CONCENTRATION OF OWNERSHIP

Concentration of regional television

Although the commitment to the regional basis of the ITV system continued with the 1990 and 1996 Broadcasting Acts, relaxation of ownership rules has increasingly allowed regional companies to merge with each other, leading to the establishment of a news oligopoly in the commercial sector (alongside a news monopoly in the public sector).

By 2000 the ITV system was mainly owned by three big companies: United News and Media, Granada Group (parent company of Granada) and Carlton Central. In 2001 the regional companies owned by United News and Media were absorbed into Granada and Carlton (see Appendix 3), and in 2003 The Communications Act enabled the merger of Granada and Carlton to go ahead.[39] This occurred in February 2004, when a single ITV company for England and Wales called (confusingly enough) ITV plc was created. ITV plc owns the same franchises as do the merged Granada and Carlton, leaving Scottish Media Group (Scottish TV and Grampian TV), Channel TV and Ulster TV as part of an ITV system dominated by ITV plc.

The creation of ITV plc and its dominant position within the ITV system led to concerns about news provision for two reasons: first, over its relationship with and use of ITN and second, over its commitment to local news (Harrison 2005). ITV plc (which owns 40 per cent of ITN),[40] moved control of ITV news, which is broadcast throughout Britain (i.e. beyond the ownership boundaries of ITV plc) from the ITV Network Centre, which is operated on behalf of all ITV companies, to its own news division (Revoir 2004a: 3). The smaller licensee for Scotland, Scottish Media Group (SMG), argued that stories broadcast by ITV's national news will be dominated by England and Wales, a claim contested by the ITV News Group (ibid.). In the absence of meaningful news agenda analysis on this issue the debate and concerns are not yet settled. Associated with the concerns over ITN were concerns over local news provision within the regions themselves. It is still unclear exactly how regional news provision will be affected, but the prognosis is not good. With the ITV system specifically charged with a remit to reflect the different regions of the United Kingdom, the decision to save £100 million of costs deriving from the merger of Carlton and Granada does not bode well for local news operation. At the time of writing, it is predicted that ITV plc will seek to reduce the cost of its news provision further (subject to OFCOM's position on this) and will move away from some regional news responsibilities altogether (Revoir 2003: 9). In combination these two areas of concern point to diminishment in the scope of ITV news.[41] Currently, ITN is the news supplier to ITV1 (previously called Channel 3) which, to put its task into perspective is eleven times smaller than BBC News, (between 2001 and 2004 ITN received £35 million a year for its news services to the network compared with the BBC which had a 'news budget' of £400 million for approximately the same period). The Elstein Report 2004[42] commented that the economic reality of the ITV system is such that it will not be able to afford to pay for its PSB obligations,[43] of which news provision is one, and at the same time retain a competitive position in the marketplace. The sole guarantor of these PSB requirements and of ensuring a reasonable level of financial provision for ITN from contractors such as the ITV system is OFCOM.

Concentration of the national press

Mergers and take-overs between newspaper titles have long been part of the newspaper industry (in Britain a competition assessment by the Competition Commission is required if a possible merger involves a newspaper organization whose average paid-for circulation is higher than 500,000[44]). As a result multinational organizations have emerged whose impact on the news media industry has been significant. Large media organizations are better able to secure control over the preparation and distribution of news content and to cross-promote stories in an attempt to maximize audiences and thereby control the market. News becomes a commodity. In addition, the reduction of reliance on other organizations in the production, distribution and market processes helps news organizations to gain advantage over competitors, making news a more efficient and profitable commodity.

Sometimes, control of large sections of the market and the ability to cross-subsidize business strategies from other parts of the company has allowed companies such as News International to use price reductions to attempt to force rival news competitors out of the market. In 1998 the House of Lords voted by 121 votes to 93 in favour of an amendment to the Competition Bill (in its report stage in the House of Lords) to try to prevent any newspaper abusing a dominant position in the market via predatory pricing (i.e. where a newspaper cuts its price in such a way that it is determined to clear the field of rivals and reduce competition). This amendment was aimed specifically at *The Times* newspaper which cut its price to 10 pence by subsidizing its losses from profits gained from News International:[45] a strategy which saw *The Times* double its circulation at the expense of newspapers such as the *Independent*. Although the *Independent* survived, it revealed how vulnerable it was to such tactics from a much larger organization. At the time it was argued that it would have been disastrous if the *Independent* had closed, since it would have seriously reduced the diversity of news provision in the, then, broadsheet news marketplace.

There is common agreement that a diverse range of information sources is important in order to perpetuate cultural and ideological plurality and to challenge established or dominant 'truth' claims. For this reason it is good that there are many different types of journalistic engagement, selection and explanation of news events, and different types and styles of reporting. However, measured by circulation, it is clear that market domination has been allowed to occur in the British newspaper market. Eighty-six per cent of the national press now belongs to four publishers. News International's *Sun* newspaper is the most popular newspaper, selling around three and a half million copies per day. The red top tabloids, the *Sun*, *Daily Mirror* and *Daily Star*, between them account for almost half of national newspaper sales, with the *Daily Mail* and the *Daily Express* accounting for more than a quarter of daily sales. The 'broadsheets' (I include the compact *Times* and tabloid-sized *Independent* in this category) therefore account for under 25 per cent of the national readership market. Similarly, on Sundays it is News International's *News of the World* which sells the greatest number of papers and *The Sunday Times* leads the 'broadsheet' market (see Appendix 4).

The domination of the British newspaper market by only four publishers cannot be viewed as a positive development. Although the newspapers in circulation may look different from each other, there is danger of a creeping homogeneity of content and a tacit consensus on which events are newsworthy and, more importantly, which are not (the so-called 'pack or herd mentality'). For example, different newspapers within the same organization can adopt a collective view (sometimes the proprietor's and sometimes senior management's) and then express that view in the particular style of the various newspapers within the organization. Coverage in Britain of Europe, asylum seekers and immigration are good examples. Thus, for example, an anti-European view in one paper can sound moderate and balanced, and yet in another newspaper within the same group, it may sound strident and jingoistic. House lines promote a news homogeneity concealed beneath stylistic differences. Problematically, concentration of ownership not only diminishes the news's engagement with the contemporary world, shaping and steering it in particular ways, it also reduces the number of possible attempts to provide a truthful, accurate and sincere account of contemporary events.

Concentration of the local press

The local press has come under increasing pressure over the past two decades. Local newspapers have been incorporated into national or multinational organizations which some critics have argued has reduced 'local editorial autonomy' (Franklin 1997: 103). Concentration of ownership at the local level is often justified as part of a news organization's drive for greater efficiency (Franklin and Murphy 1991). Such a drive often conflicts with the traditional news interests of local audiences, which as we have seen are served primarily by local newspapers which cover local events. When local newspapers are 'market-driven' and the production of news is subordinated to competitive market forces, it usually results in a reduction of the number of journalists covering local events or in newsrooms (ibid.). It has also been said that it leads to a 'sweatshop culture' (Guild of Editors 1995: 5, cited in Franklin and Murphy 1991: 16), where traditional jobs are replaced with short-term contract posts and news feeds provide copy which substitutes for detailed local reporting. Local print journalists are now expected to be generalists, able to replace a variety of specialist sub-editors and picture journalists. Alongside this development has been the restructuring away from local level to either the regional or national level of activities such as sub-editing. This also threatens a local newspaper's capacity to cover events well. If a sub-editor is not located in, or is unfamiliar with, a particular area, local coverage loses its depth and subtlety. In short, the quality of local coverage is diminished. Local content is replaced with so-called larger stories, which are prioritized by editors operating across more than one local newspaper. These larger stories are associated more closely with events at a national or international level than at a local level. In addition, as the numbers of journalists in newsrooms dwindle, those remaining experience a greater pressure on their time. A consequence has been the reduction in development of external contacts with sources and greater reliance on efficient press releases which help the time-short journalist. Problematically, the interpretive role of the journalist is neglected in the drive for efficiency as well-resourced sources continue to gain easy access to the local news media.

A further development which affects the local press is the infiltration of free newspapers into the market. This has been well documented by McNair (1996: 193). Initially, free newspapers attracted only 1.4 per cent of advertising revenue in 1970, compared with 35 per cent by 1990 (ibid.). Advertisers were attracted to the free newspapers, seeing them as a more effective way of targeting readers. The key factor for advertisers is that a free newspaper can be delivered to every household regardless of whether or not it is requested, or be distributed free at railway stations. The reach of free newspapers is a compelling idea for advertisers in an increasingly segmented and competitive media marketplace. Consequently, free newspapers prioritize attracting advertisers over and above providing news, and most of the 'news' consists of press releases and other public relations material. Here, 'audiences can be considered as products of the media, harvested by the appeal of popular commodities and sold to advertisers by their thousand' (McQuail 2002: 10). Little 'hard' local news is required which means that the paper can be very efficiently produced and, in the case of the highly successful *Metro* freesheet newspaper, be circulated around several major British cities.[46] Although *Metro* is owned by Associated Newspapers, its regional editions are run by different newspaper groups across the country. Each region's paper is produced to a template which simply leaves blank a small amount of space into which local stories or listings can be fitted. The news in the paper generally comprises several very short stories, which are often a mixture of national, international and local events, all served in a convenient and easily consumable format, conducive to being read while travelling or sitting in a waiting room.

Competition from the free newspapers began to have a serious consequence for the paid-for weekly newspapers (McNair 1996). The solution was for regional newspaper owners to buy up the free newspapers from the independent publishers who originally set them up. In this way the regional newspaper owners were able to regain control of the advertising market and use the free newspaper to advertise their own newspaper (via cross-promotions). More resources and news-gathering facilities were provided for the free newspapers, and the quality and scope of reporting increased. In this way regional newspapers have been able to consolidate their interests within the regional newspaper market and the freesheet market (McNair 1996; Franklin 1997; Allan 1999). In the regional and local press, 50 million of the 69 million papers circulated each week (more than 75 per cent of regional newspaper circulation) are controlled by the top four owners: Johnston Press; Trinity Mirror; Newsquest[47] (owned by Gannett); and the Daily Mail and General Trust, who jointly own 799 of the 1,300 titles (Bell and Alden 2003: 27).[48] Here, news is subordinated to the successful format of the freesheet newspaper and is additional to the main concerns which are focused on advertising, and the efficiency of production and distribution.

Overall, the concentration of ownership of news-producing organizations has not resulted in the calamitous ideological strait-jacket so often feared by some academic commentators and analysts. Certainly the local press is shrinking, but regulatory frameworks work to ameliorate any hegemonic tendencies by valuing truthfulness and admiring accurate and sincere reporting. While technological developments produce entrepreneurial opportunities for many new companies, the so-called large behemoths often have the most dependency on others to develop their new media technologies. Nor does the concentration of ownership itself necessarily diminish public trust (see Chapter 4 for a discussion of public trust). The private sector's concentration of ownership of news-producing organizations comes nowhere near the powers of once state-owned media producers, and fears concerning the effects of owner-ship are perhaps (certainly historically) more justified when the state owns and controls. So far, the concentration of ownership has produced, somewhat paradoxically, fierce competition, and if it is true that the natural inclination of multinationals is towards a cartel out of fear of competition, then that has not yet happened, which of course cannot be said of all industrial sectors. It is towards understanding the nature of that competition that we now turn. There is reason to be sceptical about the extent to which current ownership patterns diminish either the amount of news coverage (the opposite could be argued: BBC 24 is a direct response to Sky News and BBCi a response to Sky Active, just as Sky Sat will respond to Freeview), or its quality in these circumstances. In addition, perhaps we risk underestimating the amount of good news journalism that is still available.

COMPETITION AND THE INTERNATIONALIZATION OF NEWS

A competitive international media industry is not a new phenomenon. Books, films and music have been transported to different parts of the world by transnational corporations (TNCs) for many years. However, the sheer size and scale of modern conglomerates is notable, with News Corporation Limited generally referred to as the most global of all the media groups in the world[49] (Marjoribanks 2000: 93). Likewise, international news reporting is not new. It began with the first war corre-spondents, such as William Russell, who reported during the Crimean War for *The London Times*. But the relatively recent growth in news outlets and twenty-four-hour news has increased the amount of news in circulation around the globe and the speed of its dissemination.

It is television in particular that has been seen to be 'the defining medium of the age . . . as . . . it provides the basis for an integrated global commercial media market' (Herman and McChesney 1997: 2). Reuters Television and Associated Press Television (APTV)[50] provide most of the television pictures which are broadcast around the world and are often the first to supply pictures. Despite the increase in demand for news feeds, news agencies themselves are feeling the effects of compe-tition; whereas in the past broadcasters would take a feed from two major agencies, they can generally only afford to take one today.[51] Other important news agencies provide different types of news. Bloomberg and Reuters are major providers of financial news, Agence France Presse (AFP) still dominates parts of the world which remain strongly influenced by earlier French colonialism, and United Press International (UPI), while not as commercially aggressive as the others, is renowned for its journalistic excellence.

Domination of the news market by a few global news agencies has resulted in a common news delivery system for a great deal of international and national news, again arguably reducing the range and diversity of news available to the consumer, as many news organizations now rely upon agency material for much of their international news rather than sending news crews to cover the story themselves. The extent to which reliance on agency material occurs is directly related to the financial health of the news organization (at both national and local level) and the amount of 'investigative investment' (Williams 2002: 87) they are able or willing to make in the pursuit of original news stories.

The uncoupling of space and time by, first, the telegraph and, later, the electronic media has meant that news from distant places can be virtually instantaneously received in a variety of locations, thereby becoming 'immediate'. Simultaneous viewing of the same contemporary event is becoming increasingly common across the globe, since different nation-states have televisual access to the live event as it unfolds. The domination of international news flows by a few major news agencies has raised questions for those concerned with the lack of diversity of information in circulation and the inequality of representation of parts of the world (Tunstall 1977; Smith 1980; Wallis and Baran 1990). Despite the efforts of New World Information and Communication Order (NWICO)[52] some countries and even whole continents (such as parts of Asia, Africa and South America) are hardly covered by Western news agencies or Western news organizations. Indeed, it may be argued that when they are, they are reflected to the rest of the world in terms of dominant news values of negativity, unusual (usually disastrous) events and human interest stories, often of an exotic kind and which often have the effect of not helping different cultures to understand each other.

Schlesinger (1978) and Smith (1980) remind us that global news agencies are large commercial empires built on to colonial information systems. The British news agency Reuters, in particular, was oriented towards promoting national interests in Britain's various colonies and promoting British economic interests worldwide (Read 1992; Lorimer 1994). However, it is also important to note that a purely commercial global news market coexists with overseas news agency material on a reciprocal exchange basis via the European Broadcasting Union (EBU).[53] The EBU is an independent, non-governmental, non-commercial body which promotes cooperation in international radio and television broadcasting. It acts as a broker through which broadcasters worldwide can exchange radio and television services and, in particular, large amounts of news footage[54] and complete programmes, via Eurovision for television and Euroradio for radio. It began on a trial basis in 1958, becoming established by 1961. A daily news exchange is now held which provides its members with much of their non-domestic and European news. The Eurovision News Exchange (EVN)[55] is the only news organization which receives cooperation from countries at war with each other and therefore plays a vital role in the free flow of global news. EVN has now been supplemented by a multilingual channel known as EuroNews,[56] designed to provide Europeans[57] with world and local news coverage from a European viewpoint.[58]

Even though news exchanges like EVN and EuroNews are crucial in enhancing the accurate coverage of contemporary events, some organizations remain dominant in the provision of international news. The development of commercially driven global news media giants such as the news agencies has sometimes been viewed as a process by which homogeneity of news is inevitable, as dominant views and values are transported around the world (Clausen 2003). The large amount of American broadcast programmes which are exported has long been viewed with suspicion, as a form of media imperialism inculcating cultures with the 'American view' of the world (Schiller 1996). However, this view has been challenged over the years and Schiller has revised his initial argument. More recently, he has argued that while American media content is still dominant and is exported to the rest of the world, the investment capital needed for the production of this content is international. International money underpins the global flow of news and other media products.

Certainly, the development and growth of global satellite television and the development of cable and digital technology have changed the constitution of the global news market. Multinational news organizations are now able to broadcast opt-outs to many countries across the world, increasing their dominance in world markets. Marjoribanks' (2000) analysis of the News Corporation paints a negative picture of the ability of a particular news media organization to dominate information supplies and to package the news into an exportable commodity that can travel anywhere. Such packaging requires the use of news clichés, dramatic film where possible and simple sound bites easily translated into other languages. Marjoribanks (2000) shows that recent global developments, which are related to technology and concentration of ownership, have also affected the way in which the newspaper industry operates throughout the world. The sharing of technology by different publications in its News Corporation has allowed it to expand around the world while at the same time reducing the size of its workforce: the same stories are used in more than one paper and 'increasing use is made of syndicated stories and news services' (ibid.: 190).

The internationalization of news is complex and cannot easily be explained by a model of media imperialism. The growth and development of news organizations which offer alternative views and perspectives from western commercial news organizations is important. Their existence offers evidence that news diversity exists. Global PSB organizations such as the BBC's World Service and its World Service Television (WSTV), now BBC World, set themselves the goal of taking an 'objective' stance in their reporting. They seek to reflect the diverse range of needs and concerns of local listeners and viewers while offering a more localized or culturally sensitive account of events than other commercial news organizations. Other news outlets are also emerging which offer perspectives that often contradict what they perceive to be Western cultural and political bias. A channel like Al-Jazeera[59], the twenty-four-hour all-news channel based in the Persian Gulf state of Qatar, is a good example. This became the first news channel to provide air time to Osama bin Laden and, for a time in 2001, was the only news organization reporting from Taliban-controlled regions in Afghanistan. It is today, by and large, a well-regarded source of valuable news often denied to Western journalists. Interestingly, it has been accused by Western audiences of using unacceptable material for its broadcasts (for example, showing graphic footage of Iraqi and American casualties and fatalities in Iraq) and by Arab audiences for its iconoclastic approach to traditional news taboos (for example, interviewing Israeli policemen). Today it provides news on a global scale and is used increasingly by Western news watchers as a legitimate alternative view. The current British Prime Minister Tony Blair, as well as the current US Secretary of State (then the National Security Adviser) Condoleeza Rice, have requested and given interviews on Al-Jazeera and have been able to 'make their case through an impartial medium to a receptive Arab public' (El-Nawawy and Iskandar 2002: 24). Such is the credibility Al-Jazeera has gained in recent years that in March 2003 it announced it had signed up four million subscribers in Europe. In September 2004 it began recruiting staff for a news and documentary channel to be broadcast in English (Whitaker 2004: 23).

The internationalization of news is no longer only the domain of a few Western news organizations. In a sense, by covering events and topics that Western news broadcasters previously eschewed until they became unavoidable (Islamic-interest stories), Al-Jazeera has provided a contribution to the balancing of the global news mix, and offers some evidence for those who do not subscribe to the view of news imperialism, that diversity of news and news analysis have not been eradicated from the coverage of international news. The homogenizing of news seems to have been overestimated; clearly there is no one 'pan-world view' of events. Instead of McLuhan's (1962) global village, we appear to have several 'global villages' (Clausen 2001, 2003: 8), each of which provides international news that can then be disseminated at a national level by a range of competing news organizations. These news organizations 'domesticate' the news as it is produced according to the 'legal rules and political system of their country' (ibid.: 15).

It is at this point that censorship enters the news chain, since the nature of broadcast domestic news can be directly shaped through overt political censorship which seeks to remove any external criticism of its own national regime. For example, both the BBC's WSTV and Al-Jazeera have been censored by national governments. In 1994 Rupert Murdoch agreed to a request from the Chinese government to remove the BBC's WSTV (now BBC World) from his Star satellite (AsiaSat-1), after it broadcast a critical view of the events in Tiananmen Square and a highly controversial biography of Chairman Mao (Page 2003). On 7 August 2004 Al-Jazeera's Baghdad station was subjected to a month-long ban by the Iraqi interim government which accused the broadcasters of inciting hatred and racial tension. Critics argued that the reason for the ban was the extensive coverage by Al-Jazeera of the insurgent forces in Iraq, headed by Moqtada Sadr and his Mehdi army militia, and also its critical accounts of the interim government. In both cases, news with a global reach was subject to the dictates of national censorship (see the work of Reporters Without Borders (2003) for more examples).

Clausen's (2003) study of global television news takes the view that there is no such thing as 'global' news because news (even when news regimes take news from the big three news agencies[60] is 'domesticated' by and through nationally specific production practices and routines. The result is always a news product which is aimed at particular national audiences. Clausen cites Japan as having highly specific political and cultural influences which occur 'at many levels in the production process' (ibid.: 15). It is also argued that the domestication of 'foreign' events by national news providers is an attempt to construe the significance of these events 'in ways that are compatible with the culture and the "dominant ideology" of societies they serve' (Gurevitch et al. 1991: 207). Domestication makes 'foreign' events relevant and comprehensible to a domestic audience by being presented/written in the national language and adopting a narrative style that is familiar to both presenters and their audience (ibid.). The production process and the professional activities of these domestic or host journalists are specifically oriented towards targeting national, regional or local audiences (Clausen 2003). It is also important to note that different types of domestication may occur within the same country. In America, Fox News offers a completely different perspective of American military intervention from other national broadcasters. It has adopted a patriotic stance, which has meant an almost uncritical acceptance of official justifications and accounts of events in the Iraq war. The domestication of news for particular national, regional or local audiences means that the character of international news varies both between and within countries. Overall, the global news market is complex and the features of this complexity appear to be a few global news organizations (although rivals are emerging), who turn news into an exportable commodity and sell it, only for it to be repackaged according to the political or cultural dispositions of different news providers operating at a state or regional level.

CONCLUSION

As noted at the beginning of this chapter, the modern news ecology is understood according to sets of competing assumptions. On the one hand, it is argued that market-led competition, driven by technological change and leading to a growth in news media outlets, may be seen to encourage diversity, choice and quality of provision for the consumer. Here, competition is viewed as a necessary and positive function in providing a range of goods and services. It is consumers who choose what they want from a range of options. Today, a variety of news types may be obtained through a variety of platforms. Three assumptions exist here: first, that there is a range of options to choose from. Second, choice is real, and does not just entail choosing from a range of goods or services which are packaged differently, but which contain inherently the same or very similar content. Third, the consumer has the necessary information, knowledge and financial resources to make a discerning choice. On the other hand, a 'critical' perspective would argue accordingly: first, that a connection between competition and a positive social outcome does not occur. Second, competition drives out diversity, particularly when deregulatory policies have facilitated the further concentration of ownership. Third, choice is superficial and exists only when there are more products of the same kind to choose from. Overall, it is concluded that the modern news ecology supports a cultural and ideological hegemony because of the small number of significant news suppliers[61] and their economic activity.

Yet both sets of assumptions underestimate the complexity of the modern news ecology. Technology continues to extend the scope of news coverage, while regulation still enshrines the values of truthfulness, accuracy and sincerity. Ownership is still subject to regulation, standards of governance, shareholder accountability and limitations imposed by competition and anti-monopolistic frameworks. As for content and the positive social outcomes generated by the new news ecology, Clausen (2003) disputes the thesis that the news is becoming a homogeneous product. She prefers to talk of it as undergoing a process of domestication occurring in national, regional and local contexts (ibid.). Van Gompel *et al.* (2002: 197) on the other hand say that arguments about a positive social outcome resulting from increased competition are used to 'justify or legitimize both the dominant way in which media systems are organized and structured in contemporary (late) capitalist societies, and the everyday practices and routines of journalists and other professional media workers'.

Equally relevant to understanding the news ecology is the relationship between news and advertising. Clearly, it is often asserted that the pursuit of ratings to sell to advertisers has had a deleterious affect on programming priorities, reducing innovation and creativity in favour of 'safe' and popular programming which entertains the viewers rather than challenging them. It is a practice which Curran (1991: 47) refers to as 'common denominator provision for the mass market'. Nevertheless, there is nothing that indicates a *clear-cut* relationship between news production/reporting and advertising. News production remains in the hands of public service providers and commercial operators. As noted in the Introduction, the relationship between the two is a balancing act undertaken by policymakers who increasingly see the value of both and wish for the dominance of neither. I shall return to this issue in Chapters 5 and 6.

5

NEWS AND
SOCIETY

INTRODUCTION

Underpinning the value placed on truthfulness (accuracy and sincerity) in news production and reporting is freedom of expression (see Table 1, Introduction). Freedom of expression is a principle which, in practice, requires that it work within acceptable limits of expression. These limits serve to ban 'impermissible' speech and images: usually racial, national, religious or sexual excesses, although even here, excess is sometimes defended and judgement regarded as censorship. More formal legislation restricting freedom of expression exists in areas such as libel, defamation, protection of minors, contempt of court, official secrets and race relations. Curbs on freedom of expression can also be put in place to protect the private interest of individuals, whereby invasion of privacy must be justified and be in the public interest. Limits to freedom of expression also exist where a judgement is made over the quality of superficiality of expression. Overall the rationale for imposed limits, or sometimes obligations, is that they exist to better serve the public interest and further the best interests of society. Clearly, this is an issue of immense importance for news, and requires that those who mediate the news exercise both collective and individual responsibility. Such measures cannot ensure that the truth is revealed, but can ensure that truthfulness is valued (or aimed at), accurate journalism admired, and that both journalists and news organizations are provided with the mechanisms through which they can exercise good practice.

Of course the usual debate rages between 'critical' thinkers and liberal pluralists. For example, Lichtenberg (1995) argues that the news media do not exercise freedom of expression; rather they seek to suppress information or ignore certain views, undermining the truthfulness and accuracy of the news. Kelley and Donway (1995) suggest that limits or controls are placed on media freedom in the interest of providing news which has a disposition towards truthfulness. Furthermore, Kelley and Donway argue that the public have certain rights to receive reliable and accurate information and, if the media are not providing it, a government should intervene. In other words, regulatory intervention may be necessary to secure the range and quality of news needed to encourage the kind of public argument and debate required in a democracy.

Allan (1999: 3–4) helpfully looks at three broad ways of investigating the role of news in the context of media freedom. First, news is seen as an object of policy formation, where it is treated as an aspect of a democratic society. Here issues of truthfulness, accuracy and sincerity, law, freedom of expression and information, and avoiding unnecessary invasions of privacy are relevant, and deemed to define the scope of the public interest. Audiences are viewed primarily as comprising citizens or voters with rights, who need to be protected via regulatory authorities. Freedom of expression is justified by the argument that those being governed in a democracy give their informed consent which occurs where there is freely available information on which such consent may be based. In short, democracy carries with it the idea of freedom of information which supports the involvement of the active citizen or voter. Where truth and accuracy are valued, the news should ensure that key information is supplied to citizens concerned and interested in their own political life and the nature of the world in which they live. Second, news may be seen as an object of public opinion. This argument places the news media in the realm of the public sphere, and raises questions about its ability to foster rational-critical debate among citizens. Again, freedom of expression is crucial in order to facilitate the expression of diverse views and to enable such debate to take place. Third, news may be viewed as an object of commodification, where audience members are seen primarily as consumers. Freedom of expression can be misused in order to pursue commercial gain at the expense of the public and private interest: in other words, where the public interest is not served due to the trivial, sensational or irrelevant nature of the news, and private interest is ignored through breaches of privacy and intrusive reporting.

Where freedom of expression underpins the accuracy of the news, sincerity, it has been argued, is underpinned by journalistic practice and the exercise of collective and individual journalistic responsibility (see Table 1, Introduction). Here, responsibility is exercised in large part through the fact that journalists work within a range of 'sometimes conflicting influences, some more powerful than others and some powerful at certain times' (Harcup 2004: 13). Harcup's own experience as a journalist leads him to claim that these pressures can 'be negotiated and resisted as well as accepted' (ibid.). Despite difficulties in balancing a range of pressures, McQuail (2000) argues that there is quite a high measure of agreement on the basic ideas of how the media in general *should* contribute responsibly to the working of democratic society. This agreement may be summarized, when applied to news, in the following way:

- a free flow of accurate and diverse information
- which is reliable and is made available to all citizens
- who can use the information to challenge existing political, social, economic and cultural 'truths'
- without destroying the moral and social fabric of society
- and that citizens can ultimately use their improved knowledge and understanding to establish a stronger sense of social coherence, mutual understanding and belonging to a community.

Expressed in this form, the list represents a series of moral or normative aspirations on what the setting of news journalism should be, how it should report contemporary events and what the outcome of these reports should be. In short, the list represents the ideal news ecology or environment.

In reality these aspirations are premised on the extent to which the news media are both free and act in a responsible manner: a relationship not always acknowledged as possible. But with both in mind, four themes will structure the argument throughout the remainder of this chapter.

First, we will consider the need for freedom of expression which should allow for a free flow of information which is available to all citizens. Freedom of expression is a fundamental right in traditional liberal thought, but one which in practice raises questions about who (or which news media) can and should exercise this freedom, and who or what places constraints on those rights to free speech. These issues are crucial to the character of news that is produced (see Table 1, Introduction). As we will see later, freedom of expression also raises concerns about protecting society or individuals from harmful information, which poses a threat to the individual or group. This leads to the second theme, namely the idea that freedom of expression must be undertaken responsibly and that such responsibility necessarily produces limits. These limits operate in the interests of morality, democracy, decency and the public interest (Webster 1990), and are imposed both collectively and individually (see Table 1, Introduction). Third, the news media will be considered in relation to their role in the public sphere and the liberal democratic ideal of cultivating an informed public. Freedom of expression (at its best) can create the conditions where established political power in society is presented to the public in a transparent manner, which in theory can then allow the citizen to make political choices through voting in elections. Depending on the type, range and accuracy of the news provided, citizens can also, via the news media, become informed about a wider range of public issues beyond the political realm, such as cultural and social issues. The news media can, both in principle and in practice, contribute to both informed decision-making and greater understanding of issues. News as a purveyor of information to the public therefore has an important role to play in helping citizens make sense of the world in which they live by providing a diverse range of information to feed into a marketplace of ideas. As we saw in Chapter 3, there is common agreement that a diverse range of information sources is important in order to perpetuate cultural and ideological plurality and to challenge established or dominant 'truth' claims. I shall return to this later. Finally, I will examine the different ways in which news is regulated and the impact this has on the nature and character of news provided by different news organizations.

FREEDOM OF EXPRESSION

The classic liberal defence of freedom of expression is made by John Stuart Mill in *On Liberty* (1859). In this Mill accepted that unrestricted freedom of expression was not an ideal and that it needed to be restricted via balancing principles, themselves underpinned by Mill's lifelong attachment to the virtue of tolerance. As Isaiah Berlin (1969: 183–184) writes, Mill 'longed for the widest variety of human life and character. He saw that this could not be obtained without protecting individuals from each other, and, above all, from the terrible weight of social pressure; this led to his insistent and persistent demand for toleration.' Mill argued that it is wrong for government to silence opinion, whether right or wrong, since, he believed, it is only by having access to a diverse range of opinions and by comparing a variety of opinions or truth claims that we can make a reasonable attempt to discover the truth. Or to put it another way, since it is impossible for individuals to know whether any opinions which are suppressed are true or false, it is important to allow a variety of opinions to be heard, discussed and analysed. In addition, the suppression of opinions implies that the suppressor is infallible and is sure which claims are true and which are false, and which claims should be discussed and analysed.

However, Mill believed that each individual is fallible (and that each epoch or age is fallible), and so must be willing to listen to opinions which challenge existing views. In Mill's view, as further information is discovered by future generations, existing truths are necessarily questioned, a process which is important to the development of both the individual and society itself. Mill's defence of freedom of speech assumes that the only way in which intellectual life can flourish within a society is through the free discussion and interrogation of established truths and via the scrutiny of new views and opinions. Or, as The European Court notes, 'freedom of expression constitutes one of the essential foundations of a society, one of the basic conditions for its progress and for the development of every man' (*Handyside vs. United Kingdom* [1976]). Freedom of expression implies the right of criticism of governments and other agencies which seek to control or influence society (such as political parties, large corporations or commercial interests), and the interrogation and exploration of new cultural ideas and views which challenge and develop established norms and values. News is of course inevitably implicated in such a right, and the accurate (and sincere) reporting of contemporary events requires freedom of expression.

Whereas Mill justifies supporting freedom of expression through moral arguments, elsewhere support for freedom of expression is identified with the nature of political order. Many legal systems identify freedom of speech with the protection and proper functioning of democracy and the rule of good government. This is an idea that has been recognized in many countries' constitutions. The First Amendment to the US Constitution states that:

> Congress shall make no law respecting an establishment of religion, or prohibiting the free exercise thereof; or abridging the freedom of speech, or of the press; or the right of the people peaceably to assemble, and to petition the government for a redress of grievances.[1]

The American courts can review governments to make sure that they do not infringe the freedoms guaranteed in the First Amendment.

It is not only in America that freedom of expression is given constitutional protection; similar provisions may be found in other countries, such as Germany. Even in Britain, which has no written constitution, freedom of expression has been given protection by the European Convention on Human Rights (ECHR). Article 10 (section 1) states that:

> Everyone has the right to freedom of expression. This right shall include
> the right to hold opinions and to receive and impart information and ideas
> without interference by public authority and regardless of frontiers.

It is not only within Europe that international law protects freedom of expression. The International Covenant on Civil and Political Rights (ICCPR)[2] recognizes that in accordance with the Universal Declaration of Human Rights, the ideal of free human beings enjoying civil and political freedom, and freedom from fear and want, can only be achieved if the conditions are created whereby all citizens may enjoy their civil and political rights, as well as economic, social and cultural rights[3].

The importance of the European Court of Human Rights in protecting freedom of expression rights for the media in Britain was first exemplified by its decision in *The Sunday Times vs. United Kingdom* [1979], whereby the Court held for *The Sunday Times* to have the freedom to publish an article about the marketing and manufacture of the Thalidomide drug (a cause of various birth deformities). The British government had attempted to prevent publication because existing cases were already in litigation, claiming that a news story would prejudge issues and was therefore in contempt of court. However, given that an essential characteristic of news journalism is that it should deal in facts which may otherwise be concealed by vested interests, the European Court of Human Rights ruled that the public interest served by the freedom of expression in this case outweighed the need to protect the courts and the rights of litigants. The public, they argued, had a right to be properly informed about the drug. Because of this judgment the news media were able to convey information which was of major importance to public safety and served the public interest. Where liberal and democratic values support the case for freedom of expression, news production and reporting can and will remain open. This openness is not permissive since, as we shall now see, both news production and reporting must conduct themselves within the further requirement to exercise responsibility.

NEWS AND THE EXERCISE OF RESPONSIBILITY

It has been recognized that freedom of expression is not an unqualified 'good thing'; obligations, duties and responsibilities qualify its exercise. Mill (1859) acknowledged that the context within which an opinion is expressed must be recognized, requiring intellectual debate to be undertaken according to a code which places some restrictions upon freedom of action. Mill also recognized that freedom of speech may be harmful in certain contexts (the harm principle) and argued that freedom of speech should only be free from interference if it does not put others at risk. Mill's classic liberal defence of freedom of speech therefore takes into account both freedom and responsibility, a position which has been recognized, as noted above, by both the ECHR[4] and the ICCPR.[5] Clearly, news that is mediated can reach enormous numbers of people, meaning that the possibility of freedom of expression having consequences for individuals or societies is enhanced. Justifications for regulation of the media in general (although different media are curtailed by different levels of regulatory constraints) have been made on the grounds that they are special and must serve a democratic process, nourish the public sphere and serve the public interest and, as such, need to have some form of control imposed upon them. In particular, news and current affairs have been seen to be the most significant in democratic terms.

A dilemma arises in the careful balancing act which must be undertaken between the positive requirement for freedom of expression and the pursuit of the truth and the desire for the news media to be sincere in their intention to serve some type of public purpose through the exercise of individual and collective responsibility. This entails the restriction of the negative social consequences which may arise from uncontrolled free speech, or the pursuit of purely selfish, vested or commercial interests by media organizations. As such, in Britain and in many other democratic countries, news which incites racial, cultural or religious hatred, places a nation at risk, incites violence, invades a person's private life and so on, is proscribed either through negative regulatory requirements (something which a publisher or broadcaster must not do), or via particular laws or constitutional arrangements.[6] Proscriptive legal rules exist which are in place to restrict or eliminate activities that are seen to be antisocial, such as criminal activity. Laws on obscenity, defamation, contempt of court, official secrecy, confidentiality and libel are important proscriptive legal rules which form both an important part of journalistic activity and affect the exercise of journalism and, consequently, the nature and character of the news which is produced.[7]

The raft of legal restrictions placed upon journalistic activity reflects the emphasis that is placed on the power of the news, rather than other media genre, to have significant consequences for day-to-day life in particular, and the extent of openness in a society in general. In Britain such constraints on news reporting have traditionally been balanced to some extent by the ability of news journalists to use a defence of qualified privilege in libel cases. A precedent was established in the ruling in *Reynolds vs. Times Newspapers* [1998].[8] Effectively, this justified the publication of information where it is immaterial whether the allegations are true, false or made carelessly. However, proof of malice militates against the publication of untrue allegations. The judge in the case, Lord Nicholls, made an important observation in the Reynolds case which serves as a kind of legal view of what news should be: namely that the common law does not seek to set a higher standard than that of responsible journalism, which he believed the profession sets for itself already. Investigative journalism was given protection via this ruling, although the Reynolds defence would not protect news concerned with salacious matters. Qualified privilege can therefore be used to report to the public 'fair information of public interest', which should be 'believed on reasonable grounds to be accurate' (Barendt and Hitchens 2000: 371). Or put another way, a core quality of news is that it should sincerely attempt to be an accurate representation of the event it is reporting.

Occasionally, journalists' attempts to expose wrongdoing or injustice are constrained. Sometimes their attempt to reveal information can be curtailed through the use of the courts before it is even published. News censorship may be undertaken by the use of injunctions which are awarded at secret hearings in the High Court by judges who are asked to impose prior restraint on material to be published; these are referred to colloquially by journalists as 'gagging orders'. Such applications are usually based on a complaint that the information has been acquired in breach of confidence (Robertson and Nicol 1990) and may also be used to protect particular vested interests. In November 2003 an application for the use of prior restraint was used in an unusual way by Michael Fawcett (Prince Charles's former royal aide) after *The Mail on Sunday* outlined a series of allegations relating to The Prince of Wales's official London residence, Clarence House. An injunction was requested and granted on the basis that the allegations were libellous, an unusual action, since injunctions based on libel are rare and are usually granted only when the court is satisfied that the allegations are false and that the newspaper is not seeking to claim that they are true. One of the greatest rallying cries for freedom, 'publish and be damned', may be used by publishers and newspapers in an attempt to assert that allegations are true. While 'publish and be damned' represents, particularly in films that feature brave and bold editors and journalists, the power of the press to speak out against injustice, it also represents attempts made by some elements of the press to flout the courts. In a similar vein, press assertions of truth, which arise from a belief that a story is true when in fact it is not, may be due to a failure to examine the evidence for the story. While not necessarily doubting the sincerity of a particular belief (for example, held by an editor) that a story is true, failing to check the evidence for its veracity may lead to 'news' stories which are not news. The publication of faked pictures of the alleged torture of Iraqi prisoners by British soldiers eventually prompted an apology from the *Mirror* which declared: 'Sorry we were hoaxed':[9] an apology that begs the question of how much checking was undertaken by the newspaper before it made its very serious allegations. What becomes clear after such an incident is that unchecked events are not news simply because they are dramatic, have a grain of truth in them, or represent something that is desired. News must be characterized by more rigorous editorial demands than these.

The watchdog role of the news can easily be pushed too far in pursuit of a story that will momentarily grab the audience's attention. Regular attacks by the American news media on the value and integrity of public institutions and those who work within them, through sleaze and scandal revelations, have been criticized by those who argue that this 'scepticism has started to eat at the soul of American democratic values' (Hargreaves 2003: 7). This type of reporting has been seen by some to be particularly damaging in the area of political communication. Fallows (1996) shows how the increasing personalization of politics in the news is alienating American television audiences. In Britain too, the news media prefer to reflect the conflictual nature of politics because it makes for interesting television or good reading. A former editor of ITN's *5.40 p.m. News* (now ITV's *6.30 p.m. News*), for example, preferred to broadcast political stories when there had been a 'good punch-up at PMQs' (Prime Minister's Questions) rather than routinely cover political process and debate (Harrison 2000: 195).[10] Although Prime Minister's Question Time and coverage of actual political debate and policy issues remain popular on such channels as C-Span in America, there has been an increasing tendency by the mainstream news media to cover politics in an adversarial way, both in America and Britain. The tabloids in particular tend to treat politicians in the same way that they treat celebrities, as individuals who do not really have the right to a private life if a lucrative story is involved.

Throughout the period when John Major was Prime Minister (1991 to 1997), a long list of revelations about politicians' misdemeanours set a new low in the tone of political news reporting, with scandal and sleaze often dominating the coverage of political affairs in most newspapers (for an historical overview of the period 1987 to 1995 see McNair 1996: 162–177; Wilson 1996: 81–86). The defence of many of these invasions into politicians' personal or private lives was frequently justified as exposing hypocrisy. Thus, for example, the reporting of adulterous relationships within the Major government was justifiable on public interest grounds, as a key policy initiative of the Conservative government was the 'back to basics' campaign which championed the importance of family values. The above example reinforces the point that the teller of news helps define the scope and tone of news. Some news media organizations use the personal and private lives of politicians as a source of news rather than the policies they represent, while others do not. Using the private lives of public figures to support a story, or to be the story, dwells within the conspectus of truthfulness (obviously only if it is not fabricated), but not of sincerity. Prurience and profit may be more of a motive. This type of 'news' reporting is often criticized for being trivial, salacious in content and lacking in any educational value. Some critics go even further and lament a change in the news media organizations' news selection and news values (examined further in Chapter 6), which signal a shift from information-based reporting to entertainment-based reporting in accordance with what is perceived to be audience preferences (Barnett 1998). However, the distinction between information- and entertainment-based reporting is, as we have seen, sometimes a spurious one. Entertaining an audience has a long and legitimate history in news reporting (see Chapter 2), and claims that standards of news reporting are deteriorating and what constitutes news is becoming trivial need to be examined. It is to the role of news in the public sphere that I now turn.

NEWS AND THE PUBLIC SPHERE

The public sphere is a notional space, existing between civil society and the state (Thompson 1992). It is a social setting, frequently non-institutional, where individuals obtain information or education and undertake discussion and deliberation about contemporary events in all their diversity. It can exist formally (a town hall meeting open to the public) or in an informal setting (an internet chat site). In complex contemporary societies people take much of their understanding of the world from the news media: broadcast news, current affairs programmes, political news in the press and increasingly via news sites on the internet. The development of a range of new information communication technologies (ICTs) and the growth of global communications systems means it is no longer feasible to speak of a unified public sphere (Keane 1995: 8), but rather of several public spheres. These public sphere(s) arise in the conversational relationships people can now be part of by using diverse communication technologies. Writing to the editor, using the red button on the TV remote control and belonging to a discussion group on the internet generate different communicative relationships that are only limited by the technology deployed. Public spheres of discussion are not confined to geographical boundaries. Essentially, two views of news in relationship to the public sphere(s) are worth noting.

First, a narrow view of the public sphere(s): here it (or they) are simply seen as a means of delivering information to people enabling them to form opinions. From this perspective the public sphere is a means by which citizens can read or hear about competing political views as politicians compete for support and express this competition through the news media. The way in which politics is covered in the news is therefore important, but as we have seen, the irresponsible exercise of freedom of expression in political reporting may lead to news that becomes 'an object of commodification' (Allan 1999: 3). Understanding and responding to perceived public opinion becomes a form of news reporting which represents the dynamic between the citizen and the politician in terms of political coverage based upon 'popular interest' (ibid.: 16) rather than any deeper values. In this limited public sphere an impetus towards reporting the trivial or trivializing complex issues is established. Indeed, it is argued that news broadcasts which encourage viewers to 'phone in', ' text in', 'e-mail in' or 'press the red button' to let us know 'your views' are further confusing news with opinion. All that is established is a public sphere dominated by versions of public opinion and news coverage that claim to reflect popular interest. For news organizations, understanding public opinion and popular interests becomes the driving force for the way news is reported and packaged. Confusingly the attachment to this kind of news produces a lexicon of justification that can lead to news being further debased. 'The people have a right to know', 'it is in the public interest' and (as we have seen) 'publish and be damned' may be used to justify inaccurate and insincere news journalism as much as accurate and sincere news journalism.

Second, a more complex view of the public sphere is to see it as a *deliberative* rather than just an informational forum. Good-quality inform- ation is required to stimulate discussion, and the development of interactive communication, weblogs and other opportunities for discus- sion on the internet offers forums for active debate and discussion. These debates and discussions are generally fed by the news available through a variety of online sites as well as the traditional media and can serve to challenge mainstream versions of contemporary events by widening discussion and deepening debate. In this sense the amount of news in circulation is increased beyond that provided by the mainstream news media. Online discussion and debate resonate with the qualities of well- attended town hall meetings and gatherings in late eighteenth century London coffee shops. Habermas thought the latter constituted one of the beginnings of a bourgeois public sphere (by analogy a point which may apply to the internet) which he describes as a space that mediates between society and the state, where individuals and groups discuss and argue about public matters:

> By 'the public sphere' we mean first of all a realm of our social life in which something approaching public opinion can be formed. Access is guaranteed to all citizens. A portion of the public sphere comes into being in every conversation in which private individuals assemble to form a public body.
>
> (Habermas 1984: 49)

The bourgeois public sphere of the eighteenth- and nineteenth-century town halls and coffee shops (see Chapter 2) is not democratic in terms of its constitution and membership (male and middle class). None the less, it represents for Habermas an ideal in terms of its aspiration to 'communicative rationality' — discussion undertaken without the exercise of coercion or manipulation, whereby mutual understanding between individuals and groups in society is reached. In short, it represents a picture of balanced debate and informed discussion. While idealistic, and in terms of the town halls and coffee shops, utopian, the image is powerful enough to be an aspiration shared by those, unlike the above, who take seriously the slogans 'the people have a right to know', 'it is in the public interest' or even 'publish and be damned'.

What prevents the ideal from being the real is the commodification of news, which Habermas (1989) believed had 'refeudalized' the bourgeois public sphere replete with its aspirational communicative rationality, turning it into a pseudo public sphere within which the public behave as consumers set in their own private consumption pattern, rather than discursive citizens engaged in rational-critical debate. Livingstone and Lunt (1994) also regard the commodification of news as problematic, because the public are offered preprepared arguments in ways which do not encourage public debate and discussion. Commodified news, they argue, seeks to influence the public through non-rational persuasion, rather than to achieve consensus through rational argument. Even in this more complex view of the public sphere(s), news is seen as ultimately the product of commercial interests targeting consumers and not citizens. In many European countries a public service broadcaster has been set up to restrict the influence of commercial interests or the effects of gossip journalism. Generally funded via state subsidy or grant, public service broadcasters are expected to report news which reflects a diverse range of contemporary events and issues and is underpinned by high levels of research and investigation.[11] They are usually free to air and are remitted to provide national coverage. In this sense public service broadcasters can act as enabling agents for the establishment and nourishment of deliberative or discursive public sphere(s).[12]

News, the public sphere and pluralism

Two versions of news pluralism may be discerned. First, a traditional liberal approach argues that free competition will necessarily lead to a plurality of views, thereby serving one of the conditions of democratic pluralism; a free and varied news media offering a diverse range of news and information. Second, critics of this approach argue that this plurality of news is superficial, producing, as it does, limited news choices. In both cases the type of news provided is linked to the way different news organizations exercise their responsibility towards news. From our point of view this will establish a range of news which spans the divide between entertainment at one end and education at the other. It is questionable though to what extent a diverse and inclusive range of news is provided in a competitive environment. A study by Hargreaves and Thomas (2002), for example, found that mainstream broadcasters, in particular television news broadcasters, were failing to engage with certain audiences such as Britain's ethnic minorities (see Chapter 7).[13] Recently, the internet has been seen to offer opportunities for the inclusion of those who feel the mainstream news media do not represent them or their concerns adequately. Optimistic analysts such as Nicholas Negroponte (1996) and Mark Poster (1995) saw the internet and digitization as democratizing and emancipatory developments. Papacharissi (2002: 24) finds hope in the fact that the internet has facilitated the development of cyberspheres, where people from all over the globe, from culturally diverse backgrounds, come together to engage in a 'virtual political discussion' about issues in the news. In contrast, Curran and Seaton (2003) argue that the history of the internet underlines its contemporary contradictory nature. On the one hand, it still has a public service element through the free distribution of news, information, access to libraries, the BBC's online services and galleries and so on. On the other hand, major corporate bodies attempt to dominate and control large areas of it. Significantly though, users of the internet can bypass established centres of power and set up their own chat rooms, forming cyberspheres and discussing and challenging mediated news provided by mainstream news organizations.

The range of news provision that is now available means that it is now possible to talk about news provision in relation to different typologies of public spheres, which Keane (1995) refers to as micro-, meso- and macro-public spheres.[14]

Traditional news providers operating in the meso-public sphere (Keane 1995) such as the BBC have perceived their role to be a re-engagement of the young with politics via traditional broadcast media, but also via the internet, marrying its public service role with the potential of new media (Kevill 2002a, 2002b). The BBC has introduced a new website called iCan which seeks specifically to encourage individual citizens to connect with politics through common concerns such as speed cameras or bullying, as well as introducing a wider range of news stories than those covered by the national media. It remains to be seen to what extent this initiative will encourage web-based communities and citizen engagement. The encouragement of alternative forms of democratic engagement is particularly important if we agree that the news available in the meso-public sphere in particular is increasingly being provided by a smaller number of large and powerful organizations, as well as by organized and well-resourced groups in civil society (such as interest groups, non-governmental organizations (NGOs) and other large associations). Not only do media conglomerates generally host the most popular websites (Curran and Seaton 2003), but large, well-organized NGOs are often very successful at gaining publicity and are 'heard' by the public because they have the financial means to establish a public voice and are adept at negotiating with national news broadcasters. Gaining coverage by the news media often relies on successfully producing a 'pseudo event' (Boorstin 1964: 22–23). This is a planned event, aimed primarily at catching the news organizations' attention with the intention of achieving coverage or publicity which is beneficial. Boorstin argues that these events distort the different roles of actor and audience, as the actor actually creates a new story for the convenience of the news media, and aims to influence rather than benefit the audience.

Some voices from the private sector, the state and civil society are more likely to be successful at gaining access to the news than others. A culture of press relations has arisen whereby most organizations employ press officers (often ex-journalists) to ensure that their message is likely to be used by the news media, because they are able to write in ways that will appeal to journalists. Their aim is to influence a news agenda in the hope that journalists who use these press releases will write stories that benefit the organization from which the release came. Press officers act increasingly as intermediaries between the journalist and the organization, which restricts the journalist's access to sources and source material. Consequently, the relationship between the news media and the public relations machine may have an impact on the quality or reliability of the information which feeds the meso-public sphere. Franklin (1997: 20) observed that experts in managing politics such as Sir Bernard Ingham and Alastair Campbell have been criticized for taking control of the political news agenda too far. However, Walker (2002) has observed that, sometimes, the perceptions of Westminster journalists (such as Nick Jones 1996) that press officers or spin machines overly manipulate them may be overstated, since news media organizations may also be political actors in their own right. If this is the case, then organizations may place their own 'spin' on stories. Certainly the BBC has received constant criticism from different conservative governments for having a politically left-leaning ethos.

Overall, stories which emerge from a contest between press officer and journalist represent a power struggle between controlling sources and controlling the news product which the public receives. Although as Hargreaves (2003) observes, the more experienced journalists will probably see through the 'spin' or polish provided by a press officer, the younger recruit may not be so critically aware. Consequently, since many of the older, more experienced journalists leave the newsroom and become press officers, it would seem that the balance of power and influence is being tilted away from the journalist. If so, a problem may arise in those sections of the news media which rely increasingly on press releases as a cheaper form of news-gathering. Inexperienced journalists, or those who rarely leave the newsroom, may be tempted to regurgitate messages verbatim, acting more as a fifth column than a fourth estate, propping up rather than scrutinizing political institutions or large organizations. Political parties in particular have recognized the importance of getting the best possible coverage of their activities and are prepared in the future 'to spin messages in cyberspace' (Curran and Seaton 2003: 266). The character of news which emerges from such activities will depend very much on the way in which different news organizations scrutinize the messages. Undoubtedly there will be a great deal of material available and political parties will consistently attempt to stage pseudo-events (Boorstin 1964) or pseudo-cyber-events in order to attract the public and the news media. To date, most news organizations tend to cover staged events, since few are willing to abandon the news pack in search of a different story. Press conferences, promotions and other publicity stunts are therefore such a familiar part of the news that it is possible that the audience forgets, when these events find their way into news, that they are thoroughly contrived.

If powerful voices, such as politicians', can be said to dominate some sectors of the news media, then at least two other sectors may also be said to be in a position to defy domination. First, news media organizations themselves, which in theory have the resources and the will to resist attempts to impose vested interests upon them. This includes public service broadcasters (particularly the licence fee-funded BBC). Second, news sites on the internet which enable access to non-mainstream views and have even threatened (in some countries) to break through official censorship. However, it is important not to overplay the role of PSB or the internet. As public service broadcasters come under increasing pressure in the multi-channel environment, their future role, remit and funding are unclear. Furthermore, Curran and Seaton (2003: 270) argue that inequality of resources and power structures in the real world structure and affect the online world. None the less, Curran and Seaton offer some possibility for the development of a deliberative and discursive news public sphere, pointing out that while 'alternative voices tend not to be heard in the main square of the electronic public sphere . . . they still get heard in some online backstreets'. Curran and Seaton see this situation as an improvement on media–citizen relationships in the real world, since 'market censorship remains less developed and effective in the online world than it is in the off-line world' (ibid.). Websites such as <http://www.openDemocracy.net> offer citizens the opportunity to scrutinize the activities of some global organizations, whose activities may be seen arguably to be stripped of their PR and spin. Consequently, alternative news sites, weblogs and personal journalism offer areas of contestation alongside areas of control by corporate and political interests. Potentially, such sites offer possibilities for the development of micro-public spheres or cyberspheres which may allow alternative voices to challenge the 'meso-public sphere' (Keane 1995: 8). News provided by the mainstream news media may be questioned or challenged in a way which was not previously possible, by audiences accessing news that is not defined by the traditional news organizations.

The ideals and values behind a deliberative or discursive public sphere exist in tension with the lived reality of journalistic activity, the exercise of power by large organizations and the pressures of the news media marketplace. What news should be and what news is may be understood as expressing a gap based on two limitations. First, freedom of expression must be considered in relation to social responsibility and second, the informational and educational value of news and information must be assessed in relation to the reality of the production context and the pressures under which journalism operates. The limits placed upon the ideals of perfect public spheres and perfect news pluralism represent the mundane reality of news, a reality which both values PSB and the anarchic and democratic impulses of the internet and yet encompasses an ever-deregulated news environment within which large-scale news organizations, which regard news as a commodity, can operate more widely and freely.

UK REGULATION OF THE NEWS

Self-regulation of print news

Gibbons (1998: 64) points out that the first Royal Commission on the Press (1947) did not judge the newspaper industry to be an 'agency for political education in a democracy'. In fact, the Royal Commission recognized that it would be unwise to allow the press to pursue its commercial interests without limit, since this would have a negative effect on the character of the news provided. A series of reports and Royal Commissions on the press have been undertaken,[15] with the main focus being on preventing unjustified press intrusion into people's private lives and the abandonment of responsible reporting. In 1990 the first Calcutt Report[16] concluded that the newspaper industry should continue to be self-regulated, but a new body should replace the Press Council. The Press Complaints Commission (PCC), which came into existence in 1991, differed from the Press Council in two key ways: it comprised editors from a variety of newspapers, and it published a new code of practice for journalists. These codes aimed to curb some journalists' instinct to follow the story at any expense and refocus them on the core qualities of news such as accuracy and a disposition towards truthfulness. Calcutt also recognized that increasing competition between newspapers for readers had led to greater intrusion and a change in news agendas had affected the character of news, as increasingly stories were being selected on the likelihood that they would provide competitive advantage over their rival news organizations and not for their inherent news value.

Harcup (2004) describes a trend in which television programmes and the activities of all types of celebrities who appear in them has become a source of news for the press. In particular, stories about celebrities' private lives and problems have become increasingly common, as have stories about politicians' private lives (exacerbated further today by the free availability of gossip on internet sites).[17] The rationale appears to be that once individuals have become 'celebrities' by appearing on television, they waive their right to privacy and become public property. The prurient interest, whipped up by the tabloids, in the activities of numerous celebrities has changed the character of press news. While famous film stars, the aristocracy and royalty have long been a source of news, the status of celebrity has changed over recent years, meaning that some news reporting thrives on the activities of people who are minor, or 'B' or 'C' class celebrities. These people are generally made famous through appearances in television programmes such as reality TV shows, and they retain their notoriety through further news media interest in their affairs. By creating 'news' through press coverage of the activities of television celebrities, organizations can successfully cross-promote their media interests, often at the expense of the privacy of the individual concerned.

In response to concerns about invasion of privacy and accuracy of reporting, the PCC has, on several occasions, amended its rules.[18] These rules, however, have not tended to be particularly effective in controlling the behaviour of some elements of the press. During the 1980s and 1990s the character of press news began to change, as the British tabloid press became obsessed by anything that Diana, Princess of Wales did (we have seen similar levels of interest since in celebrities such as David and Victoria Beckham). The problem of harassment of individuals was revisited in 1997 after Princess Diana died in a car crash in Paris while trying to escape from pursuing paparazzi. Clause 4 of the PCC's Code of Practice was amended to advise that material obtained through 'persistent pursuit' should be published only if the editor is convinced it does not breach the Code.[19] This provision was extended to include material obtained by freelance journalists. A significant amendment to the definition of a private place was also made, which included both public and private places 'where there is a reasonable expectation of privacy'.[20] Consequent curbs on news-gathering practice have attempted to refocus the tabloid newspapers' definition of news with little success.[21]

In order to safeguard press freedom of expression, the PCC's public interest section gives details of the occasions when an editor can argue for breaches of the PCC Code.[22] Using the public interest defence, an editor can argue that breaches of the Code were justified to protect the public's right to know (freedom of expression rights). Problematically for those concerned about the nature of news which emerges, the public interest threshold used to justify intrusions into privacy appears lower in the press than in the broadcast sector (see also Gibbons 1998: 86–87).[23] In this vein, Franklin (1997: 17) argues that the decision to continue 'press self-regulation will be a significant factor in ensuring that newzak [news converted into entertainment] flourishes'. He considers that invasions of privacy and inaccuracies, trivialization and sensationalism, perpetrated in the main by the tabloid press, will not be curbed by elements of a self-regulating industry which prioritize commercial interests above standards of content.

A disadvantage of self-regulation is that there is nothing in an informal system to prevent people from taking complaints against the press to court. In contrast, statutory regulatory bodies generally appear to be able to deal with complaints in a manner which satisfies the complainant. It appears that in the absence of privacy legislation, redress for invasions of privacy by the press will be increasingly pursued through the courts,[24] regardless of whether PCC-enforced apologies from the newspapers in question are published. Problematically in Britain there are few ways to achieve redress for invasions of privacy without endangering wider press freedoms. The increasing pursuit of celebrity stories is a circular activity, since the celebrity culture on which some newspapers largely feed is spread and nurtured by television and newspapers themselves. As celebrities retaliate, editors are increasingly finding themselves fighting in battles for the principles of press freedom in court, although the story or material over which they fight is often trivial and unlikely to serve the public interest. Even so, the principles over which these court cases are fought are important ones, since they circumscribe press freedom and need to be retained to ensure that the 'serious' news media can continue to operate and fulfil their news remit. It is significant that Rupert Murdoch, owner of the two bestselling newspapers in Britain, the *Sun* and the *News of the World*, claims that his newspapers are unashamedly 'in the entertainment business' (cited in Harcup 2004: 86) signalling, perhaps, his continued willingness to fight for the right to publish the trivial at whatever cost. And of course he is absolutely correct to suggest that the freedom of expression is not limited to worthy or serious publication, but applies equally to the freedom to publish or show trivia.

The activities of some elements of a self-regulated press appear to be a factor in the low levels of public trust readers have with the print medium as a whole, particularly when the press is compared with broadcast news (Sanders 2003). A MORI survey carried out for the British Media Association in 2000 showed that 78 per cent of those surveyed believe that journalists do not tell the truth.[25] In 2003 Eurobarometer reported that only 20 per cent of British people trust newspapers, which is less than half of the EU average (46 per cent), whereas 75 per cent of the British public say they tend not to trust the press. Despite a great deal of evidence showing the lack of trust the British have in their print news, more Britons read a newspaper every day than the EU average (48 per cent in Britain compared with 40 per cent in the rest of the EU).[26] We have seen how the self-regulation of the print medium has not prevented the reporting of stories which can be challenged as both inaccurate and as an unjustifiable invasion of privacy. The abandonment of the pursuit of truth, accuracy and the exercise of responsibility, alongside a further narrowing of the news agenda to focus largely on the world of the celebrity, means that what appears in some newspapers today is little more than entertaining gossip. The pursuit of gossip simply to sell newspapers has not escaped the notice of the audience who may enjoy reading such stories but do not necessarily believe them to be true.

Regulation of broadcast news

Broadcast news has traditionally been carefully controlled and regulated in response to a belief that it is of a different nature from print news. In particular, the protection of impartiality, standards and quality in news is vested in PSB, a position which has been reinforced in the 2003 Communications Act (Appendix 5) and the duties of OFCOM. In the multi-channel environment the special status of the BBC as a licence fee public service broadcaster is to be retained, at least until the Charter renewal in 2006. [27] The retention of PSB obligations for news providers is important, because the public trust highly regulated broadcast news to be a truthful and accurate account of contemporary events. In Britain, trust in radio and television (65 per cent and 71 per cent respectively) is significantly higher than trust in the press and higher than the EU average of 62 per cent (figures reported in the *Guardian* 24 April 2002). During the war with Iraq in March/April 2003 the public stated that they trusted television coverage the most (MORI 3, April 2003). [28] Broadcast news is subject to statutory regulation which has imposed both negative regulations (those which prevent the broadcaster from doing something) [29] and positive regulations (those which charge the broadcaster with a duty to undertake specific tasks and functions and to provide certain types and amounts of content, in particular news which is accurate, reliable and impartial). [30] Regulations placed on news have been relaxed over the years. [31] The ITV sector was allowed to move *News at Ten* from 10 p.m. in 1999 to later time slots, finally moving it permanently to 10.30 p.m. in 2001. According to Richard Tait, the failure by the ITC to enforce PSB obligations on ITV1 to broadcast news at a consistent time led to the BBC taking advantage of the gap in the schedule, to launch its own *News at Ten* programme in October 2000, a tactic which was also adopted by Sky News. [32]

As we saw in Chapter 3, the fortunes of ITN are irrevocably linked to the ITV system, which itself operates in an increasingly commercial and competitive broadcasting environment. In practice, ITN today has to reconcile being a public service news organization alongside the need to be a versatile and flexible company operating on smaller budgets while supplying more outlets and broadcasting more hours of news for a wide range of contractors.[33] With the exception of *Channel 4 News* which ITN describes on its website as an 'innovative approach to news reporting, aiming to think more laterally than other television news programmes' and providing 'intelligent analysis', news provided for ITV1 is characterized as 'up-to-the-minute' news coverage offering 'a popular approach' which is 'accessible and relevant'.[34] The latter approach has long been part of the ITV remit, but it can sit uneasily with PSB obligations as ITV becomes increasingly competitive (Harrison 2000). The character of news provided by ITN for ITV1 has to fit into a purely entertainment-oriented channel and cannot be allowed to disrupt the flow of programming in a way which would cause audiences to switch channels. In practice ITN has had to ensure that news is accessible, not too challenging and, above all, entertaining in character, a characteristic which it extends to its twenty-four-hour news channel.

ITN sees its ITV news channels as putting 'the drama back into news with an emphasis on live events, breaking news, live pictures and agenda setting interviews'.[35] Since ITN operates under public service obligations it has to marry ITV's need for audience-grabbing stories (an emphasis on the contemporary via liveness and drama), while retaining the core values of accurate and sincerely reported news. This marriage is best summarized by ITN's *Tonight* programme which is broadcast at peak time (8 p.m.) twice a week and (at the time of writing) presented by ITN's most famous face, Trevor McDonald. *Tonight* aims 'to make a more accessible current affairs programme (fusing human interest stories with major political interviews, using the American news magazine format as a model) without jeopardising journalistic integrity, depth and objectivity'.[36] The programme's breadth of interest is reflected in the wide-ranging interviews undertaken with both celebrities and politicians as entertainment is mixed with both informational and educational subject matter: an approach which which may be described as 'cosy'. According to this view the audience for this kind of news programme is addressed in a familiar style, where their understanding of events is anticipated in terms of a general emotional response rather than an intellectual one (for example, being told what is coming next and how 'shocking', 'disturbing' or 'funny' the next item is – see in particular ITV's *6.30 p.m. News*). Indeed, it is assumed that the audience is not disposed to think too deeply about the items reported. Yet grouping together different types of subject matter is, according to Tunstall (1993), where the three goals of PSB merge to form ed-info-tainment. This merging of goals is not new and is evident in programmes such as *That's Life* or the *Antiques Road Show*, and has also appeared before in a quasi-news programme, also called *Tonight*, broadcast by the BBC in 1957 as a flagship programme. *Tonight's* informal style of presentation broke sharply with old BBC traditions (Briggs 1995). Although the news programmes broadcast by ITN have changed in recent years, popular approaches to news delivery are not new, nor simply a feature of a non-PSB environment.

We have seen that in practice many types and styles of news can exist in a statutory and self-regulatory news environment. While news journalists from both the print and broadcast media have common concerns with regard to freedom of expression, there is a crucial difference between the two types of news media with respect to issues of 'quality of programmes and publications' (Gibbons 1998: 64). This is due in part to the different types of regulatory constraints within which they work and the professional culture they inhabit. Both affect the character of news they produce.

According to Feintuck (1999), press journalists operate with a libertarian approach to their job while broadcast journalists operate according to a model of social responsibility. Press journalists combine a culture of systematic doubt with herd instinct and a solitary approach to their job. Their 'pack animal' description points towards an established consensus on a news story, not their individualism or desire for exclusives. By contrast, broadcast news journalists are inculcated in the careful and sensitive handling of broadcast material (even if that impinges upon freedom of expression (Gibbons 1998)). Feintuck (1999: 41) summarizes the difference between the two approaches accordingly: the libertarian approach is associated with the 'free marketplace of ideas', and the social responsibility model expects the broadcaster to respect moral and cultural mores and values, be mindful of public levels of tolerance and make a contribution to the education of the viewer. Gibbons (1998) argues that the press has not concerned itself with identifying 'quality' in news reporting, but has let the market dictate the level of sophistication that the readership is willing to purchase. In practice, this has meant that whether the press is 'quality/broadsheet' or 'tabloid', the news it contains has still focused on following the preferences of their differentiated readership (giving readers what they want) rather than pursuing a more serious-minded news agenda. As we have seen, in this regard the press has long defended its need to exercise freedom of expression in news reporting in order to provide information which is uncensored. Even were censorship seen to be for the public good, or to protect the privacy of individuals in the spotlight, it is anathema to the press's rationale. Policymakers and lawyers have concerned themselves with infringements of individuals' privacy rights, sometimes calling for the introduction of privacy legislation in Britain. However, there has not been any serious attempt made to regulate the press in terms of standards of quality of content, even though criticisms have often been levelled at the degree of sensationalism that exists in certain sectors of the press. News in the press has therefore become very variable in style and quality, whereas television news has more often drawn criticism relating to its increasingly homogeneous content (see Chapter 3).

UK STATUTORY REQUIREMENTS FOR IMPARTIALITY IN BROADCAST NEWS REPORTING

The BBC and independence from government

An important element of the BBC's public service role has been grounded in the constitutional independence it holds (in theory at least) from politicians, and in particular from the government of the day. In theory this independence has allowed the BBC to be impartial when reporting controversial matters such as politics (Briggs 1961). Despite attempts to separate the BBC from vested interests, the BBC's relationship with the government of the day has from time to time become very tense. Although its news reporting was expected to be conducted in the public interest, an interest not regarded as synonymous with government or the state, such a clear distinction was blurred during the General Strike of 1926 when Reith and the BBC explicitly supported the government (Scannell and Cardiff 1991). At the beginning of the Second World War the BBC 'took the policy decision to tell the truth, as far as the truth could be ascertained, rather than create propaganda' (Crisell 1997: 56), in order to attain independence from government. The question of the BBC's 'loyalty' to government has arisen many times over the years. In recent times where war has necessitated the deployment of troops to the Falkland Islands, Kosovo, Kuwait and Iraq, the BBC has always viewed it as an occasion to give an impartial account of events, which may mean that it reports events which may reflect negatively on Britain and its troops.

During the 1991 war with Iraq, the BBC was given the nickname the *Baghdad Broadcasting Corporation* for following its own guidelines on impartial news reporting and showing pictures of civilian Iraqi casualties caught in NATO's bombing of the Al Amiriya shelter. The BBC's news had a different character from most other print and broadcast media, leading the the *Sun* newspaper to criticize the BBC on the grounds that the pictures could elicit sympathy for Iraq (Taylor 1992). During the

2003 war with Iraq, the BBC was also criticized by then Broadcasting Minister John Reid, who claimed publicly that the BBC was 'acting like a friend of Baghdad' (Bell and Alden 2003: 2). However, during the 2003 war, the BBC was further criticized for being too cautious because it did not show enough graphic pictures of the war and its consequences. The Director of Editorial Policy at the BBC at the time acknowledged that the exercise of discretion and moral sensibility in the current broadcasting environment is becoming more of a challenge, given that broadcasters such as Al-Jazeera, whose channel is now available in Britain, will show far more graphic pictures of the consequences of war than will British broadcasters (Whittle 2004). Any caution in the reflection of the true nature of a war can easily elicit criticism from those taking an anti-war stance and lead to accusations of support for the government. Consequently, the BBC has often found itself in a difficult position in relation to the way it reports war in particular, and its ability to claim to be impartial.

The manner in which the BBC covered the 2003 war in Iraq caused disquiet at No. 10 and laid the seeds for the development of an increasingly antagonistic relationship between the BBC and No. 10. The demands of impartiality that more than one side of the story is told can result in news coverage of dissenters to war or those who criticize the government's actions. Similarly, the need to show the consequences of war and any atrocities or mistakes committed by allied forces generally contradicts the propagandist instincts of the military and the government of the day. Showing the war in terms of its full horror, or allowing dissenting voices access to the news media, can be problematic for those trying to rally support for military action. Consequently, the military and the government try very carefully to manage the news agenda. In America there has been particular sensitivity about showing the arrival home of soldiers' coffins as similar scenes during the Vietnam War helped to further turn public opinion against the Johnson administration. Producing the news during wars therefore presents enormous challenges to journalists, particularly as the public tend to have an increased interest in the news during such times. The desire for less impartial news has been clearly illustrated in America with the advent of Fox News which was deliberately supportive of the Bush Administration's pro-war stance and the American troops (see Chapter 6).

The BBC's reporting of the 2003 war in Iraq and the justification which the Blair government used to go to war attracted criticism, particularly when BBC journalist Andrew Gilligan claimed that the government knowingly used inaccurate intelligence (see Appendix 1).

The Hutton Report criticized two interrelated aspects of regulation in particular at the BBC: its editorial systems and its governance. Here we will briefly consider the issue of BBC governance by referring specifically to the measures it took to maintain impartiality as the key characteristic of its news output. The more detailed implications for the editorial systems governing news's character at the BBC and also the relationship between the Board of Management and the Board of Governors will be considered in Chapter 5. Following the release of the Hutton Report, the BBC acknowledged that one of its mistakes was not to launch an internal inquiry at the time of Alastair Campbell's original complaint. However, Campbell, the then Director of Communications for No. 10, was seen by the Director General of the BBC to be 'running a campaign to try to influence the BBC's coverage of the war' (Dyke GMTV, 30 January 2004). The BBC's resistance to pressure from any government is centred on its belief in the need for an independent and impartial relationship and a fourth estate role for its news, and has long had an impact on the character of the news it broadcasts. Problematically, the level of trust between the BBC and the government in this instance was so fragile that a denial by the government was not recognized as legitimate by the BBC because it had come under so much pressure in the past to change its news reporting. Following the Hutton Inquiry, the BBC's Neil Report (2004: 7) once again stressed that for the BBC independence was a core editorial value and consequently, 'whatever groups or individuals may wish us to say or do, we will make all decisions based on the BBC's editorial values'. For the BBC the character and integrity of its news rests on being independent of both state and partisan interests.

Impartiality as a statutory requirement

The BBC

Although the BBC has a particular constitutional position with regard to its editorial independence from government, the rules of impartiality in news reporting are a key element of regulation of all broadcast news programming. In theory, the quest for impartiality implies serving all interests and ensuring that minority interests are represented because different views must be reflected, an idea which echoes Mill's (1859) view that comparing a variety of opinions or truth claims can aid the pursuit of truth. At the BBC the maxim is that good journalism (which is impartial) will help people to make up their own minds. Achieving impartiality in news reporting has an impact on practice via the use of particular journalistic devices and skills which we will discuss in Chapter 5. The requirement to provide impartial news is a legal one, conveyed by the Communications Act 2003, and in the BBC's Licence and Agreement. The BBC had, and still has, to comply with the terms of its Charter and its Licence and Agreement, forming the basis on which it can broadcast. Over the years the BBC developed its own internal rules about taste and impartiality which 'were so strict there was no call to subject the Corporation to statutory duties or to obscenity law' (Robertson and Nichol 1990: 770). The BBC codifies these requirements in its *Producers' Guidelines* which are circulated to correspondents, producers, programme-makers, editors and managerial staff at the BBC, and are also available on the BBC website.[37] The BBC is forbidden in Clause 13(7) of the Agreement from broadcasting its own opinions on current affairs and matters of public policy, and the BBC's *Producers' Guidelines* are very clear about the relationship between fact and opinion in regard to news reporting, stating that:

> Programme makers should be at their most scrupulous in factual areas. . . . Reporting should be dispassionate . . . (good reporting) . . . should offer viewers and listeners an intelligent and informed account that enables them to form a view. A reporter may express a professional judgement but not a personal opinion.
>
> (http://www.bbc.co.uk/info/policies/producer_guides/, accessed 12 January 2004)

The evidence emanating from the 2003 Hutton Inquiry illustrated that the forensic scrutiny of Andrew Gilligan's professional methods of reporting revealed in this case a shortfall in his accuracy and precision. In his defence, this is a particular pitfall when the facts themselves are unclear or are complex in nature. Gilligan admitted subsequently that 'my error was to ascribe that statement to him [Dr David Kelly] when it was actually a conclusion of mine',[38] highlighting the problems of being accurate, fair and impartial in reporting when a reporter's own judgement is presented as neutral fact. In short, the application of judgement, essential to good news journalism, is constantly fraught because of the requirements of accuracy. The Neil Report (2004: 7) examined the lessons to be learned from the Hutton Inquiry and Report, and reiterated the importance of getting the delicate balance between facts, judgement and opinion right, stating that 'BBC journalists will report the facts first, understand and explain their context, provide professional judgements where appropriate, but never promote their own personal opinions'. This is an issue we will return to in Chapter 5.

The commercial sector in Britain

All commercial broadcast news in Britain is regulated by OFCOM. The news regulator has taken the existing regulations in the Broadcasting Act 1990 and the ITC's interpretation of those guidelines as its current policy. The Impartiality Code relates specifically to Section 6(1)(c) of the Act and is drawn up in accordance with Section 6(3), 6(5) and 6(6). It is published under Section 6(7). The Broadcasting Act 1990 states that:

> Any news given (in whatever form) in its programmes is presented with due accuracy and impartiality; that due impartiality is preserved on the part of the person providing the service as respects matters of political or industrial controversy or relating to current public policy.
>
> (*Broadcasting Act* 1990: 6(1)b)

In the case of news provision (3.4) the due accuracy requirement relates to news on all topics, and to appearances by politicians and other political activists.

A variety of views exist about journalistic pursuit of impartiality in news reporting. The regulators and lawyers have drafted legal requirements in the view that impartiality encourages a plurality of views (Gibbons 1998). The audience relates impartiality to the level of trust it can accord to the news media reporting (Goodwin and Whannel 1990; Gunter and Winstone 1992). Journalists view impartial reporting as a central tenet of their professionalism (Tuchman 1978), although as Cottle (2003: 18) points out, 'we can encounter journalists and investigative reporters who are reflexively aware of the philosophical difficulties involved as well as the pragmatic conventions and artifices they and their colleagues deploy'. In this respect Cottle argues that journalists are often patronized by academics who seem to assume that 'they alone have an omniscient insight into such difficult representational issues' (ibid.: 18). Such a view masks the simple fact that both academics and journalists share in a fundamental way a concern for the particular virtue of truthfulness. Academic criticism of news journalism is more serious when concerned with the way news journalism justifies itself, by claiming to be objective when in fact it is being partisan or tendentious (Glasser 1984; Collins 1990).

CONCLUSION

Media policy has established the social, political and economic environment for news to be regarded by large media organizations as a commercial product and subsequently sold as a commodity. However, there still remains the view that some of the news media are also expected to serve a wider public interest and purpose, namely to contribute to the effective functioning of a democratic society. In the twenty-first century, these parallel and often contradictory forces go to the heart of the tensions which many newsmakers face when trying to reconcile competing objectives. Perhaps nowhere is more susceptible to the stresses and strains of a media policy, which seeks to promote both the social value of the media and the virtues of a deregulated media environment, than current European audio-visual policy. Although Pottker (2003) has argued convincingly that mercantile interests and the journalistic ethos are not diametrically opposed and that the two are not necessarily irreconcilable, many are worried that in some cases the balance can tip too far towards the commercial interests of the media industry or news media owners, rather than the interests of the wider public.

The risk facing contemporary news analysis is that too often the relationship between news as a product of the public service broadcaster and news as a product of a private sector news organization is seen as good versus bad. Too often assumptions are hidden as these analyses try to justify that one is better than the other, or that they undertake their orientation towards news in irreconcilable ways. For 'critical analysts' of the news, freedom of expression, responsible news production and reporting, and a pluralist public sphere are myths that need to be exposed. For liberal pluralists the myths are real. In both cases articulation of an understanding of news is determined by the intellectual assumptions made. Put another way, we expect the news to reflect its relationship to wider forces which seek to influence or regulate its practice and output, and recognize that these expectations are inextricably linked to the views we hold on freedom of expression and pluralism, and the need for quality and public service in broadcasting (Gibbons 1998: 307). Furthermore, as we have seen it still remains the case that these expectations are managed via a variety of regulatory and legal requirements and also by journalists themselves reflecting varying degrees of individual and collective responsibility. In this context chapters 5 and 6 go on to explore the way the character of news is determined by how it is selected and produced, and how its content is packaged and sold to its audiences.

6

NEWS PRACTICE

INTRODUCTION

This chapter continues the analysis of news by looking at what or who makes the news, how it is organized, selected and processed in the newsroom and in its wider organizational context. News is generally produced by journalism professionals (of which there are different types with different journalistic subcultures, for example, reporters, producers, technical staff and managerial staff) working in a routine day-to-day manner within a news organization. In many fictitious accounts of newsrooms (especially in films) we see the fearless and usually maverick investigative journalist, standing up for journalistic integrity against the organization's determination to prioritize profit or their own interests above the truth.[1] The day-to-day reality is rather different since news is shaped by a multitude of influences: combined, these influences may be judged in two ways. The first way is that they are ideological in the sense that they are formed within an existing system of meanings, values and beliefs within which we all live and within which news journalism operates, and here the room for mavericks is small. Thus for example, Williams (1977: 109) argues that ideology is a 'relatively formal and articulated system of meanings, values and beliefs' which comprises a more or less organized 'world view'. The second way is derived from a critical theoretical approach which argues that news media organizations are ideological insofar as they have the power to *define* a world view which supports their particular interests and values, by controlling what we see and by making it appear 'natural' or 'obvious'.

Here the room for the freedom-loving maverick news journalist remains embarrassingly large. Accordingly, the ideological character of the news media can either refer to the adoption of a particular shared (relatively) 'world view', or to the way news reports are used instrumentally to help establish and maintain a particular set of power relationships.

In either case, and however it is judged, it is recognized that the presence of daily beliefs and values in the news cannot be avoided. It is the significance and motivation behind the adoption of these beliefs and values that is at issue. Either the presence of these beliefs and values is explicit, established through systematic processes and routine work practices, or they are replete with hidden and encoded messages that legitimate and justify certain views. In the former case it is recognized that both the viewer and the journalist live in a social world which they more or less share and make sense of. As such, embedded in the language of reporting are news values and taken-for-granted assumptions which are well understood by the audience. According to this view, mainstream news values are explicitly constructed within a common framework of understanding which ranges from formal editorial and producer guidelines to informal taken-for-granted assumptions such as the legitimacy of capitalism and the value of democracy. In the latter case, reporting news is deeply political: not in the sense of merely backing a candidate or a party, but justifying certain ways of life as better than others, certain values as superior to others, certain differences worth perpetuating, certain power relationships worth protecting. News journalism is encoded with these beliefs and justifies them. The point here is to analyse both the way these messages are produced (their values and material/economic base) and the way they are articulated (their linguistic and symbolic structure). Once this is articulated, news will be seen for what it is; that is in its deep ideological and therefore political role.

As we saw in Chapter 4, news is selected, produced and presented within the context of the particular news ecology within which it is located. News is constrained by a variety of laws and regulatory requirements, made within a particular political, social and cultural order, which reflect variously located expectations about the role of the news, the codes of conduct and the professional practices of journalists. It is also constrained by a range of organizational influences which reflect the role and remit of different news organizations and which allow different types of mediated news to emerge. The organizations within which journalists work have a range of aims, from primarily making a profit to prioritizing the public interest, with shades of grey in between. Increasing competition for audiences has encouraged new approaches to news presentation and, sometimes, news content. Technological developments have increased the nature and scale of news-gathering which can be undertaken and have influenced both news presentation and the speed of dissemination of the news. News arises and is reported within a sea of influences, some of which may affect journalists' freedom to report, or the accuracy and depth of their reporting. Journalists therefore have to balance their desire to exercise their professional journalistic values alongside a variety of external and internal pressures and logistical constraints; all shaping the character of the news which emerges.

REPORTING NEWS: A BALANCE OF FORCES

Observational studies of news organizations have given us greater understanding about the way in which news is selected, processed and presented within a range of pressures and tensions (Burns 1969; Epstein 1973; Altheide 1976; Tuchman 1978; Gans 1979; Golding and Elliott 1979; Fishman 1980; Schlesinger 1987; Ericson et al. 1991; Cottle 1993; Harrison 2000; Kung-Shankleman 2000). McQuail (2000) argues that there are a number of different relationships within and across the boundaries of organizations and researchers have attempted to identify which groups have the most power and influence on the final news product. However, there is little agreement about the degree of agency that journalists exercise in this regard. Gans (1979) believes that news organizations operate a tug-of-war between sources and consumers, whereas Altschull (1984) argues that advertisers have most influence on the news organization which subsequently affects journalistic practice. Entman (1989) identifies consumers as the most important influences on news. For Turrow (1984), control of journalists and the news process is predominantly imposed by owners, and for Bagdikian (1990) and McManus (1994) it is the large corporate investors who exercise control. As we have seen, those who take a critical approach to theorizing the news media see them as an instrument for perpetuating an unwelcomed capitalism, since the interests of media owners and ruling capitalist elites coincide (Miliband 1969; Herman and Chomsky 1988). A more moderate position is that the rules of the marketplace determine the increase in competition, concentration and conglomeration of the news media (Murdock and Golding 1974). Equally, but from a different perspective, the argument goes that the journalists themselves are free enough to control and shape the news independently of any ideological rectitude and for this reason it is necessary for them to try to put across their side of the story. At the same time, and as if to prove the point, journalists now claim that they are finding it increasingly difficult to resist the spin exercised by politicians (Jones 1996), a contention which Walker (2002) questions, arguing that news media organizations and their journalists are not value neutral and may be political players in their own right. The extent to which journalistic practice allows journalists to act as interpreters rather than conduits of information is something we will now turn to.

News: distinguishing interpretation from allegation – The Hutton Report

As argued earlier, the core values of news accuracy and sincerity in reporting can be undermined by a variety of factors. The news's obsession with contemporary events means that journalists are continually pursuing stories which they can report immediately, live, and preferably first. Often the time for double-checking may be short, particularly when the periodicity of the news cycle demands regular updates on events. Broadcast journalists in particular are increasingly spending so much time doing live updates to the newsroom that there is less time to '*go out into the action*' and research the story. Feeding a hungry news production cycle means that journalists often have to think on their feet and answer questions or make statements directly to the presenter, for which they may not be entirely prepared. When the news story concerns a sensitive issue which will incur reprisals, such as government wrongdoing; or a complex story where there are many views, the journalist, as we saw in the Introduction, has to try to ensure that facts and his or her own judgements are distinct and signalled as such. All organizations reported in the news will attempt to ensure they are portrayed in the best light. The recent battle between the BBC and the Blair government (in particular the No. 10 press office), which culminated in the Hutton Report (2004), indicates the lengths to which two powerful institutions may go to try to control the character of the news which is reported to the public. Negative statements about political parties arise continually and of course politicians try to respond in a way which refutes any negative press they may have had. Dramatic negative statements about the government of the day in the press are often to be expected, and some newspapers, such as the *Sun* or the *Daily Mail*, will take up particularly adversarial positions. The disappearance of the left-wing press after the Second World War left Britain with a newspaper industry which was prone to sympathize with Conservative governments. For the Labour Party this became particularly problematic in the 1980s. As Alastair Campbell observed, 'the chances of ever winning were greatly diminished by the fact that, day in and day out, newspapers attacked the Labour party – and Neil Kinnock in particular – virulently' (cited in Greenslade 2003a: 607–608). In particular the *Sun* was seen in the Thatcher and Major years as anti-Labour. Today its editorial rationale is one of strident (sometimes militant) independence. It makes a virtue of campaigning for or against particular political leaders and political parties as well as criticizing policies according to their intrinsic merit (as the *Sun* sees it) and not from which party they originated.[2] It revels in the rhetoric of a free press and sets itself up as the benchmark for freedom through its fearlessness to tackle any subject. In short, it has become iconoclastic.

In contrast, as we saw in Chapter 4, broadcasting organizations are under a statutory duty to produce impartial news which places them in a completely different position from the press, particularly when covering political issues, since political parties closely monitor broadcast news for evidence of bias or unfair reporting of their party and its policies. The BBC has long occupied a difficult position in relation to various governments, and has been the news provider which has come under greatest scrutiny and pressure in relation to its political reporting. Furthermore, the BBC has set very high standards for its news, with truth and accuracy identified as some of the core journalistic values at the BBC (see The Neil Report 2004), seeing these, alongside the requirement for impartiality, as fundamental to the relationship of trust which it establishes with the licence fee-paying public. The new and higher editorial standards which the BBC has set for itself following the Hutton Inquiry and Report and its own internal review by Ron Neil shows how a thorough scrutiny of news reveals the core qualities required to ensure that a 'news report' can actually claim to be 'news' rather than speculation or gossip.

On 29 May 2003 the BBC's Defence Correspondent, Andrew Gilligan, broadcast several reports on the BBC's *Today* programme which questioned the accuracy of a dossier published by the government in September 2002. The dossier, entitled *Iraq's Weapons of Mass Destruction*, made the case for Britain to go to war with Iraq. Gilligan's initial broadcast at 6.07 a.m. took the form of a live two-way (an interview with John Humphrys the presenter). During this broadcast Gilligan raised questions about the claim made in the dossier that Iraq had weapons of mass destruction which were ready for use in forty-five minutes, alleging that the government knew it was using intelligence which was wrong. The following words had a huge impact, and exacerbated the political will to obtain a retraction and an apology:

[What] we've been told by one of the senior officials in charge of drawing
up that dossier was that, actually the government probably erm, knew that
that forty five minute figure was wrong, even before it decided to put it in.
(Hutton 2004: 6.07 a.m.:see Appendix 1)

Gilligan followed this statement in the same broadcast with the words:
'Downing Street, our source says, ordered a week before publication,
ordered it to be sexed up, to be made more exciting and ordered more
facts to be er, to be discovered' (ibid.). The harsh condemnation of
Andrew Gilligan made by Lord Hutton in the Hutton Report released
on 28 January 2004, namely that Gilligan's allegations were 'very grave'
in his first broadcast on *Today* at 6.07 a.m., has been criticized. The
National Union of Journalists (NUJ) took pains to point out that,
although Gilligan made other broadcasts on the morning of 29 May 2003,
in which he never repeated the initial claim, it was in fact one sentence
from the one report at 6.07 a.m. which particularly attracted the attention of the government and Lord Hutton. According to the NUJ, no
credit was given for the fact that Gilligan dropped, in subsequent scripted
broadcasts, his claim that the government included information in the
Iraq dossier, knowing it to be wrong. Furthermore, following the release
of the Butler Report in July 2004,[3] which questioned the intelligence on
which the government's forty-five minute claim was made, Gilligan
appeared to have been somewhat vindicated.

However, as the BBC itself notes in its Neil Report, there were problems with the way in which the story was gathered: 'The notes of the
meeting with the source [Dr Kelly] were not complete and did not
support all the allegations that were reported on air', nor were 'the allegations made . . . put to Downing Street on the night before the
broadcast' (Neil Report 2004: 10). The story was clearly a complex one
and in the interests of fairness there should have been 'a proper opportunity to respond' (ibid.), and 'the 6.07 broadcast should have been
scripted' (ibid.) to allow proper preparation and clarification of any
judgements Gilligan may have made. As we have already seen in the
Introduction (this volume), an accurate report of events requires that
facts and judgements are signalled clearly. Transcripts from Gilligan's
broadcast at 7.32 a.m. on the *Today* programme showed that he had
slightly changed the tenor of his comments later on, now saying: 'what
I have been told is that the government knew that claim was *questionable*,
even before the war, even before they wrote it in their dossier.'
However, BBC's *Panorama* journalist John Ware argued that 'the allegation of conscious wrongdoing by No. 10 remained implicit in a number
of Gilligan's other broadcasts on Radio 2 and Radio 5' (Ware 2004: 14),

but were not supported by accurate reporting and scrupulous and rigorous note taking. Others inside and outside the BBC have also criticized the unscripted and rather casual nature of the 6.07 a.m. broadcast (transmitted while Gilligan was sitting on his bed at home), feeling that it seemed to lack clarity and coherence (BBC correspondent 2 April 2004) and that the myth of 'mostly right' was perpetuated by Gilligan himself (Ware 2004:14).

Gilligan's problems were compounded when the Hutton Inquiry revealed that his comments about the forty-five minute claim were, at the time actually, inaccurate because the intelligence report was not received by the government in time to have it placed in an earlier draft dossier. In his Report, Lord Hutton explicitly pointed out that:

> Therefore, whether or not at some time in the future the report on which the 45 minutes claim was based is shown to be unreliable, the allegation reported by Mr Gilligan on 29 May 2003 that the Government probably knew that the 45 minutes claim was wrong before the Government decided to put it in the dossier, was an allegation which was unfounded.
>
> (Hutton 2004: Section 467, ii)

Lord Hutton also took the view that the implication that the government had acted dishonestly was actually made by the BBC, rather than the source of the story. Such an assertion breaks the rules of impartiality whereby a journalist's own conjecture should be separated from fact. In his 6.07 a.m. report Gilligan appeared to attribute the forty-five minute claim directly to his source, Dr Kelly. Indeed, when giving evidence to the Hutton Inquiry on 17 September 2003, Gilligan admitted that:

> The error I made here was in expressing the understanding I had that the views had been conveyed to the Government as something which Dr Kelly had told me directly. It was not intentional, it was the kind of slip of the tongue that does happen often during live broadcasts. It is an occupational hazard, which is why it would have been better to have scripted this one.[4]
>
> (ibid.)

The fact that the specifically worded allegation, which caused so much offence to No. 10, was broadcast only once at 6.07 a.m. and yet had such an enormous impact, says a great deal about its provenance and the Blair government's sensitivity to the power of the BBC's news to influence both the public and the political classes. The BBC was exposed to government ire paradoxically because of the following. First, the BBC's particular status as a trusted source of accurate news and information both in Britain and abroad meant that the story could have had a high impact throughout the world.[5] Second, Radio 4's *Today* programme itself is generally said to 'set the news agenda' for the day in Britain, particularly in relation to political news, which would then subsequently be reported by the press and other news media outlets. Third, it is the 'forum where the top story of the day is discussed by the key protagonists' (Luckhurst 2004: 6), and other journalists and politicians generally listen to it. Consequently the story was consumed by those who would be most likely to react strongly and effectively to the allegation which was made. It is worth considering how strong government reaction would have been were it not for these three key factors, since it seems reasonable to conclude that it is not always *what* the news actually says that has the impact, but it is *with what organizational authority* it is said, and who is listening.

To this end, the BBC is especially keen to ensure that its journalists understand the difference between reporting events that have happened and providing an original investigative scoop. Both can be viewed as news, but many pitfalls are evident in the latter. Harcup (2004: 75) observes that a great deal of journalism is 'reportage', a practice which may be viewed as ultimately descriptive. Investigative journalism is different, and, as we discussed in the Introduction, is often classed as a feature rather than news. This is because it involves allowing journalists to develop a point of view and marshal evidence to support a claim. It requires 'original research . . . involves wrongdoing or negligence for which there is no published evidence . . . [which] someone is trying to keep . . . secret . . . [and] the stakes are high' (Randall 2000: 99–100). Importantly, where investigative reporting exposes serious wrongdoing, or injustice, it is often praised for fulfilling the role assigned to it by describing it as the fourth estate. If 'investigation' is going to occur in the news, Randall cautions the journalist to avoid making assumptions and to 'report only what you know, not what you think you know' (ibid.: 5). Retaining an impartial approach can be difficult. A former Director General of the BBC argued that there 'is no such thing as pure fact which can be separated from "comment"; this is one of the myths of journalism' (Birt and Jay 1976b). Carl Bernstein, putting it rather better, said, 'the best available version of truth exists . . . [and] . . . the commitment to fairness and accuracy and context has to be the guiding principle' (Lloyd 2004: 10).

The influence of the news media organization

The news values of different news organizations differ. News selection and presentation is adapted according to the designated style of each organization and represents only one way of doing the job. To put it another way, reporting style is not universal (Harrison 2000). Or, as a journalist puts it, the journalistic culture which exists in a newsroom 'sets what editors and their executives regard as a good story or dismiss as "boring" and determines the subjects they think of as "sexy" and those that are not'; it also 'creates the moral atmosphere of a paper [or broadcast newsroom]' (Randall 2000: 16). On any 'normal' newsday not dominated by a major story, it is evident that a variety of priorities exist in different news organizations which result in different judgements about what is newsworthy. British audiences have access to a wider range of news judgements than ever before, with the broadcasting sector in particular expanding notably in the era of twenty-four-hour news channels. Alongside Sky News, BBC News-24 and the ITV News Channel, other twenty-four-hour news channels now provide news which can be accessed in Britain (and by other international audiences) such as CNN International, EuroNews, Bloomberg and CNBC, with the last two providing business news. Other twenty-four-hour news channels originate from overseas and provide very different perspectives on the news such as Fox News (USA), Al-Jazeera (Qatar) and CCTV-9 (China). The sheer volume of channels and perspectives means any evaluation of the ideological character of news, news values and news agendas can no longer consider only Western news providers. The diversity of news organizations (as well as new communication technologies) now needs to be taken account of before we can talk of dominant news hegemony.

Furthermore, the role which a particular news organization recognises itself to have is equally important in understanding the character of today's news. When a particular channel or newspaper describes itself as the 'voice of' or 'representing the people of', it is using a descriptor that captures certain audiences' disposition to watch, listen or read. Just as the nineteenth-century British national newspapers, with the exception of some Sunday newspapers, were intended to be 'journals of influence' (Hodgson 1989: 50), so these channels and newspapers also seek to be influential. Of course all news organizations seek to attract the reader, viewer or listener. It is a vital element of their function. However, motives vary. For some news organizations, influence lies in attracting mass audiences to support advertising revenues. For others, influence is being involved in political and cultural debates, and for some it is both. Two examples will suffice. In the case of News International's the *News of the World*, the paper has long distinguished itself from its competitors by adopting a campaigning tone and undertaking investigation into a criminal's activities or social problems (Hodgson 1989). As such it has achieved healthy sales and secured advertising revenues accordingly. Equally, but for entirely different motives, the BBC's PSB remit demands that it provides news that is distinctive from its competitors' in order to serve its audience (Kung-Shankleman 2000).

Looked at another way, the capacity for a news organization to achieve influence also depends upon the ability of its journalists to identify a news story in the first place. Typically, news journalists are expected to exhibit personal qualities which will help them to 'get the story' or to deal with a story responsibly (note the earlier distinction between so-called libertarian print journalists and socially responsible broadcast journalists). Veteran BBC journalist Vin Ray (2003: 3–15) identifies the vital qualities: curiosity, enthusiasm and passion, courage, radicalism, membership of 'the awkward squad', team work, 'a rat-like cunning', stamina, humility, a way with words, a flair for storytelling and a 'good bladder'. All these personal qualities, alongside rigorous skills training, knowledge of the audience and a desire to be original, helps to make, he argues, an excellent journalist who can sniff out the news and report it well.[6]

In a less subjective vein, some researchers explain how contemporary events become news. They argue that the explanation for newsworthiness resides in the properties inherent in a contemporary event itself and not in the news organizations' predispositions or value system. Rather than focusing on the context of journalistic practice within news organizations as an explanation for news selection, we should concentrate on news values. This approach is becoming increasingly influential and is now taught on many journalism courses. Basically it regards news selection as something that occurs because of the essential news value within an event. The event 'tells' the journalist that it is newsworthy. News is considered as a set of identifiable values located within an event and recognizable to a trained journalist. However, as persuasive as these inherent or eidetic values may seem, ultimately news value analysis is a form of content-based research which makes judgements about the production process by attempting to identify the way in which 'a property of an event . . . increases its chance of becoming "news" ' (Sande 1971: 222). A significant attempt to identify factors which define the intrinsic news value of an event for news organization was made by Galtung and Ruge in 1965.[7] They used the metaphor of the world as an enormous set of broadcasting stations, each continually emitting a signal (ibid: 64–91). From this they formulated a list of factors which illustrate the criteria that have to be met before an event is selected and turned into a news story by a typical news organization. Galtung and Ruge identified twelve factors (sixteen if their sub-factors are counted).[8] These were recently updated by Harcup and O'Neill (2001)[9] and are discussed in some detail by Harcup (2004: 30–9). Scholars working within this perspective have tended to concentrate on identifying news factors which they believed were inherent in an event and which would influence journalists making a choice about which event to select. To summarize this approach, identification of these factors has allowed scholars (see Galtung and Ruge 1965; Ostgaard 1965; Sande 1971; Tunstall 1971; Rosengren 1977; Sparkes and Winter 1980; Bell 1991; Harrison 2000; Harcup and O'Neil 2001; Harcup 2004) to conclude that news events are more likely to be selected if:

- there are pictures or film available (television news);
- they contain short, dramatic occurrences which can be sensationalized;
- they have novelty value;
- they are open to simple reporting;
- they occur on a grand scale;
- they are negative or contain violence, crime, confrontation or catastrophe;
- they are either unexpected;
- they contain things which one would expect to happen;
- the events have meaning and relevance to the audience;
- similar events are already in the news;
- they provide a balanced programme;
- they contain elite people or nations;
- they allow an event to be reported in personal or human interest terms.

Interestingly, journalists themselves do not explicitly refer to these types of lists when articulating news value or giving an explanation of news selection. Indeed, as Harcup (2004: 34) observes, 'recruits to journalism tend to pick up a sense of newsworthiness and develop their "nose" for a story by consuming news and by absorbing news values from senior colleagues', via a process of socialization (Bantz 1985). Indeed, this process of socialization helps us to understand better how journalists can move between different news organizations and accept and understand different organizations' news policies and agendas.

Several scholars have explored how a news organization can control journalistic activity to ensure that they conform to its own particular news policies, while at the same time allowing some degree of journalistic autonomy and creativity. Breed's (1955) study of how organizational news policy is maintained by an organization's leaders, and how an organization ensures that conformity in news selection and presentation is achieved from journalists, led him to identify socialization as a key element in explaining how journalists accept and understand organizational news values without actually explicitly being told what they are. He argues that news journalists understand a news organization's news policy and news values by consuming the output provided by their own organization, and this helps them to copy the techniques and styles and to understand what is newsworthy. This understanding is then reinforced by editorial decisions and meetings, as well as by the rejection of stories if something occurs which contradicts the organization's news policy. Often the passing on of organizational policy may be implicit rather than explicit, although codes of practice also exist which contain guidelines. As journalists want to get their stories published they soon learn how to conform to organizational policy and provide the 'right' kind of news. Similarly, as managers do not always tell journalists explicitly what the organizational news policies are, they do not appear to be enforcing editorial control from above, allowing journalists to feel they have some editorial autonomy and freedom to be creative. For Breed, the process of learning policy in this way masks a means of social control in the newsroom, whereby journalists realize that more opportunities will probably be given to those who conform to organizational news policy, a concern which is reinforced by feelings of obligation and esteem for superiors or news veterans.

Bantz's (1985) analysis of television newsroom culture introduces conflict to our understanding of journalistic practice. Newsroom conflict exists primarily in the tiered relationships between the three different levels of personnel in a news organization: the news journalist, middle management and upper management, executives or owners. Conflict, he argues, fundamentally exists in the constant clash between organizational policy demands and journalistic ideals. However, as he further notes, conflict is part of a shared system of symbolic organizational meaning in a newsroom and is a common and constant element across all news organizations. In this sense, conflict in a newsroom is seen to be part of routine behaviour, which appears as a natural or normal part of journalistic activity. The news journalist's 'natural' orientation towards conflict can actually work in the news organization's favour and shapes the way journalists interrogate news events and people's accounts of them. Journalistic professionalism focuses on a degree of scepticism or distrust of individuals who try to force a particular point of view upon them, allowing them in principle to reject attempts at manipulation by sources or the use of spin. The exercise of journalistic agency in this way challenges the idea that news's character is entirely shaped or determined by forces beyond the journalist's control. However (and as noted in Chapter 3), the degree of agency exercised by journalists may be diminishing in some newsrooms through the loss of older, more experienced journalists in some news organizations (Ursell 2001, 2003), raising questions about the ability of younger journalists in practice to interrogate and interpret source material.

A key part of news's character derives from control of the news agenda. The practical mechanism by which control is exercised within an organization is via the editorial system which expects liaison between different levels. Sometimes this system can fail and result in conflict or a breakdown in procedures. At the top of the pyramid of control is the proprietor, owner or, in the BBC's case (at the time of writing), a Board of Governors. The degree to which an owner interferes in the day-to-day running and shapes the news agenda appears to vary greatly. Lord Beaverbrook in the persona of and following the *modus operandi* of Evelyn Waugh's Lord Copper in *Scoop*, interfered in all areas of production of the *Daily Express* newspaper, including its content and the way in which stories were written (Greenslade 2003a). Others, such as Rupert Murdoch, are clear about the policy of their paper and the type of news agenda they want it to follow, and therefore shape the character of news that is reported. Replying in the 1970s to a question regarding the extent of current affairs coverage in the *Sun,* Murdoch is reported to have said, 'I'm not having any of that up-market shit in my paper' (Page 2003: 83). As such the *Sunday Correspondent* and the *Independent on Sunday* were easily able to attract journalists away from the Murdoch press at Wapping into an environment less constrained by proprietorial interests, where journalistic integrity could better flourish (Greenslade 2003a).

Sometimes journalists working in the newsroom may be less aware of the levels of control exercised by an owner, as the latter will generally speak directly to the editor. None the less, the journalist has to be aware of a general policy on particular issues. In newspapers which are partisan this can be quite clear-cut, but in television or radio news this simply adds a 'flavour' to the news which is not always clearly articulated. For example, although policy meetings or conversations with owners occur in news organizations, they are generally witnessed only by senior editorial staff. And yet it is usually during such encounters that policy issues – such as the manner in which the organization will handle Northern Ireland, Europe, how elections are covered and so on – are discussed. The formula then becomes part of the common currency of the newsroom until it is a taken-for-granted response and underpins the culture of the newsroom and news practice. The editor liaises between journalists and the top levels of the organization, and needs to maintain control in the newsroom and make sure that journalists adhere to and follow organizational news policy without necessarily making it explicit that the policy message came from the management (Harrison 2000). Communication of organizational policy is achieved via meetings with reporters, correspondents and producers which establish the character and style of news that is reported, perhaps overtly stating how particular stories are to be covered, or, with more senior and experienced journalists, perhaps by placing nuances on how a story might be shaped. Here, although the news agenda to be followed has been established, responsibility then rests on the news journalists themselves to go out and pursue stories and report them using their creativity and skills. The degree of leeway in this regard obviously depends on the nature of the story, the news organization's particular policy, the complexity of the story and the seniority and experience of the journalist. The character of news in this scenario is nevertheless deeply entrenched within the parameters of organizational practice and culture.

There are many different types of news culture. They range from an aggressive culture that pushes journalists to provide campaigning stories and 'investigative scoops', and often strains at the boundaries of rules, or even flouts them, to a passive news culture dominated by pursuing the bottom line, where journalists never leave the newsroom and find themselves simply reprocessing material which comes in as press releases from a variety of sources. As Sanders (2003: 128) observes, 'the economic realities of the media business can be one of the greatest obstacles to ethical journalism' and the ambience of commerce over culture can produce news which lacks the core qualities of accuracy and sincerity. Even the BBC[10] is constantly reviewing its news style and the cultural precepts it is based upon (BBC 2003). In its bid to be distinctive the BBC's Radio 4 *Today* programme moved away from being a programme of record, towards actually seeking to break news stories. This change in editorial focus meant that the programme pursued a more investigative or aggressive style of journalism than it had in the past as it sought to actively manage the news agenda of the day. According to Luckhurst (2004: 6–7), this attempt resulted in senior ministers being advised by the No. 10 press office to stay away from the programme and to aim for programmes or outlets with less antagonistic interviewers. In 2001 to 2002, the strategy of the editor Rod Liddle was to change the production culture of the programme by appointing 'hard-news reporters – including Andrew Gilligan – to dig up exclusive stories' and to take a more investigative slant, breaking stories rather than analysing them (ibid.). In Luckhurst's words, 'he created the culture in which Gilligan pushed the envelope too far' (ibid.). The Neil Report (2004: 21) subsequently recommended that the BBC's editorial system must control the urge to create news, saying that 'programmes need to be careful to apply normal journalistic standards in assessing the significance of stories that we originate ourselves'. The BBC still intends to produce investigative elements in its news, but as we have seen, these have to be carefully balanced against achieving accuracy and impartiality.

News and the routinization of practice

The job of the news organization is to deliver, within the constraints of time and space, the most acceptable news product to its audience in the most efficient manner. As we saw in Chapter 2, historically there has been a need to maximize news-gathering and reporting skills which value efficiency, time management, forward planning, succinct writing or good storytelling, impartiality, and which work within legal and regulatory requirements. These skills must be balanced against the organizational interests in achieving high levels of readership or ratings which in turn attract advertising or return circulation revenue. Routinization of journalistic practice thus helps to maximize a successful outcome. The routines inherent in journalistic practice (which structure journalists' relationships with their sources, audiences and their adoption and interpretation of impartiality requirements) enable journalists to retain their professionalism (and integrity) while meeting many of the needs of the organization (Tuchman 1978). Eliasoph's (1988: 313) study of a community radio station in America (KPFA-FM in Berkeley) found that the routines and conventions of journalistic practice may be used as an 'oppositional tool' rather than one which perpetuates status quo news reports, or which uncritically supports a profit-driven news culture. In contrast, some analysts see routines as limiting journalistic freedom, insofar as journalists will be influenced by particular conventions (Schudson 1978) which operate within any given news organization. For Sigal (1973: 66), this loss of freedom leads to 'standardized newspaper content'.

The routine use of sources

Information can enter the newsroom in a variety of ways: news agency material via the wire services or news agencies, press releases, from reporters and correspondents out on location, via other news competitors and tip-offs (see Harcup 2004: 46 for a list of potential sources of material for journalists). For some researchers the production process of news is about the exercise of power. It is shaped by those sources who are adept at gaining access to the news media and who are able to set the 'tone' of the news. This can result in groups in society being variously labelled as insiders or outsiders. It can also lead to some outsiders becoming stigmatized (Goffman 1963). The use of labels is instrumental in creating moral panics (Cohen and Young 1973) or producing 'a reality'. The view that realities are constructed or generated from linguistic forms and their social settings has been influential in the study of news, particularly where news is seen as producing 'realities' which are determined and subsequently confirmed by those who hold power (Cohen and Young 1981). However, explaining journalistic practices this way ignores their ability to resist the powerful. In the words of *The Times* political commentator Peter Riddell, lobby correspondents can in the same day act as 'tame lapdog, alert watchdog and fierce fighting dog' (Sanders 2003: 113). Yet as we have also seen, news journalism relies upon the routine use of sources. Fishman (1980, 1982) sees the world in which the journalist gathers news as predominantly bureaucratically organized. News journalists operate within particular 'news beats' to obtain most of their stories: the police, courts, politicians and large businesses; a practice which helps determine what events are seen to be newsworthy and what are not. Indeed, according to Fishman (1982: 215), journalists use 'schemes of interpretation' to understand and report events. They do so by adopting and tracking the same 'phase structures' (ways of seeing the beginning, middle and end of an event)[11] as those organizations which form a journalist's particular 'news beat' (ibid.: 215). In this way routinized practice follows the patterns necessary to gain access to particular sources of news. However, the word 'follows' does not imply passive reporting, or simply acquiescing to the whims of the powerful.

Innes (1999) provided an interesting insight into the balance of power in 'news beat' routines in the form of how the police/journalist relationship operates, when he undertook a study of how the police handle high-profile murder stories. In his study, local and national news journalists took quite different approaches to the police's attempts to control them. He quotes a senior investigating officer who observed that:

> You tend to find two different camps, the local media and the national media and the local media are very much easier to keep in your camp. The national media have no rules because the national media are only trying to sell more newspapers than the next. . . . They're not concerned, although they'd argue they are, they're more concerned with selling more newspapers than helping you the SIO to clear the murder. If they can rake something up on the deceased person or on the family. . . . It's always the unusual that attracts national publicity. Local publicity and the local media are much more

responsible because I think it's happened in their area and they do think that
they have a key role to play in trying to catch the person.

(Innes 1999: 274)

Quite simply, local journalists are more dependent upon local police for stories and briefings (on and off the record) than are national journalists, hence their cooperative relationship. The point is that working cooperatively with regular sources is the norm. It is a relationship which has been described as exhibiting a 'constant tension between nurturing trust and maintaining scepticism' (Sanders 2003: 105). Who has the upper hand in this relationship is debatable. Gans (1979) and Cohen (1963) argue that powerful sources generally have the most control over the story, Hess (1984) argues that journalists have the most power, and Bantz (1985) has expressed concerns that some television journalists, such as the political reporter or the police reporter, may go native (i.e. the political reporter can become a political actor). Consequently, some researchers have argued that the relationship between journalists and their sources is a complex and constantly changing dynamic (Schlesinger and Tumber 1994; Jones 1996; Negrine 1996), a form of symbiosis where both use each other (Sanders 2003: 108). A global survey of journalists by Weaver (1998) showed that British journalists are three times more likely to pay sources for information than are their peers in other countries. This practice, it has been argued, encourages embellishments or distortions in reporting a story, or omissions in court evidence in order to retain a story which can be sold as an exclusive (Epworth and Hanna 1998). Weaver (1998) highlighted the journalistic belief that the protection of sources is an important ethical journalistic principle. Although British journalists are slightly more likely to break agreements of confidentiality and to reveal their source than are their counterparts in other countries, the disclosure of the identity of the source is generally viewed as bad practice. In part this is expedient. If sources knew they were likely to be revealed, they would be less willing to come forward. In the main, courts have claimed 'to recognize that there is a public interest in journalists being able to protect their sources' (Greenwood and Welsh 2001: 286), but none the less, disclosure of sources is ordered when the court has considered it to be necessary.[12]

As far as the use of sources and the character of news is concerned, the following points apply. The relationship between sources and journalists varies. It is not fixed in a particular power or indeed financial format. It is information-based and as such requires managing by both. The techniques for managing the relationship cover the spectrum of interpersonal relationships; in that sense they are no different from other social arrangements. But the purpose of the relationship is always about the disclosure of information judged by the source or the journalist or both to provide insight and understanding of a particular event. It is the extent to which the source is believed in and the journalist is free to interrogate this information that determines the quality of the news report. Buying a source produces news which has to repay the cost of purchase by attracting extra readers (or viewers). Here news is loudly promoted, and excitingly written or presented. Passively accepting the official line produces news which is acquiescent. Both may be true, but the styles of reporting vary with the relationship the journalist has to the source.

The routine acceptance of impartiality as a professional journalistic value

Within their different news organizations, and working to different pressures and versions of the public interest, journalists in the broadcasting sector are under a statutory obligation to ensure that they are producing news which will be *judged* to be objective and impartial. Because news journalism requires judgement and is a product of the extent to which an event is analysed, objectivity is better understood to mean balanced, or judging both sides of an argument equally. As argued throughout, news is certainly not value free; indeed, it has core values (see Table 1, Introduction). Most journalists recognize this and prefer to describe their intentions as trying to produce fair and balanced reporting which meets the regulatory requirements for impartiality (Harrison 2000). Impartiality has been adopted as one of the routine norms of good practice (Boyer 1981; McQuail 1992: 184–185). It is via these norms that the journalist claims to be able to achieve an objective account of an event. Impartiality represents the way journalists try to remove their own personal opinions or feelings from a news report and present a balanced and accurate account. In this way they seek to protect themselves from accusations of bias and untruthful reporting (Tuchman 1978). Using a particular set of 'strategic rituals' (Tuchman 1972: 660), journalists attempt to fulfil their responsibility to be impartial and therefore objective.

These rituals are:

• The verification of facts, whereby facts are checked and made to 'stand up'. This is generally done via triangulation, checking with other source material and assessing the credibility of sources.

Sometimes a single source is seen to be so reliable that a journalist will accept his or her truth claim.

- To make a story stronger, journalists will try to present supporting evidence. This may be in the form of a picture, a film or an official statement.

- Presentation of conflicting possibilities: in order to protect themselves and keep their opinions out of the story, journalists routinely use two or more spokespersons to present different sides of the story. The acceptance of certain 'official' spokespersons' comments is defended by journalists as a way of producing objective coverage of events. Therefore a truth claim made by source 'A' may not be true, but it can then be balanced against a different truth claim made by source 'B'. By reporting these truth claims as 'facts' even though they are not necessarily true, journalists can report allegations without appearing to make them themselves.

- The claims or comments made by sources can be directly reported using quotation marks in press reports and by specific attribution in broadcast news. If source 'A' is reported as saying something specific, then the journalist can use a direct quotation from that source, which effectively removes the journalist's own comments from the report. For this procedure to be followed effectively there needs to be a verbatim recording, or shorthand note taken of the source's exact words. As we have seen, the lack of verbatim notes was one of the failings of Andrew Gilligan which was picked up in the Hutton Report.

In short, it is argued that objective news reporting is achieved through impartiality, as impartiality is merged into daily routines which support the journalist in an attempt to write accurate news stories. Both objectivity and impartiality are fused in journalistic practice. Journalistic training in Britain supports this view by ensuring that such routines are taught.[13] Such training and the acceptance of routines help a journalist to turn an event or series of events into a news story (Bell 1991) in a manner best suited the news medium in which it is being told, and the requirements both of the organization which is underwriting it and the audience which consumes it (see e.g. Boyd 1994; White 1996; Holland 1997; Yorke 1997; Hicks 1999; Randall 2000; Pottker 2003). The use of professional rituals and routines helps journalists to cope with the logistics of newswork and its unexpected nature, and to claim that the news they have produced is impartial. However, there are problems with this analysis. First, objectivity and impartiality do not mean the same thing (see below). Second, routines and rituals are not a foolproof way of ensuring that the core values of news, accuracy and sincerity are achieved. Harcup (2004: 69) observes, 'despite such routines, journalists frequently publish things that turn out to be untrue. Inaccuracies might appear because sources do not (yet) know the full story', and sources may lie or embellish. Third, some academics criticize the employment of objectivity norms by journalists as facilitating a way in which power and control in society may be hidden or masked (Glasser 1984; Collins 1990). Although Lichtenberg (1991) cautions us that even if it is not realistic to believe that anyone can be objective, we still need to assume that objectivity as an ideal is both possible and valuable.

Academic criticism about the use of 'objectivity' as a criterion for news reporting

Academic criticism about the use of the term 'objectivity' arises from concerns about the so-called 'objectivity defence' used by journalists and news reporters to describe what they are doing. For journalists the claim to be objective is supported by routines, which, it is argued, turn news reports into impartial accounts of contemporary events. For television journalists, the practice of impartial reporting is a legal requirement and has led journalists to develop a set of guidelines which they can follow when selecting and producing news. Yet the problem remains that too often journalists use the words 'impartiality' and 'objectivity' to mean much the same (Wilson 1996: 45). The concept of impartiality is different from objectivity, but they are both guiding principles of British broadcast journalism (McNair 1996). However, objectivity in news reporting has broader demands than those of impartiality. Here, objectivity means the elimination of subjective values from a news report, an impossible requirement for reporting a news event, which is supported by *in situ* judgements as the event unfolds. News reporting is concerned with assessing, analysing and judging contemporary events. The requirement for impartiality means that journalists 'must try to report events in ways that will survive scrutiny' (ibid.: 46). In this sense we cannot expect news to be value free, and, as already argued, the production and reporting of news can only *aspire* towards the truth through the constant disposition towards truthfulness (see Table 1, Introduction). As such, objectivity and impartiality are at best qualities which should be aspired to. In point of fact it would be better if both of these terms were replaced with the more consistent and helpful terms *accuracy* and *sincerity*. At least these terms tell a far more human story about the task of news journalism and provide a logical consistency to what news reports should aim for.

Sociological studies of news have been concerned with 'establishing that [news] information [is] produced, selected, organized, structured, and (in consequence) biased' (Collins 1990: 20). Lichtenberg (1991) even points out that the aspiration to objectivity contains its own biases. The use of established sources or the use of artificial, arithmetical balance between views (for example, where the same amount of broadcast time is given to different political parties during an election period) does not produce an objective account of events. Using facts to achieve accuracy and balance is relatively straightforward since it is possible to check and verify facts. Being accurate about more complex events and issues obviously exerts greater demands. As we saw in Chapter 2, journalism, historically, has made accuracy a guiding principle of its own professional practice. Then, as now, it was understood that accuracy under certain circumstances is difficult to achieve but can be managed. It is often overlooked that news reporters will often report their own incomplete and partial understanding of events, or allow spokespersons to do so. However, ignoring or denying facts can sometimes look absurd. Saddam Hussein's Information Minister, Mohammed Saeed al-Sahaf, was named 'Comical Ali' during the 2003 war on Iraq because of his cheerful denials that there were no Americans in Baghdad. As he made his claims on live television, viewers could see American troops waving behind him. In a sense balance was achieved here because two sides of the story could be seen by the viewer. However, balance should not be confused with accurate coverage. The more or less completeness of coverage does not alter the responsibility of the journalist to be both accurate and balanced.

News reporting also requires subjective judgements to be made. An assessment about which facts are more important than others, prioritizing which questions to ask, will inevitably involve the exercise of the journalist's understanding of an event. Similarly, subjective judgements are also made when establishing the running order for a news broadcast, or which page the news story will appear on, how much time or space it will be accorded, and on which page it will appear. In this way journalists are constantly deciding what constitutes newsworthiness. Yet of course, this judgement will operate in accordance with their own particular news organization's news policy and news values. At each stage of the production process journalists make considered decisions. Selection of news stories to be told requires the exclusion of other events from the news agenda. Not all voices are given equal access. Some sources of information are prioritized above others because they are adept at obtaining access to journalists, thereby getting their views across at the expense of those who are not (Altheide 1984; Ericson et al. 1991; Schlesinger and Tumber 1994). Finally, a professional adherence to objectivity can mean that a journalist could avoid taking responsibility for independent thinking. For example, 'spun facts' may be reported uncritically and this is a particular risk where news organizations do not have the resources to employ experienced journalists who can interrogate and challenge press releases and press statements made by the sophisticated.

To summarize, both objectivity and impartiality are well-established ideals in the history of and training in news journalism. Impartiality is embedded and maintained in good professional practice and objective news reporting is seen by journalists to be the outcome. However, the suggestion that objectivity can be achieved through the routinization of particular reporting techniques is misleading. Certainly good practice can and does produce balanced and fair news journalism, and in this sense these are more real and better descriptors of good news journalism than 'objective' and 'impartial'. To describe a news report as 'balanced' and 'fair' is to commend it, but these descriptors do not go far enough to capture the character of what news journalism should be. News journalism should be disposed towards revealing the truth about contemporary events and because of this it should be accurate and sincere. These terms depict the deep character of news journalism (see Table 1, Introduction), and they do so in all settings and within any set of ideological constraints. To substitute a disposition towards truthfulness with 'balanced' and 'fair' misses the point as far as news is concerned. Contemporary events have to be revealed for what they are, and as far as possible that means getting to the truth of these events. The extent to which a journalist can get to the truth of contemporary events is via accurate and sincere reporting and not aspirations towards objectivity and impartiality, even if that means balanced and fair reporting is subordinated to truthful reporting. The mantra of balanced and fair reporting is most definitely subordinate to the principle of truthful reporting no matter how one-sided that is.

The expansion of the news genre

Technological change has brought new opportunities for the development and expansion of the news genre. In particular the growing desire to offer alternative news reporting by so-called native reporters (Atton 2002) can bypass or improve upon mainstream reporting processes, to include more voices, encourage personal journalism and to experiment with new forms of production. Atton uses the example of Independent Media Centres (IMC) or 'Indymedia' (ibid.) to show how independent journalists with an interest in the global anti-capitalist movement can circulate their work, which concerns local issues, via the internet, achieving global circulation to 'global citizens' (ibid.). Indymedia currently comprises around eighty IMCs in over thirty countries, resulting in a decentralized organization of groups and with little attempt at editorial control.[14] The use of the internet, its informality and lack of regulatory constraints produces some compelling examples of innovation and control over (or freedom from) the news production process (see Chapter 3).

In contrast, the mainstream broadcast media have regarded technological change as either a necessity to keep up with their competitors, or as an opportunity to expand news content produced by their existing news-gathering department across a variety of channels or media platforms. The process of digitization of the newsrooms has been uneven, and by 2003 ITN had progressed furthest down the path of digitizing its newsroom when compared with the BBC and Sky News (Garcia Aviles et al. 2004).[15] In the mainstream media, the enthusiasm for technological change has been patchy. Technology is clearly a factor in the changing news production environment, although there is little theoretical or empirical evidence to help us to understand 'the complex interactions between changing news technologies and journalist practices' (Cottle 1999: 26). He argues that while on the one hand journalists are more computer-bound and pressurized by multi-skilling and multi-media working practices, some journalists welcome the increased control over work processes and the news product which mastery of the technology can bring.

The effect that new technology and newsroom practices may have on the quality of news and the nature of news journalism is subject to both optimistic and pessimistic research findings. Pavlik's (1999: 55) analysis of the news coverage of the Oklahoma bomb in 1995 led him to argue that thanks to new technology, news reports are 'put in better context, accuracy is increased and [the] lead, sources and story angles are more quickly identified'. Garcia Aviles et al. (2004) found in their comparative study of newsrooms in Spain and Britain that in the main, news journalists are gradually discovering the benefits of technology – the opportunity to write scripts to the images they had selected, to edit their copy personally and to put voice-overs to their own pictures were seen as beneficial. Such multi-skilling is gaining momentum as younger broadcast journalists join the profession and current journalists welcome the opportunity to retrain.[16]

Other researchers raise concerns about the impact of new technology on news. Hardt (1990) argues that new technology is primarily a management tool rather than a news tool and is used in part to deskill the workforce and to underpin some of the economic and social battles fought between management and journalists. Bromley (1997) offers a critique of the deleterious impact of news technology on journalists' working practices. MacGregor (1997) raises concerns that the growth of technology, which allows news transmission to be live and instantaneous, may result in sacrificing depth of reporting for immediacy. Marjoribanks' (2000) analysis of News Corporation in a comparative study of Murdoch's newspapers in the UK, the USA and Australia puts technological innovation into a global context. He argues that the introduction of computerized systems has resulted in a modification of the journalistic skills required in a newspaper environment. He found that technological innovation was more likely to benefit the management than the journalists. Murdoch's ability to bypass print unions and establish a newer, more efficient, streamlined production process has allowed the News Corporation to develop a 'global strategy of technological innovation, in which different organizational sites in the company are able to benefit from the experiences of one another' (Marjoribanks 2003: 74). In practice this has meant that different news organizations owned by Murdoch produce similar news to each other.

As early as 1994, John Tusa, in his James Cameron Memorial Lecture, raised concerns about the nature of news reporting in a technologically developing news environment. He said that a reporter had recently commented to him that 'we're not correspondents any more. We're scarcely even reporters. We have become re-processors. There is no time for digging up the news' (Tusa 1994: 4, cited in Harrison 2000: 120). As newsrooms have become increasingly computerized, we have witnessed the development of the 'mouse monkey' or the journalist who is entirely computer-bound (Garcia Aviles et al. 2004: 89). The computer-bound journalist can reprocess and repackage incoming news feeds and agency news stories into stories for a variety of different news programmes without ever leaving the building (MacGregor 1997). This is problematic, since it means that journalists cannot go out and follow up or deepen a story. For Ursell (2001), this represents a reduction in quality in the production process. Garcia Aviles et al. (2004) quote one journalist at the BBC who claimed that reporters have to work much harder and cannot go out on the stories as they used to, because they have to service a live output of twenty-four-hour news. This led to a huge emphasis on processing and, as one journalist put it 'an element of write it down and whack it out' (ibid.: 96). The ability to process and reprocess news stories very quickly using digital technology has become increasingly necessary, as the number of news outlets increases and news is broadcast twenty-four hours a day, where the demand for news packages in some newsrooms is continuous and relentless. This often means that the editing process is not as scrupulous as it would be for scheduled programmes when there is longer to prepare. Sometimes headlines and the spoken words do not match, or the presenter simply does a voice-over of some pictures without any natural sound.

Working to a deadline, and working quickly, has always been a feature of journalism (indeed, the provincial printers of the eighteenth century were under enormous pressure in this regard: see Chapter 2). Schlesinger (1987: 84) has called this aspect of news journalism 'a stop-watch culture'. However, while the growth in continuous news broadcasting and ever-hungry broadcasting outlets requires a speedy turn-around of news feeds into stories, it is the sheer volume of content required today which makes gathering as much news as quickly as possible into a key newsroom priority. This in turn has led to an increase in the use of live pictures broadcast directly from the scene. These priorities affect journalistic practice and some critics have expressed concern that speed, immediacy and volume are being prioritized above accuracy (MacGregor 1997), allowing very little time for some of the basic tenets of professional journalistic practice to be applied (Ursell 2001). A very significant development, enabled by technology, was the live two-way, where a journalist at the scene, or even in the studio (in the case of radio broadcasting), talks directly to the presenter. We will return to this practice in Chapter 6, but a key concern among journalists themselves has been the tendency to do two-ways with people before they fully know the story. As we have seen, at its worst, this can encourage journalists to engage in an unscripted two-way about complex issues and make assertions or even allegations that can subsequently prove to be problematic.

Four things emerge that are worthy of note when looking at the consequences of new technology and its relationship to broadcast (and to a lesser extent print) news. First, in current broadcast news emphasis is switched to rolling news where updates are an integral part of reporting the story, rolling banner headlines, which speak of breaking news are commonplace, while news announcers speak constantly of coming back to the story when they know more. Incomplete reports are part of the process of on-air reporting. They are presented as exciting, firsthand, embedded in a lexicon of revelation as viewers are treated as witnesses to 'unfolding events', and too frequently 'history in the making'. Clichés aside, the video camera as noted above is now also beginning to make its mark on news reporting, further encouraging the rolling news style. The second consequence of new technology is less well reported. News journalists (print and broadcast) now have access to superb databases, research facilities and global networks. The newspaper morgue has been replaced with online databases that can be semantically searched for information that deepens news coverage of any story. For example, international events can be presented against deeper cultural and historical understanding, complex technical stories against networks of experts, online libraries and so on. Checking and rechecking facts is easier now than ever before. Third, as news journalists become more familiar with new technology, so they absorb and accommodate it in ways that facilitate traditional practices, and the mobile phone, the lap-top and the video camera all militate against the need for journalists to be completely desk-bound. Fourth, the presentation of broadcast news has moved from the talking head to news packaged in graphics, animation, split screen and interactivity. Visually the news is more compelling than ever. It can be more explanatory, and the use of such aids as 3D maps, mock-ups and animation are probably helpful to viewers. Indeed, the digital curriculum will probably use for lessons much of the visual packaging that is currently used by the news broadcasters.

CONCLUSION

News journalists operate within a professional and organizational framework through which and by which they participate in the understanding and interpretation of contemporary events. This participation is premised on the assumption that they understand what news is in a generic sense. This understanding is gained through the adoption of a range of particular professional and historical practices. These include:

- interviewing,
- notetaking,
- research,
- and being able to make a judgement about the relevance or importance of a contemporary event within particular organizational contexts.

They are further supported by the adoption of:

- formulae (using the inverted pyramid to tell the story),
- routines (managing the logistical constraints of time and space/place),
- and normative assumptions (about the value or importance of news and the need to provide a truthful, accurate and sincere account of events).

Moreover, journalists are often responsible for maintaining myths about their own profession (for example, they are the only people who 'have a nose for news'). The historical and professional consciousness of journalism is passed down to new generations of journalists through a process of training and socialization. As most journalists work for news organizations which demand adherence to their news policies and news agendas, they must, if they are to be successful, adopt the particular news organization's rules for producing news. However, this in no way impairs news journalists who continue to move from one organization to another from adopting house styles on the way. The continued expansion of a market-driven media environment alongside technological changes has led to an increasingly competitive news environment. Sometimes new practices have replaced older ones, while at other times new technology simply enhances traditional skills. It is via these developments that the character of the news provided and the way it is produced, packaged and sold (McManus 1994; Hume 1996; Franklin 1997; McQuail 2000) is currently being worked out.

Overall in the multi-channel, multi-media news environment, where audiences are fragmenting, where internet access is growing in popularity and newspaper circulations continue to decline, the fight to interest the audience has led to an unprecedented era of competition among 'traditional' news providers, alongside the growth of new types of news provision. Consequently, we shall turn our attention to what the audiences for news want. How sympathetic are they to the type of news produced by mainstream broadcast news organizations and what do they regard as newsworthy events? Or, to put it another way, what is the relationship between what is wanted by consumers and what is shown or printed by news providers?

7

NEWS

Character and audience

INTRODUCTION

Today we inhabit an increasingly competitive and market-driven news
environment where the need to attract and retain audiences has become
an important determinant of the character of news. For critics such as
Bourdieu (1998: 27), concentrating on attracting audiences has meant
that ratings are now the journalist's 'Last Judgement', having consequences for the type of news that is provided, the way in which
journalists work, and the relationship between the audience and the way
that news is packaged and sold. In order to understand this point more
fully, I propose to focus in this chapter more on television news than on
press news, since this has drawn the greatest amount of comment and
criticism in recent years due to its position in 'the commanding heights
of the UK news system' (Hargreaves and Thomas 2002: 5).

The ubiquitous presence of television in people's homes has reinforced its position as the prime source of news and information for
several decades (it is still regarded by the advertising industry as an
opportunity to target both mass and niche audiences). All the main
terrestrial TV channels in Britain recognize the importance of news in
helping to define the look of their channel. Whereas news used to be
independent of the programmes around it, today the style of news
bulletins is designed to fit into the programming profile of different channels (OFCOM 2004).[1] At the moment, news is a vital part of television
programming and it is television, above all, that is still defining news as
a package of different items, placed together in a stream of information

which creates a 'news agenda' (much of which is then reported by the newspapers the following day, thereby reinforcing a consensus on what is newsworthy).

CHANGING PATTERNS OF NEWS CONSUMPTION

The consumption of news is changing, and those providing it have to be aware of the nature and consequences of those changes in order to retain a competitive edge in an increasingly crowded news market. This has entailed a re-evaluation by news providers of the role and importance of the audience to their task. As we saw in Chapter 1, early theories of audiences were based upon the assumptions that they were passive and that media messages could have a direct impact on them. This is a view which still underpins some of the legal and regulatory restraints placed on broadcast images.[2] Later academic research has been sceptical about this view of audiences, focusing instead on the question of 'what people do with the media' (Halloran 1969: 18–19). In turn this approach was contested in a debate over the extent to which audiences may be regarded as free to critically interpret messages (Ang 1996). Today, audience research is an ongoing dialogue between those trying to 're-establish the notion of the power of the media to shape peoples' knowledge, beliefs and attitudes' and active audience theorists, who see audiences as being highly involved in their use of media and interpretation of its messages (Williams 2003: 209).[3]

Those working in news take the view that audiences are active and discerning. Consequently they tend to see the decline in audience figures as evidence of dissatisfaction with traditional news formats and a desire on the part of audiences to have more control and selection of options (Neuman 1991). To this end, news presentation styles and content are, as we will see below, consistently being developed to become more agreeable to perceived audience tastes. Increasing numbers of news providers and competition for viewers, listeners and readers appear to be producing audiences who are less interested in news provided by the mainstream news providers. As more information sources open up, particularly on the internet, offering specialist and transactional services, audiences can follow contemporary events from the worlds of culture (film, music and events), sport (all sports), health (as it concerns them) and the latest news from a variety of categories which constitute a range of personal preferences (for example the latest in a particular job market). All of these services amount to a personal diary of news interest, most of which will not (or cannot) be covered by a mainstream news provider.

The evidence that news consumption habits are changing is manifold. Hargreaves and Thomas (2002) found that there has been an attitude shift among younger viewers. This group in particular said that they were more likely to watch news or buy a newspaper only when they already knew that something would interest them. Hargreaves and Thomas refer to this group as 'spotlight chasers' (ibid.: 5) who, although interested in major or significant events, will not make a regular effort to watch the news on television or buy a newspaper (interestingly a habit prevalent among non-voters). Despite the difficulties in doing so, the BBC, in its public service capacity, has adopted a policy of trying to re-engage younger viewers and non-voters with the political process through a re-evaluation of political programming and the way in which politics is portrayed in the news (Kevill 2002a, 2002b). Other points to note about changes in news consumption include the following: national newspaper circulations are around 25 per cent lower than in the 1960s; regional and local newspapers have either closed or downsized the scale of their operations; and local commercial radio is increasingly popular (Hargreaves and Thomas 2002) mainly due to the expansion of music content with little or no news provision.

More importantly from our point of view is that viewing figures for television news have also dropped by more than 10 per cent since 1994 (ibid.: 10–11, 62). Whereas viewers in 1994 were watching national television news for an average of nine hours per month, this fell to eight and a half hours in 2001 and to eight hours in 2002 (ibid.: 24). The fall in viewing figures has been felt most seriously by the ITV network which has experienced a 23 per cent decline in news viewing between 1994 and 2001; a problem which was exacerbated by moving ITN's *News at Ten* from its regular 10 p.m. slot in 1999 (ibid.: 29). Regional television news viewing has also fallen sharply, probably as a result of unfavourable rescheduling following the move of *News at Ten* and increased competition for viewers from a range of other channels and platforms. Viewing of regional news fell from a high point of 1.27 hours per month in late 1997, to a low of 0.47 hours in May 2001 (ibid.: 32). Significantly, viewers in multi-channel homes watch fewer hours of television news than those who do not have so great a choice of alternative entertainment and sport programming. This decline in viewing is not compensated for by those viewers watching the same amount of news on twenty-four-hour news channels (ibid.: 35). At the same time, the internet is growing in importance as a source of news, with the number of people using it at home estimated to have increased from 7.1 million in November 2000 to 10.6 million people per month in the first half of

2002 (ibid.: 42). The figures for those using the internet at work for non-work interests have not been systematically gathered, but would probably swell the above figures considerably. Analysis of the demographics of those using the internet for news shows that the user is most likely to be male, have a high socio-economic status and be young (Norris 2000), whereas television news still has a more extensive reach across a range of all demographics due to its availability. There is also emerging evidence to show that those using the internet for news are also more likely to read newspapers and listen to radio news than non-internet users, but as yet there is no such clear-cut relationship between internet news users and television news watchers (ibid.: 133).

The variation in use of news sources emphasizes the differences in the types of news provided by television and the internet and the different ways in which they are used by audiences. Television provides two broad types of news (see Appendix 6):

1   Appointment bulletins which are broadcast at specific times of day on the five terrestrial channels.
2   Twenty-four-hour news.

The appointment bulletins are prepared over a relatively long time period (in broadcasting terms) and the news packages are carefully crafted to the extent that the later evening programme is often referred to as the 'flagship', exemplifying high journalistic standards (particularly the BBC's *News at Ten*). Appointment programmes are usually concerned with the coverage of contemporary events in a highly prepared manner. Live links to reporters outside the studio are used, but these are generally to reiterate what has already been said in the prepared package. In contrast, although preprepared packages do appear on twenty-four-hour news, this type of news programme more often covers events as they unfold. This generally entails the presenter talking over pictures transmitted direct from the scene. While internet news varies enormously in quality and veracity (see Chapter 3), it offers new opportunities for news consumption. As noted above internet news can offer breadth, depth and immediacy, with news sometimes appearing on the internet first in a form which is used almost verbatim by Ceefax or Teletext services. For example, football websites sometimes carry an exclusive interview with the manager, or a press release from the football club. Here the website is a mere channel for the press release, but also provides 'news' for journalists looking for new information about the club, which often then finds its way on to Ceefax or Teletext.

When using internet news, audiences can pursue their own interests and ignore those areas which do not engage them. In contrast, an appointment television programme is a linear data stream which is designed with the expectation that the audience will sit through the whole programme. Increasingly, broadcasters have tried to make such programmes seem less linear, offering more inducements to the audience to stay tuned. Terrestrial channels such as Five, which only broadcast appointment news programmes, have introduced hourly headlines to keep the audience up to date and tuned to their channel. Here, news is presented as a series of short pieces read by the presenter (news bites). News programmes now make a point of telling the audience what is coming up in the programme through a type of in-programme advertising, particularly before an advertising break. The BBC, which does not have advertising breaks copies the style used by ITN and Sky News, and announces after about fifteen minutes what is coming up later in the programme. A variety of other methods are used to keep the audience watching: new presentation techniques, live two-ways, an increasing focus on different news values that are of immediate relevance to that audience; such as crime, leisure, lifestyle, as well as the use of 'special reports' sometimes carried out by amateurs for the BBC's *Six O'clock News*. Innovations such as short headlines on the hour, on screen banners giving information about breaking news, improved text services and alternative screens offering immediate access to headlines (via Sky Active and BBCi News) presuppose that in an 'ambient' news environment (Hargreaves and Thomas 2002: 44) audiences want to have the latest news available immediately and are no longer willing to wait for scheduled news programmes.

A poll conducted by MORI in April 2003[4] illustrates the difficulties that traditional news organizations may face in trying to retain different audiences' attention. The poll identified new distinct 'breeds' of news audiences. These illustrate the different types and levels of use of available news outlets. One breed is 'All-rounders', who have a general interest in all news and tend to be tabloid readers. This group comprised 32 per cent of those interviewed. A group identified as the 'Ho-hums' comprised 21 per cent of those surveyed, and these were uninterested in every type of news with the exception of celebrity news and the *Metro* newspaper. This group mainly tended to be unemployed females. The 'Newshounds' (14 per cent of those surveyed) in contrast had a very keen interest in the news and watched breakfast news, read broadsheet newspapers and were not interested in celebrity news. The 'Early birds' (13 per cent of those interviewed) mainly accessed news at breakfast time from both the press and television and were interested in local, national and international news. 'Technos' (12 per cent of the sample) used the internet, mobile phone and teletext to access news at all times of the day. Members of this group were interested in local, national and international news and were in full-time employment, mainly male and aged between 22 and 44. The final group identified were the 'Night owls' (8 per cent of those surveyed). This group tended to access news via magazines, newspapers, the internet, teletext and radio in the evening. News programme-makers over the past few years have provided the news, knowing that many viewers will already be aware of the top stories of the day before the appointment programmes are broadcast (OFCOM 2004). Consequently, appointment programmes have to offer 'added value' (ibid.) via analysis or by developing a distinctive character, especially in their main evening programmes.

Clearly the ambient character of twenty-first-century news means that diverse audiences now use it in distinct ways. The review of PSB undertaken by OFCOM (2004) showed that 63 per cent of those surveyed said that they still rely primarily on the main appointment terrestrial programmes for their news needs, even in digital homes (over 60 per cent of households). They also said they did not believe that twenty-four-hour news channels or the internet were adequate replacements. Despite their stated attachment to appointment programming, audiences do now generally seem to use other sources of news to supplement these programmes, with 33 per cent of interviewees with satellite television, and 24 per cent of those with Freeview, using twenty-four-hour news channels or the internet first to check on breaking news. In contrast only 8 per cent of those in terrestrial television-only homes were likely to turn to the internet. Regular appointment television news on mass audience channels is used the least by younger viewers,[5] ethnic communities and those from social groups III(M), IV and V[6] (Hargreaves and Thomas 2002: 5). These groups in particular now get their news from other sources which they dip into when they feel it is necessary, such as twenty-four-hour news, the internet and through 'word of mouth' (ibid.). Currently, those watching appointment television news programmes on the mainstream channels have a higher age profile, but there is no indication that they can or will be replaced by younger viewers as they get older. It seems likely that viewing figures for appointment programmes will continue to decline in the future. The changes in viewers' habits and preferences will lead to continued fragmentation of the mass audiences where, as we have seen, audiences use different news sources to serve their own particular needs and interests, accessing information about particular contemporary events which interest them, which may not be covered (i.e. not deemed to be news) by the mainstream news organizations.

Not surprisingly, competition between the mainstream news providers to attract audiences to sell to advertisers has increased further. Increased competition has, according to several researchers, led to more entertainment-centred news which competes with other forms of media entertainment (Blumler 1999; Murdock and Golding 1999; Franklin 2003). Some news providers are trying to make news more enjoyable in the hope of improving its marketability (see below) and acceptability to audiences (Buchman 2000). In this environment 'the market is accepted more and more as a legitimate means of legitimation' (Bourdieu 1998: 27). Or, to put it another way, success is measured in relation to popularity. Competition to maximize audiences has led to the use of entertainment values when defining potential audiences. Unlike a public service rationale where audiences are regarded as citizens, a market-driven news environment considers the audience as consumers who need to be entertained (McManus 1994; Murdock and Golding 1999; Chalaby 2000; Franklin 2001). Alternatively expressed, this is akin to either viewing the individual as a person to be governed or to be exploited economically (Fraser 1989). Regarding news as entertainment and as a commercial product entails its separation from other news areas such as politics and culture, and, according to Habermas (1989), such a separation results in a transformation from a culture-debating public to a culture-consuming public. As previously noted, Habermas refers to this as the refeudalization of the public sphere. This process has, according to Thompson (1992: 113), turned the public sphere 'into a theatre and . . . politics into a managed show in which leaders and parties routinely seek the acclamatory assent of a depoliticized population'.

These pessimistic views do not tell the whole story. Broadcast news has in the main resisted some of the pressures of commercialization by not submitting to a tabloid news agenda (see below). Although, of course, news agendas have changed over time either in direct response to changing audience attitudes or wider social changes. News-programme makers quoted in OFCOM's (2004) review of PSB sum up these changes as follows:

> News agendas have changed. But so have the agendas of broadsheet newspapers. Lifestyle issues are more important to all of us. Society has changed. You're no longer old at 40. . . . We must get away from the idea that news is about white, middle-aged males. There are different news agendas

for different audiences. Let's not be too snooty. For many people, David Beckham is more important than Gordon Brown.

(Section 7.1.1 News <http://www.ofcom.org.uk/ consultations/past/psb/psb)

Views such as these have been used to point to an inevitable decline in the quality of news. Those who take a normative approach to television news believe that it should engage citizens in the social and political culture. In particular, the inability of the still very popular television medium to engage some viewers' interest and trust has led to questions about the breakdown of trust between the media, politics and the people (Phillis 2004). Hargreaves and Thomas (2002) argue that people feel they are poorly informed about their localities and international affairs, and in part place the blame with the news media. While it is in part the responsibility of educators and politicians to create the conditions for improving people's knowledge of these areas (Grice 2004), the fact that most people still get most of their news from television (ibid.) means that television news providers, serving mass audiences (especially those with PSB obligations), should also shoulder responsibility. This view assumes that the character of news on television is somehow different from that of other news media insofar as it is expected to educate its audience: a view shared by some but not all broadcasters or their owners.

In the OFCOM review (2004: Section 7.1.1) some programme-makers argued 'that news programmes have a responsibility to engage viewers in serious and important issues, even if they are not immediately recognised as such by viewers'. Where television news retains its traditional agenda it is praised for fulfilling its public purpose, even though this agenda has its own problems. Chief among these is the phenomenon of 'me too-ism' as journalists flock to the same sources and cover the same stories. As we saw in Chapter 5, the routinization of practice exacerbates this phenomenon. In particular, television news media are highly susceptible to being used by politicians and celebrities to attempt to boost their own popularity through the staging of 'events' to which all are invited. Few journalists would risk ignoring such an event in favour of a 'hunch' that required them to be somewhere else. With the increasing communication skills of sources (public and private), has also come a tendency for staged events to exploit the propensity of news journalists to view something as newsworthy because the rest of the news media are also covering the story. 'Me too-ism' may well be a response to audience fragmentation where taking risks with a particular news agenda is regarded as potentially damaging to ratings.

As audiences go to a greater variety of sources, so they stretch the definition of news. From the Britney Spears website (she once boasted the most visited website of any celebrity) through to Opendemocracy. com, visitors are generally looking for something different from the news provided by the mainstream news media (e.g. different types of inform-ation, a network, a chatline). However, some audiences do not have the option to visit alternative news sources due to lack of appropriate means of access, knowledge, interest or skill to use them, or lack of the finan-cial means to pay for them. Such unequal access to a variety of news means that further pressure is placed on mainstream news providers to compensate for this. Frequently such compensation results in news programmes which appeal to popular tastes and interests.

Using Halberstam's (1992) theories of newsworthiness we can begin to understand the way news reporting differentiates itself for its audi-ences. Halberstam distinguishes between the way news story selection can focus on either what is of interest or what is important. Interest is associated with a tabloid- and audience-dominated news agenda, and with the idea of 'grabbing people's attention' or 'making them take notice'. Interest is not regarded as an essential quality of the event itself but is associated with the amount of attention it is perceived to get from an audience. Importance is associated with ideas such as consequence; significance; weight; gravity; seriousness, or solemnity. Importance is defined as an essential quality of a contemporary event that makes it worth reporting. As I have shown elsewhere (Harrison 2000), news for the BBC is in the main shaped like this. Despite the impression of a changing ethos towards a more populist news agenda, a post-Hutton BBC is prioritizing the exercise of scrupulous standards in journalism (see Chapter 5). Overall, the essential differences between interest and importance highlight the distinction in the character of news at the BBC when compared with ITN, Sky News, Fox News and other commercial news providers.[7] The BBC still prioritizes matters of public interest, international news and coverage of economic events, and will often lead on a different news story from its competitors. It must be remembered, however, that importance and interest are also generated through the work of the journalist: news journalists still maintain that the way in which the story is told and presented is crucial for holding the audience's attention. Different news organizations and news programmes will make different assessments and weighting of the levels of interest and importance a story generates in relation to what they know about their audiences. However, as audiences have increasingly been able to go elsewhere for information, such clear-cut decisions about how to address and meet audience preferences within traditional news programmes

become more difficult to achieve, and the evaluation of audience priorities may equally be said to either reflect or create audience interest in
a programme.

THE NEWS ORGANIZATION AND ITS
AUDIENCES

News, as a means to attract audiences for advertisers, has long been
recognized as a potentially lucrative product, particularly in the newspaper sector. Broadcast news has often required high levels of
investment, as the history of ITN shows (see Chapter 3). Equally, Sky
News has been a drain on resources for BSkyB which raises the question
of why BSkyB would go to the trouble of providing news, when, unlike
the BBC, ITV1, Channel 4 and Five, it is not required to do so. The
short answer is that Sky News gives BSkyB greater credibility and status
as a serious broadcaster. Sky News's increasing popularity has gradually attracted larger audiences, justifying the original investment in the
station. In the broadcasting sector, news has impact and importance for
the status of the channel and company that provides it, and this helps
organizations to attract advertising revenue. In America, some advertisers will only place their advertisements on affiliates that provide a news
programme in their schedule, as news distinguishes the channel from
purely entertainment-oriented competitors.

News organizations need to know their audience in terms of its size
and viewing or reading habits, as well as its attitudes, so that they can
effectively sell their audiences to advertisers. Knowing the audiences'
preferences helps news programme-makers to make decisions about the
feasibility of launching new initiatives and changing the style of news
presentation. A recent success story is Fox News in America. Fox uses
a different approach to news from its main competitor, CNN. It is
'populist, politically partisan (despite its claim to be "fair and balanced")
and aggressively patriotic' (Tait 2004b: 12). As far as its owner, Rupert
Murdoch is concerned, Fox is a 'really objective news channel' (ibid.),
in comparison to the liberal approach taken by CNN. The channel now
attracts more viewers than CNN and those staff who have left the station
have alleged 'that the story selection and editing made stories more palatable to right-of-centre tastes' (ibid.: 13). Certainly the opinions and
uncritical position with regard to the Bush Administration expressed by
Fox News seem to strike a chord with their viewers, particularly when
contentious issues are dealt with, such as support for the 2003 war on
Iraq. Perceptions of Fox News's 'truthfulness' provide an interesting
insight into the way in which news can shape or reinforce an audience's

views. A series of polls from the Programme on International Policy Attitudes (PIPA 2003)[8] showed that those who primarily watch Fox News are significantly more likely to have misconceptions about events than those who primarily listen to NPR or watch PBS. PIPA lists these misconceptions as:

- the belief that weapons of mass destruction had been found by American troops in Iraq;
- that Saddam Hussein and Bin Laden were in alliance;
- that Iraq was directly involved in the attacks on the World Trade Center on 11 September 2001.

For British broadcast news organizations, attracting a loyal news audience is not so easy, as traditional news scheduling decisions and the requirement for impartial reporting mean that there is currently little editorial freedom to mirror audiences' political values and prejudices. Certainly, in the quest for audiences, broadcasters may begin to look at the possibilities that providing populist partisan news brings (Tait 2004b: 13).

How organizations get to 'know' their news audiences

News organizations get to 'know' their audiences using a variety of measures: for example, they can measure audience size. In Britain this is achieved through the measurement of ratings, which for television is undertaken by the Broadcasting Audience Research Board (BARB)[9] and for radio by Radio Joint Audience Research (RAJAR).[10] The press measures its circulation figures via the National Readership Survey (NRS). As well as measuring the numbers of people using a news media product, audience reaction may be acquired through the use of appreciation indices (AI). While ratings simply concentrate on the audience's exposure to the media, research can be conducted to measure the emotions that people feel in relation to their exposure to the media. More specialized research is also undertaken by news organizations using focus groups, although these findings tend not to be released into the public domain because the information gathered is usually commercially sensitive. Specialized audience studies are also commissioned by regulators. The ITC and the BSC (as well as the BBC) have undertaken studies about public opinion towards different broadcasting related issues[11] and the 2003 Communications Act has given a significant audience research role to OFCOM. These studies are often qualitative in nature and may be undertaken by the research division of the regulator or may sometimes be commissioned from academics (see, e.g. the report by Hargreaves and Thomas 2002). Some types of media lend themselves to different sorts of direct interaction with the audience which can provide further useful information. The BBC provides its news journalists with daily 'news online statistics' which on 1 April 2004 gave information about the total number of page views for each story.[12] 'Immigration Minister resigns' attracted the most page views (351,301) alongside 'Horrific Iraq death shocks US' (313,237) and 'US vows to catch Falluja killers' (267,369). In this way the BBC online news team is able to see precisely which stories are popular and which are less so. Information about audience views may also of course be elicited via e-mail, online voting, weblogs, readers' letters, telephone calls and so on.

With this level of knowledge about user preferences, the news providers are in a position to adapt and change the type of news that is selected and the way it is presented. In this case the character of the news and the news agenda that is pursued could in principle be directly shaped in relation to user demands and levels of usage. While it is not possible to outline them all, it is clear that a number of changes are occurring both in the broadcasting and the print news sectors in response to audience data. Print news organizations make regular changes to the layout in their newspapers, add magazine supplements or new sections, and sometimes even change their masthead.[13] Often such changes are accompanied by a relaunch of their newspaper, particularly in the increasingly aggressive Saturday newspaper market.[14] In the television sector relaunches generally involve the introduction of new, colourful, technologically impressive-looking sets in television studios; increasing the tempo and pace of presentation on television and radio; increasing the use of live news links; using visually interesting graphics and even involving changing the news's position in the broadcasting schedule.[15]

Following restructuring of the BBC in 1996 to 1997,[16] the BBC initiated a Programme Strategy Review in 1998[17] and made changes to its news programmes in response to audience comments. The Review attempted to refocus and reinforce the audience's relationship to BBC news in an attempt to give the audiences more of what they wanted. When audiences were offered a choice of possible roles for BBC news and asked to identify the most important, they chose 'a wide variety of news to appeal to all audiences'.[18] The review showed that increasingly people wanted news to be warmer and to use clearer language and to cover a broad range of stories, including (but not only) personally useful news (such as consumer and health issues, or explaining the implications of a tax change) and topical issues (such as trends in employment or family life). As a consequence of the review news bulletins began to take on particular discernible characteristics. *The Nine O'Clock News* (now *The Ten O'Clock News*) became the BBC's showcase for foreign news coverage, while *The Six O'Clock News* was more strongly linked to the BBC's regional network through the inclusion of a regular 'Live From . . .' report from the regions outside London and had a more domestic news focus, deliberately reducing the amount of international news covered. In 2000 the BBC initiated a further two-year review of BBC news, claiming it to be one of the most extensive research and public consultation exercises ever undertaken in broadcast news. The BBC's study included a survey of 2,000 adults, detailed analysis of viewing figures, focus group research, research into social change and an analysis of its main competitors' performance. The BBC's key findings mirrored the earlier survey, showing that audiences want news programmes to be more relevant and engaging, with clearer language and a broader story range, and that younger audiences are less likely to be loyal to BBC news.[19] Following this review, the BBC has aimed to 'make complex ideas understandable through the use of compelling storytelling to draw people in', and sometimes devotes a day to covering a single subject (such as NHS Day, Cracking Crime Day and Hey Big Spender!), across a wide range of BBC programmes including the news (BBC 2004: 10). The BBC uses both regular scheduling of appointment programmes and special broadcasts from BBC News-24[20] to cover breaking news. The continuous news coverage on BBC News-24, BBC online, as well as news on new digital channels and radio channels (e.g. BBC 3, BBC 4, BBC Asian Network, 1Xtra and 6 Music, as well as plans to provide ultra-local television news), is the BBC's way of keeping up to date with new news technologies and meeting what it believes are the requirements of a diverse range of audiences.

Other news organizations undertake research and produce programmes on the basis of their understanding of their particular audience profile. When ITV relaunched its *News at Ten Thirty* on 2 February 2004 the venture was carefully researched and specifically targeted at a predominantly male audience of around four million viewers. In an interview with the *Guardian*'s Jason Deans, Head of ITV News, David Mannion talked about how the target audience and the consequent news values and presentation style are interlinked:

> We've done a lot of work on the audience at 10.30 p.m. It's skewed towards men. Slightly upmarket, older, we're adding sport every night, making it a

slightly more upscale product, a bit more foreign news, business news, a touch on the tiller.

(David Mannion, quoted in Deans 2004a)

Mannion also provided an example of how ITV's *News at Ten Thirty* follows a slightly different news agenda from its other ITV programmes. Although the same story would be covered by all the ITV news outlets on the same day, there would be a different focus on the story by different news programmes. He cites the recent health scare about salmon:

On the 6.30 p.m. evening news it would lean towards the consumer angle – is the fish safe to eat? By 10.30 p.m. it would tilt towards a Scottish industry under threat.

(ibid.)

Alongside the attention to news values, the use of expert 'personality' correspondents and celebrity presenters, the relaunch also involved a total studio revamp: a new big, curved news wall with a video screen behind it, a current fashion in television news presentation (Brown 2004) and, in the ITV's case, modelled on Imax cinemas (Deans 2004a). The new curved news wall screen allows a reporter to call up four video sources at one time and tell a story by walking from one side of the semicircular studio fixture to the other. The dramatic studio and presentation style is seen to be essential in an era of ambient news. The Chief Executive of the ITN News Group recognizes that 'appointment programmes must work much harder and deliver added value if viewers are to continue to feel that watching terrestrial news programmes is worth their time and commitment' (Jones 2004: 19). For him, the theatre of news with its semicircular floor-to-ceiling wall means that 'a presenter's walk across the arc of the studio is now a compelling illustrated walk into the story of the day . . . a science correspondent no longer needs to describe the surface of Mars, he can walk on it' (ibid.). The purpose of the revamp is to set the standard for modern news presenting by staging the news in a new and exciting visual way in a bid to interest and retain viewers.

Journalists make numerous judgements about an audience's tastes, sensibilities, what might distract or interest and so on. One story has it that female news presenters were ordered to wear trousers rather than skirts in case the audience was distracted by the sight of their legs which traditionally were hidden under desks. Audiences are also protected from scenes which broadcasters judge will be too horrific. The BBC take care not to show blood-stains in the aftermath of a disaster (see the

BBC's Producers' Guidelines). ITN and Sky News will often show more dramatic events. ITN will often warn viewers about the nature of the images which will be broadcast, sometimes adding a qualitative judgement that 'you will find the pictures in this report particularly disturbing'. In an era when graphic images are available via the internet, on news channels like Al-Jazeera, or may suddenly appear while showing live footage of events, attempts to protect the audience may seem quaint and overly cautious. The BBC's mission to protect the audience was illustrated clearly in their coverage of the Bosnian crisis in the mid-1990s when the correspondent Martin Bell said, 'what happened here can frankly not be shown in any detail – there is a roomful of charred bodies and they died in the greatest of agony' (BBC1's *One O'clock News*). The audience was denied any glimpse of the reality of this disaster, whereas ITN showed the burned bodies, particularly after the nine o'clock watershed (Harrison 2000).

Broadcasters often avoid showing the actual event taking place even if footage is available. For example, BBC1's *News at Ten* reported the story that twelve Nepalese workers had been executed in Iraq on 31 August 2004, showing a still picture of bodies placed in a row. The manner of the executions (shooting and beheading) were mentioned, but the presenter commented that 'these pictures offer only a suggestion of the full horror being shown on the internet'. Undoubtedly more and more graphic images are available and could be broadcast to the viewer, either as a matter of editorial judgement or by accident. During the 2003 war on Iraq, BBC correspondents reported live from battle scenes, with the attack on John Simpson and his crew captured in a memorable way, culminating with blood dripping down the camera lens, an image that was reprinted in newspapers the following day. Reaching out to the audience via on-the-spot reporting does present difficulties for the mainstream broadcast news media. Audiences may be attracted to the excitement of the event, but may switch channels if the scenes become too graphic or upsetting. The BBC in particular is placed in a difficult position. Its mission – to protect its audience from what it views as unnecessarily tasteless scenes – may be criticized for providing overly sanitized versions of events, but if it strays too far into showing graphic events it may be criticized for being overly sensationalist. Using a variety of devices such as graphics, slightly delayed 'live' footage and constant contact with correspondents at the scene, broadcast news organizations, to different extents, seek to capitalize on the live nature of the event and exploit the excitement and interest this brings, while recognizing the need to be responsive to audience sensitivities. The question for news organizations in the future is how far this balancing act needs to be undertaken in a contemporary multi-channel news environment, and to what extent therefore are the regulatory restrictions on television news becoming redundant.

Despite the amount of time, money and effort that news organizations spend on audience research, and subsequent adjustments made in the light of their research findings, there are several instances where an organization gets it wrong and either offends or alienates substantial sections of their audience. Two examples will suffice: the *Daily Mirror* and the *Sun*.

In May 2002, in an attempt to reinvigorate falling circulation figures, the *Mirror* newspaper was rebranded. Both the newspaper's appearance and news content became more serious. The *Mirror's* red masthead was replaced with the renamed *Daily Mirror*[21] which had white lettering underlined in red against a picture that took up the whole of the front page. The *Sunday Mirror* also adopted the same new look. The editor of the *Daily Mirror*, Piers Morgan, was quoted at the time as saying that the revamp was 'a very long-term branding exercise based on great journalism and not tits' and it was about repositioning as 'a serious paper with serious news, serious sport, serious gossip' (quoted by Byrne 2003a online).[22] The change in news values, however, proved to be less popular than expected with the readers (Morgan 2003). It was revealed by the Audit Bureau of Circulations that on a day when the newspaper led with a story about a famine in Malawi, its sales were down by between 3 and 4 per cent (Byrne 2003a). By August 2002, three months after its relaunch, the *Daily Mirror* was experiencing a 4.5 per cent fall in sales when compared to August 2001, and a fall of 5.34 per cent to 2,095,125 when September 2001 was compared to September 2002 (Byrne 2002). Problematically for the *Daily Mirror*, the reduction in circulation had occurred despite a substantial cut in its cover price from 32 to 20 pence in a price war with the *Sun*, and seemed to indicate a gap between the editorial position of the newspaper and the expectations of a tabloid newspaper's readers. Indeed, circulation figures increased when the newspaper returned to its more tabloid values upon acquiring an exclusive deal with Paul Burrell, Princess Diana's former butler, in November 2002 (Byrne 2003a). In February 2003, the *Daily Mirror* took a wholehearted and campaigning anti-war stance in the buildup to the war in Iraq. However, the anti-war position coincided with the continued decline in the newspaper's readership. In April 2003 the *Daily Mirror's* average circulation dropped below two million for two consecutive weeks at the start of the war in Iraq (Byrne 2003a). Although the *Daily Mirror* has returned to some of its traditional tabloid values and style, its circulation figures, like those of most of the press, are falling.

Sometimes decisions about a single story can cause long-term audience anger and rejection of a newspaper. Following the death of ninety-five Liverpool fans at the Hillsborough football stadium in April 1989, the front page of the *Sun* on 19 April 1989 carried a banner headline 'THE TRUTH', which reported unnamed police officers claiming that drunken Liverpool fans had hampered the rescue workers and robbed the dead. The reaction in Liverpool was intense as people refuted the story and publicly burned copies of the newspaper (Chippendale and Horrie 1992). Fifteen years after the disaster there are numerous people in Liverpool who still refuse to buy the *Sun*. The decision by Everton and England footballer Wayne Rooney to give a series of exclusive interviews with the *Sun* caused outrage. On 7 July 2004 the *Sun* printed a front-page apology, accompanied by a full-page editorial describing its coverage of the Hillsborough disaster as a terrible mistake. In its editorial the *Sun* said that Wayne Rooney did not deserve to be vilified for associating with the paper. The apology angered some and was criticized heavily in the local press in Liverpool, which saw it as a cynical move, along with the interview with a popular celebrity figure, to attract readers back to the paper. The original decision to cover the Hillsborough disaster in the way that it did means the *Sun* has still neither recovered nor regained a positive relationship with its audience within the Liverpool area. In both of the above cases relationships with an audience broke down due to editorial misjudgement. For the *Daily Mirror* it was forgetting its own tabloid values, for the *Sun* local sensibilities in the face of a tragedy were ignored.

CONCERNS ABOUT NEWS STANDARDS

Industry programme-makers and commissioners know themselves that the agenda of news programming has changed and is continuing to change. Overall these changes are a general decline in the amount of political news, and an increase in lifestyle, crime and consumer stories (OFCOM 2004). These changes feed debates about the quality of British journalism, and familiar ideas such as 'dumbing down', 'tabloidization' and 'commercialization' are still used as accusations against news coverage in Britain. Taking a different view entirely, McNair (2003: 42) argues that, if anything, British journalism is 'braining up', a phrase which McNair notes 'was first used by Jonathan Freedland in *The Guardian* in March 1998'. News journalism, according to McNair, now 'interacts with and necessarily adapts to an increasingly choice-rich market of sophisticated, media-literate consumers'. In a mature news market, quality and depth of news coverage has its advocates. Indeed, in

The State of the News Media 2004, undertaken by the Project for Excellence in Journalism (affiliated with Columbia University),[23] it was argued that maintaining profits by cutting costs and reducing quality will accelerate audience loss. Despite views about the ability of the audience to be discerning and active, concerns remain about the decline of standards in news provision. Increasing competition for audiences and readers is held to have a negative impact on the news, producing populist agendas which inevitably lead to a reduction in the standards and quality of news output (McManus 1994; Hume 1996; Franklin 1997; Blumler 1999; McQuail 2000; Bell 2002; Frost 2002).

There has also been a concern that the attempt to win back audiences for news has led to 'tabloidization'. While the word 'tabloid' actually refers to the size of a newspaper page (half the size of a broadsheet page), it has increasingly come to reflect a particular style of journalism. This constitutes a particular mode of presentation and the prioritization of a particular set of news values, which, in the case of some newspapers, has pioneered new definitions of what constitutes 'news' and 'news journalism'. In contrast, the original intention of popular journalism was to provide information in a fashion which did not bore the reader, by presenting stories in an accessible way, or by concentrating on elements of the story which would interest the audience. Carl Bernstein, one of the reporters who investigated Watergate in the early 1970s, argues that the risk facing contemporary popular journalism is that it can too easily slip into lowest common denominator journalism, or exhibit the worst excesses of some tabloid journalism: popular journalism and tabloid journalism are distinct and different from each other. Bernstein notes:

> Good journalism is popular culture, but popular culture that stretches and informs its consumers rather than that which appeals to the ever descending lowest common denominator [which provides a] lack of information, misinformation, disinformation, and a contempt for the truth or the reality in most people's lives.
>
> (Bernstein, quoted in Allan 1999: 185)

'Popular' journalism which engages the audience has increasingly become the currency of most television reporting, treading, as it must do, a careful line between pursuing news which interests the public and news which serves the public. As Hargreaves (2003: 137) observes, news has always been reported in a variety of styles and forms (see Chapter 1), and problems with tabloidization only arise 'if it drives out other types of journalism and diminishes diversity'. This point is quite different from Bernstein's with its emphasis upon truth. In point of fact problems arise from 'tabloidization' when it disseminates a disregard for truth just as much as if it were to become the dominant approach to news. Indeed, Britain has a very broad type and range of newspapers which fall under the general category of 'the press'. It is, broadly speaking, stratified into specialist journalism, broadsheet journalism, popular journalism and tabloid journalism. It is fiercely competitive, often riven with price wars and spoiler stories, does not operate as a homogeneous mass and yet pursues some broadly shared versions about the newsworthiness of events. Generalizations about 'the press' are usually wrong since within itself it is so varied, and yet concerns persist about the extent and significance of the 'tabloidization' of the press.

The label 'tabloid' has also been applied to television news. The prototypes of such news programmes may be found, according to Hume (1996), in local American television news shows. These programmes concentrate on entertaining audiences via sensationalism, human interest stories, crime and disasters. They use qualitative judgements (often outrageous) about what it is believed will distract, interest, entertain or upset the audience. Hume argues that these news programmes reduce comprehension, reflection and viewer engagement. The use of 'tabloid' news formats, such as those which emphasize drama, violence, celebrity gossip and sex, can boost ratings temporarily. Evidence from the USA shows that ultimately 'tabloid' coverage weakens the news producers' link with their audience and viewing figures will decline if the programme does not deliver increasingly salacious content – the 'false promise of tabloid news' (ibid.: 144) is that it may not always be successful at retaining audience interest. Despite claims that British television is becoming more tabloid in orientation, Winston (2002) found that there was no evidence to support the view that television news had resorted to tabloid news values in Britain. His findings show that the television news channels still reflected a broadsheet news agenda in 2001 when compared with 1975, although crime and human interest stories had also increased during this time. Hargreaves and Thomas's analysis of a range of academic studies into trends in television news quality leads to the tentative conclusion that on balance, 'it is difficult to deny that British television still supplies a broadly serious news agenda, albeit one that is devoting rather less space to politics and international news (in some studies) and more to crime than in the past' (2002: 18). The type of tabloid news still visible in some American local news programmes therefore remains, in Britain, the main staple of some elements of the press rather than television news (see below).

There is always an exception to a rule. The 'serious' media sometimes stray into tabloid news territory, in particular when they report the actions of famous people. A case in point is the reporting of David Beckham's alleged affair with Rebecca Loos which was extensively represented in the British news media in April 2004. Or, in August 2002, when the serious media followed the rest of the press news pack into Soham to report in great detail the disappearance and murder of Holly Wells and Jessica Chapman.[24] The mobilization of emotions by the news media's coverage of the murder of children can, according to Bourdieu (1998: 52), 'almost qualify as symbolic lynching'. It can also result in trial by media before the offender even enters the lawcourts. The reaction of the tabloids, broadsheets and broadcast news media to the death of Diana, Princess of Wales, in August 1997 illustrated how, in certain instances, different types of media can 'come together' (Hoggart 2004: 62). All the media again picked up on the emotional dimension of the event; they registered the public reaction to the tragedy and 'ran with it' (ibid.: 63). On this occasion the 'main job and purpose was to validate and sustain the emotional outpouring, to assure people that even the most excessive reaction was a proper response to the event' (ibid.: 64).

In Britain it is the tabloid newspapers that have been singled out as going further than other news media in the pursuit of news stories to excite the audience's interest. While many elements of tabloid journalism show high levels of skill, writing expertise and ingenuity, Hargreaves (2003) reports that the prioritization of particular story types by some newspapers remains questionable. He cites the example of Rupert Murdoch, who took over the *Sun* in 1969, and advised his staff 'that he wanted the Sun to focus upon "sex, sport and contests" ' (ibid.: 111). Stephenson and Bromley (1998: 1) see newspapers like the *Sun* reflecting a 'populist conservatism' through a 'preoccupation with sex, sport, chauvinism, celebrity, competitions, free offers and more sex'. And yet, the circulation figures for the tabloid newspapers in Britain remain far higher than for the broadsheet press (see Appendix 4); testament to the fact that sex and celebrity alongside sport sell newspapers. Indeed tabloid journalism not only dwells within these areas, it has also, according to Stephenson and Bromley (1998: 1) pioneered a new style of reporting: one which has been described as merging fact and fiction, and as 'intrusive, offensive, quasi-pornographic, arrogant, inaccurate, salacious and unprincipled'.

International news

Recently, concerns about 'dumbing down' of the news have focused not only on the coverage of domestic politics but also on the coverage of both international and local events (I will deal with the latter in the following section) and the audience's subsequent lack of information in these areas (Hargreaves and Thomas 2002). The importance of international news coverage is, according to Wallis and Baran (1990: 253), that 'by remaining ignorant of the world we have created we remain ignorant of ourselves'. Concern about the levels of international coverage was also raised in the Lambert Report (2002) in relation to the BBC's News-24, and reductions in international news coverage have been identified at both the BBC and ITN in some studies, although these could be attributed to annual fluctuations (Harrison 2000, 2002a). A report by The Third World and Environment Broadcasting Project (2000) showed a significant decrease in international factual programming on British television. In 1989 to 1990, 1,037 hours were shown, whereas in 1998 to 1999 only 728.6 hours were shown, with commercial channels evidencing the greatest decline. Barnett and Gaber's (1993) analysis of a week in 1993 showed that ITN's *News at 5.40 p.m.* and BBC1's *Six O'Clock News* devoted 11 per cent and 22 per cent, respectively, of their programme coverage to international news. These findings led Barnett and Gaber (1993) to suggest that in 1993 ITN was moving towards a more domestic agenda.

More recently, Barnett *et al.* (2000), in their longitudinal analysis of news from 1975 to 1999, reveal more positive findings. While the amount of international news coverage of the media has fluctuated over time, there has remained a relatively stable level of foreign news on BBC and ITV. In 1999 the BBC's late evening news programme (*Nine O'Clock News*, now broadcast at 10 p.m.) had the greatest commitment to international news coverage and the BBC's late evening news (*News at Ten*) and *Channel 4 News* still provided an important balance in the otherwise more domestic news agenda shown by the other programmes. Norris (1999) also found that both the BBC and ITV provided a good range of coverage of the European Union when compared with other European broadcasters. This may be seen as a positive finding, since it indicates that British television news offers viewers a more balanced and alternative view about European affairs than the British press, a significant sector of which has tended to take a Eurosceptic approach to coverage of the European Union.

Anderson and Weymouth's (1999) analysis of the coverage of European issues in the run-up to the 1997 election is indicative of the negative approach adopted by some newspapers. Using Peak and Fisher's (1997: 45) observation that eleven of the total nineteen daily and Sunday newspapers took a right-wing position and accounted for twenty-one million of the twenty-six million newspapers circulated, Anderson and Weymouth argue that a particular type of Eurosceptic newspaper journalism has developed in Britain in relation to both content and style. They identify two reasons for the dominance of Eurosceptic voices in the British press. First, the concentration of press ownership has allowed the domination of right-wing views in the newspaper sector, and second, the 'inexorable commercial drive of the press sector to sustain itself at all costs has influenced the quality of the discourse . . . [which in the case of some titles] has become highly conversationalized, emotive and often strongly xenophobic' (ibid.: 61). In particular *The Times* and the *Daily Telegraph* are identified as taking a Eurosceptic stance, especially in relation to the single European currency and the Social Chapter, emphasizing rivalry with Germany and France and expressing distrust of New Labour's willingness to give away 'traditional British rights' (ibid.: 76). The blacktop tabloids, the *Daily Mail* and the *Express*, raise fewer issues than the Eurosceptic broadsheets, mainly concentrating on a 'mythical British way of life' which is under threat (ibid.: 82). the *Sun* was identified by Anderson and Weymouth as a 'special case' (ibid.: 83) and while its coverage of Europe is actually relatively low in quantity, its tone when discussing European issues is entirely anti-European, with headlines playing upon the extent to which European rules interfere with British affairs, corruption in Brussels, the socialist tendencies under-lying the Social Chapter and a distrust of the intentions of European institutions (ibid.: 90).

Regional news

Consumption of regional news has fallen sharply. In the television sector viewing has fallen from almost one and a half hours per month in late 1997, to around three-quarters of an hour a month in May 2001; sales of regional newspapers have similarly declined and the consolidation of regional newspaper organizations has led to fewer titles. Moreover, commercial regional or local radio tends to concentrate on successful music formats with little or no news provision (Hargreaves and Thomas 2002: 62). Several trends are working against the reinvigoration of regional news provision by the mainstream media. As we saw in Chapter 3, concentration of ownership in the television and local newspaper sector tends to reinforce the news interests of the large-scale news providers, and as we have further seen, their subsequent national news agendas. There have been repeated reports about the reduction in spending in the local news sector; while at the same time the growing news sector of twenty-four-hour rolling news is national and to some extent international in focus. In the ITV sector the appointment of an editor of ITV's regional news marks a new period in commercial regional news provision, as it is the first time a single editor has had overall control of the eleven regional news services in England and Wales (now all owned by ITV plc). The *Guardian* regarded this measure as part of a move to centralize news operations and cut jobs in some of the regions. It was also believed to be an attempt to emphasize the ITV brand rather than the individual franchise names such as Anglia or Yorkshire TV (Deans 2004b) so that each regional franchise 'has a similar look and treatment of news' (Revoir 2004b: 5).

There is also a question mark over just how informative regional news is. Often the rationale of the regional news programme is to cast the presenter as a friend in the living-room. One of the key criteria, here, is to be entertaining and humorous; for example, BBC's Look North's weatherman consistently engages in banter and sparring with the presenters, and the presenters also like to share a light-hearted joke or two, particularly when presenting lighter items or at the end of the programme. After reporting flooding in the Yorkshire region in August 2004, the presenter asked the weatherman to 'tell us' what the weather was going to be like over the next twenty-four hours. He smiled at the camera and said to the viewers, 'and remember, whatever the weather – it isn't Paul's fault'. The programme seems to be saying, 'come on, chin up, smile through adversity, there's always a funny side to life, it's not going to get us Yorkshire folk down'.

What emerges in the informal approach to regional TV news has been described as middle-ground popularism (Cottle 1993). There is a mission to report major events and happenings in line with generalized news values which constitute respectability alongside a populist appeal, seeking to engage audiences by trying to implicate and involve them via a lexicon of personal references to 'your area', 'near you', and personal chat and asides. This means deliberately finding and telling stories in such a way as to heighten their human interest value and their parochialism. In short, these are stories which include the views and experiences, hopes and fears of so-called 'ordinary people' (Harrison 2000). This approach attempts to affirm local viewers' preoccupations and concerns combined with the private world of their family, leisure and consumption. It does not adequately deal with the political or social issues of the area (Cottle 1993). Hargreaves and Thomas (2002: 63) found that the main source of local news continues to be television followed by an ever-shrinking local press. The majority of people see themselves as only 'fairly well served' or 'not very well served' in terms of local news provision. As one journalist said:

While news can be defined as the first disclosure of a fact or an event, there is no absolute scale of value by which it can be measured. For the purpose of selecting news for the readers, an editor takes into account the geographical and personal factors of each story and then qualifies these by relating them to the special interests of the paper and its market.

(Hodgson 1989: 11)

Overall, local news is characterized by a range of opinions that seek to reflect and reinforce a given cultural, social, economic and political identity. As members of a local community (village, town, city or region) first; members of the nation, second; and of world regions such as Europe, third; local news prefigures our identity and citizenship as primarily grounded in the local. Local news is parochial because it seeks continually to foster a sense of identity and belonging. Problematically for local and regional news, national public service broadcasters such as the BBC tend to conceive of public service values in national terms: that is, in relation to serving the whole nation in the national interest. Although the BBC divides England into twelve regional television stations as well as BBC Scotland, BBC Wales and BBC Northern Ireland, it is questionable just how representative these can be of diverse cultures within sub-regions and smaller levels of community, a problem that the BBC is seeking to address.[25] Clear-cut regional delineations made by national news providers mean that localities have tended to be represented in the news in a rather stereotypical manner: keeping ferrets in Yorkshire; border disputes between Lancashire and Yorkshire (the War of the Roses); cheese-making in the Dales and so on. As Scannell and Cardiff (1991: 16) point out, early coverage of national affairs claimed to 'embody the educated, south-east English variety', whereas the most likely task of the BBC's regional centres, if they could not meet the standards and quality of London's cultural output, 'was to give expression to the everyday life and variety of the areas served by the regional stations – culture "as a way of life" in Raymond Williams' [1976] phrase.' This patronizing and inferior view of PSB is still with us today.

Coverage of local democratic institutions and local public services is often limited by the tendency to focus on local crime and human interest stories (Harrison 2000). This approach belies the fact that one of the main 'problems' for regional television news providers is that they say there is not enough news to fill their programmes. However, this is not the complete picture. While academics argue that the regions are under-representing local politics, local journalists often bemoan the fact that frequently there is not enough 'hard' political news available. Hard local news, they say, more often consists of crime, negative human interest stories and local accidents and disasters (ibid.). Since disengagement with national politics can begin with a lack of understanding at the local level, it seems unlikely that regional PSB television news will be able to strengthen citizens' engagement with local affairs if local news providers continue to believe in the superiority of the standards and values of London metropolitan culture, social affairs and coverage of politics. As Hargreaves and Thomas (2002: 65) argue, 'for many people, politics lacks meaning because it is not rooted in a real, local context' (ibid.: 65), and in this local news journalism is failing.

Format changes

A tendency adopted by all news organizations is to package and sell the news more and more aggressively. They are trying continuously to grab audiences' attention. One way of doing so is by adopting certain material formats for news. Newspapers, for example, use headlines which may be written in different sizes and widths. Tabloid-size newspapers often use a banner or streamer headline which crosses the top of the page. Its size and prominence signals clearly that this is the lead and the most important news story for that particular newspaper. Tabloid-size newspapers also tend to use a sanserif[26] style of type which is a generic name for a typeface that bears no cross-lines (serifs). As the following example shows, the letters are unembellished (compare **THIS STYLE OF TYPEFACE** with THIS STYLE OF TYPEFACE). Headlines can be white type on a black background white-on-black (WOB) or black type on a grey background black-on-tone (BOT), or headlines can be overprinted onto pictures, becoming a 'compo'. In the case of tabloid size newspapers, headlines are usually dramatic and often describe the full extent of the story itself. The *Independent* (now tabloid size, as is *The Times*) has recently taken to producing dramatic front pages, using a group of words printed in red serif type. The *Independent* has also started to use long sentences or quotations as the entire front page more frequently, since becoming tabloid size. The serif typeface uses letters which possess a cross finishing-off face on each stroke (AS SHOWN ABOVE, THIS STYLE IS MORE ELABORATE THAN THE SANS SERIF TYPEFACE).

The ability to lay out a newspaper page and to clearly signal the importance of the story has changed over time. Early newspapers often started all their stories at the top of the page and reported them in columns. Today, the term 'tops' is still used to describe stories with headlines in the top half of the page, but their importance and news value are now signalled to the reader in a much more dramatic way. Trainee journalists are taught that headlines are extremely important and must be written in a way that makes the reader want to read the story. Journalists are advised to use active verbs in order not to date the story, not to provide too much information, or to write a headline that needs a tag-line (a secondary line) to explain it. Headlines, page design and use of pictures are designed to grab readers' attention.

Broadcast news and radio news similarly use headlines to draw their audiences in. Broadcast news in particular can use music or show dramatic footage from the day's events (such as a scene of violence or the aftermath of a dramatic event), using it like a preview to whet the viewers' appetite. Coupled with strident music or the 'bongs' of Big Ben and dramatic scripting, broadcast news organizations seek to persuade their audiences that the forthcoming programme is unmissable. Broadcast news organizations also use a variety of devices to hook the audience into the programme by showing live footage whenever possible or going straight to the scene live, advertising forthcoming stories, providing moving strap-lines and interactive options.

Of course strategies for grabbing the audience may also alienate audiences, and with the increasing fragmentation of audiences this is becoming more and more likely. Audience(s) now divide into groups with a range of interests and levels of engagement with their own version of how the news should be presented to them. For those who want their news immediately and in brief, linear appointment style, broadcast news programmes which last for thirty minutes are not for them. Similarly, for those who want deep analysis and comment, devices used to maintain interest or announce what is coming next can get in the way. Television news devices aimed at retaining viewers' attention give the impression that the news programme is in competition with other news broadcasters (as well as entertainment programmes) and not in competition with other media such as newspapers or radio. In short, television news programmes compete with each other and with other television programmes, newspapers with newspapers and radio with radio. Broadcast news does not pursue a print agenda (other than text information as a supplement) and it is highly likely that broadcast news will probably keep itself distinct from internet news provision. The differentiation between media is well established in marketing, with competition (in this case) limited to like with like. Television news has to remain televisual, just as print news is constrained by the medium within which it is presented. Unlike the *Daily Prophet* in the Harry Potter series, magical moving figures are not an option in a newspaper format. The character of the news remains constrained by the medium in which it appears.

Newsroom styles are subject to design and fashion. As we have seen, particular presentational styles have grown in popularity. The use of the so-called 'live two-way' device, where the presenter in the studio and the reporter at the scene discuss events with each other, or in a journalist-to-journalist conversation (Djerf-Pierre 2000), are particularly popular today, and the use of them is one way in which news programmes currently seek to differentiate themselves from their competitors (Tuggle and Huffman 2001). Concomitant with their use is the use of the journalist or correspondent as the expert at the scene, a technique that raises concerns about the nature and quality of some of the information provided for the audience. A live two-way from the scene of a dramatic event can make the news appear more authoritative and truthful, even if viewers cannot always see the event taking place and are only privy to the immediate aftermath. Problematically, the information may in fact be unreliable if the journalist has not had time to verify the facts. The accuracy of immediate live coverage of events is of concern. In addition, live two-ways can be used primarily to fill out a news programme without actually passing on new information, a device which is particularly useful for twenty-four-hour news programmes, and gives the illusion of the development of a story. In a way, the use of live two-ways can be a tactical attempt to excite and entertain the viewers to keep them watching.

Another device to entertain is making the news seem more friendly and accessible, usually achieved through a growing tendency for news presenters and correspondents to be on first name terms when talking to each other, to joke and to mildly chide each other. Phrases such as 'Well Peter, this event has shown that . . .' or 'As you were just saying, Steve, this event has caused considerable disruption . . .' make news sound more like a chat in the pub than a formal and serious matter. This range of techniques has the effect of making news programmes seem more like a friend in the living-room than a rather formal educational event that demands our total attention in order to understand what is be said or shown. Even if there is little to report, a live link to the scene allows news organizations to intensify the drama of an event without necessarily providing any useful information. Sometimes this technique can backfire and be exposed as an unnecessary addition to the story. *Private Eye* (a satirical magazine) recently picked up a 'Going Live' feature in *Channel 4 News* when a presenter went live to a correspondent standing outside the Football Association (FA) headquarters in Soho Square to follow up on a meeting held somewhere else in London, only to be told with some humour that 'I am where the news isn't happening today' (*Private Eye* 2004: 9).

CONCLUSION

This chapter has explored why news organizations have to package and sell their news in an increasingly audience-centred way, and the concerns this raises about the quality and standards of news provision; in short, its contemporary character. As we have seen, evidence to support concerns about dumbing down are mixed. Studies have shown that there have been some changes in news agendas and an increase in the coverage of crime and human interest stories by some television news channels, as well as fluctuations in the provision of regional and international news. However, it appears that tabloid news values and reporting techniques remain restricted to certain sectors of the press, with television news media and broadsheet newspapers more likely to follow either a popular news style or a predominantly broadsheet news agenda. According to Djerf-Pierre (2000: 257), the adoption of a popular news style has involved the following:

- the construction of reality because it uses popular and dramatic narrative;
- the increasing use of journalists as experts and media personalities;
- the development of image-driven stories;
- the emphasis on increasing interaction between journalist and journalist;
- the encouragement of the integration of facts and commentary;
- the growth in the use of brief news items or bulletins.

Consequently, while analysis of different content categories has generally pointed to the continuation of a largely serious news agenda, the changes in news presentation styles allow the serious to be made more entertaining, and the contemporary nature of events to be exploited through live links and live coverage, actions which have attendant risks for accuracy.

The argument for the inevitability of the commercialization of news leading to a purely entertainment-oriented news is becoming less and less convincing in a multi-channel news ecology. While some traditional news providers have recognized that more entertaining news may attract more audiences, this does not mean that what they provide constitutes a generic definition of contemporary news or an accurate description of the potential for news in its multi-channel ecology. Indeed, the tendency seems to be for news organizations to try to serve the audiences' needs through providing news in the style and manner that they believe best suits the patterns of news consumption for their audience. Alongside the response to audience fragmentation, there is also the recognition that audiences can sometimes be homogeneous in their requirements. The ITC's Report *Conflict around the Clock* (Sancho and Glover 2003) reviewed coverage of the war in Iraq, showing that when a big story is breaking, twenty-four-hour news channels are generally the first place to which viewers turn. Both BBC and ITV1 have recognized this trend and since the events of 11 September 2001, have increasingly allowed their own twenty-four-hour services to cover stories which break into terrestrial schedules (ibid.). Later, the same television news audiences will probably turn to other sources for further news.

Uncertainty exists about what the consequences might be for news providers as news audiences increasingly change their news habits. As audiences turn to non-traditional sources for news, what is news for audiences becomes different from what is news for conventional news providers. One response to this has been for news channels, such as Fox News, to tune successfully into the views (predispositions or prejudices) of certain audience groups, by being uncritical of certain events which they know those groups support in a partisan way. This development may well be copied elsewhere and perhaps foretells the development of a partisan news agenda for some broadcast news programmes in Britain. As news audiences become increasingly fragmented, radical rethinks about news provision are inevitable. It is to the possible character of news in the future that I now turn.

8

POSSIBILITIES AND PROBLEMS

Trends in the future of news

INTRODUCTION

News is a phenomenon worthy of study because it is the pre-eminent way we understand our contemporary setting in all its diversity and complexity. Whereas an eighteenth-century encyclopaedist or perhaps even a nineteenth-century polymath may have been able to set themselves the not entirely unreasonable task of understanding everything around them, today's great thinkers are more likely to be specialists. To have a general and familiar understanding of the world in its bewildering range of developments and expressions – science and technology, medicine, engineering, the environment, culture, arts, sport, international and domestic politics, economics and commerce – it is necessary to rely on journalism of some kind or another to explain those things we are not specialists in, or indeed much interested in. Our reliance on accurate and sincere news reports is taken for granted. It is part of the furniture of the world.

Throughout, it has been argued that the core values of accuracy and sincerity should underpin reports of contemporary events (see Table 1, Introduction). These values are central to news and news journalism. They provide the basis for how news journalism seeks to be truthful. Without a disposition towards truthfulness news producers and news reporters are either apologists or propagandists: in both cases we are profoundly misled. Underpinning news production and reporting (attempting to tell the truth about contemporary events) is the *realpolitik* of the conditions under which, and from which, news and news journalism are generated and subsequently read, listened to or viewed. It has been shown how the practical world of news journalism is constantly subject to change and evolution. There is not one news journalism, news-producing organization or news agenda, but many. Central to the concerns of this book has been PSB, not for nostalgic reasons, but because of its role in securing an open and informative public sphere(s) of discussion and debate. Equally, it has been argued that journalists judge what is newsworthy and operate within news production settings and editorial views that are usually clear to them, if not always agreeable. The view that contemporary news is nothing more than the legitimization of ruling elites, distorted market relationships or injustices has very limited value. More and more, the news reveals rather than conceals. As for standards and trust, the former, as always, is both high and low; trust is easily and sometimes lost, but is usually found when it matters (especially when reporting so called news mega-events such as 9/11 or the December 2004 tsunami disaster in the Indian Ocean).

This book began by reviewing some of the approaches that may be taken to analyse news. Subsequently, it showed that news has generally been addressed as an ideological problem. That is, a problem relating to what or who makes news, and what meanings and power relationships are therefore inherent within the messages conveyed by news providers. Others have considered the news in normative terms by asking what role it should play in society and how this should be achieved. Because both of these perspectives require value judgements about the condition of news, the terms 'optimistic' and 'pessimistic' have occasionally been used to summarize their approaches. The latter has arisen more frequently, for that is the prevailing scholarly attitude. Many regard the decline of news quality, due, they say, to its perceived tendency in a competitive news media environment to dumb down to lowest common denominator levels, as inexorable. Some optimistic views may also be heard, particularly when assessing the growing range of news which is being provided through the following: new opportunities brought by the internet and via other technical advances in television (particularly interactive digital television); the continued protection of public service news via regulation; and the development of more active and discerning news audiences. The debate between optimists and pessimists continues.

Some issues are agreed. Twenty-first-century news providers operate in a rapidly changing media environment characterized by deregulatory policies, which have allowed news organizations to be owned by global entertainment organizations. At the same time, technological change has increased the amount and range of news in circulation and the number of channels available. It has also enhanced some elements of news journalism and altered others forever. Technological change has also contributed to changes in audiences' habits and preferences with regard to their news consumption. For some this has meant that they access and rely upon news that is not provided by news organizations or professional news producers. An increasingly competitive multi-channel news environment is being created. In many developed countries there has been an increasing acceptance of a commercial or free market value system, which serves as a way of operating news services. At the same time many developed countries maintain a public service broadcaster, funded entirely or partly from public subsidy.[1] In a competitive news environment the need to attract audiences has grown in importance. Getting to know the audience's likes and dislikes is a trend which looks set to continue and to be a central feature of news provision in the future, particularly as consumers are increasingly coming to expect instantaneous, customized and even personalized news products.

Competition between news suppliers is also undoubtedly exacerbated by the growth in news available. There has been an eightfold increase in the supply of television news provided by the commercial sector in the past decade, with about 243 hours a week now available to viewers (BBC 2002) compared with about thirty hours in 1989. Norris (2000) has found that between 1971 and 1996 the amount of news and current affairs broadcasting on public service television in twenty OECD countries grew from 1,168 hours per week to 3,042 hours. In addition, access to the internet has increased, so that at the time of writing, more than 20 per cent of all Europeans are online. The range and type of news available in the television broadcasting sector alone reinforces MacGregor's view that technological development has resulted in an unprecedented diversity of news 'where to speak of "the news" is anachronistic' (1997: 3). Pavlik observes that technological change has affected 'the nature of the relationships between and among news organizations, journalists and their many publics' (2000: 229). Yet, as we have seen, the differentiation of news and audience is not a new phenomenon. News is a 'cosmopolitan genre' (Crisell 1997: 5) and will continue to grow and develop further as different media or opportunities to publish news emerge. Today this 'cosmopolitan genre' is being mediated through new information and communication technologies. The application of these to news-gathering, reporting and packaging is occurring all around the globe at an unprecedented rate. Issues of location have been utterly transformed by these new technologies, as events are now reported from just about anywhere on the planet almost (and often sometimes) as they occur.

Some analysts have focused upon the importance and significance of the mediation of information in general and regard it as being on such a large scale that it is currently and usually understood as a force of major social change (Bell 1973; Masuda 1990; Castells 1997; Leadbeater 1999). Again both optimistic and pessimistic views exist in the attempts to understand the significance of the increase and scale of information flows, and more importantly from our point of view, its relevance to news. For technological determinists (and others), the internet has more than any other form of communications technology been seen to have created its own world – the virtual world which, it is argued, serves to recast the real world in greater transparency. They argue that the internet allows injustice, cruelty and oppression to be more easily exposed, cover-ups more easily revealed and non-mainstream news more widely circulated than ever before. However, Barnett (1997) sees the development of new news media outlets as retaining the same system of power and control evident in the traditional news media. Similarly for Garnham (1998), the dawn of the so-called information age, identified by Castells (1997), does not transform society but reinforces existing social and economic inequalities. Currently debates centre on whether the internet is just a distribution system that operates and moves content between platforms, or is an intrinsic agent of increased political and legal openness, a force for greater democracy.

It is a mistake primarily to assume that any given technology is a free-standing force which can lead to particular outcomes. There is always a 'balance of forces pushing and inhibiting the technologies' (Winston 1998: 2); and news operates within a complex set of forces of which the particular impact of changing technologies is only one (Majoribanks 2003: 60). None the less, as we have seen in Chapters 2 and 3, the importance of technology must not be underestimated. As Curran and Seaton (2003: 269) point out, 'if the technologically determinist argument is questioned accordingly – does technology make a difference? – the answer is clearly yes'. In particular, they argue, internet technology opens up a range of new opportunities, enormous amounts of information, access to new areas, as well as enabling unprecedented levels of interactivity (via e-mail, chat rooms and conferencing). As Gunter (2003) observes, the internet has had implications not only for the economics of news organizations, but also for the practice of journalism itself. Online journalism or journalisms are developing exponentially in conjunction with the interactive audiences that consume their products, and it is the opportunities offered by communication technology's profuse array of outputs that are having the most effect on the contemporary character of news (see Chapter 6). The view that the new news

outlets retain traditional systems of power and control and that they reinforce existing social and economic inequalities is only partly true.
Certainly most internet news is now part of the offerings of a traditional
news provider, including public service broadcasters, but there is some
journalism which is unique to the internet (see below). Consequently,
it is not true to say that the internet is solely in the hands of a particular set of a few powerful news providers, or suffers from an ideological rectitude placed upon it by such a group.

Many aspects of contemporary news journalism have antecedents
which can be traced back through several centuries. Principles of acceptable journalistic behaviour have emerged and evolved from this history
to become the professional standards which are still valued and aspired
to, even in today's multi-channel news-saturated environment. Most
significant are the professional journalistic requirements to be impartial
and responsible, and to respect and defend 'free speech'. The history of
western journalism is, I would argue, located within the specific history
of freedom of expression, its constitutional setting and the legal-political
and moral environment surrounding it, just as much as it is in technical and cultural changes (see Chapters 4 and 5). Policymakers, regulators and many journalists have long agreed, and seem set to continue to
do so, that news freedom has sometimes to be curtailed through the
exercise of a public service obligation, or via a variety of regulatory
requirements and legal constraints which serve certain special needs (for
example, restrictions on material which may cause harm). None the less,
attempts to influence and constrain 'news freedom' are also often
contested, disputed and sometimes, though rarely, ignored by the press
or, even more rarely, by a broadcaster. These disputes almost invariably
concern the exercise of freedom of expression, which remains for news
journalists a *sine qua non*. To put it bluntly, news journalists (in all their
roles) regard any form of regulation with deep suspicion and scepticism.
Today, broadcast news providers find themselves located within a set of
commercial conditions (through deregulation), which enable news to be
packaged and subsequently sold as if it were a commodity. Yet this still
goes hand in hand with the expectation that these news providers have
to produce a product that serves a general public interest and has some
form of public purpose or utility. This results in the further expectation
of policymakers that news providers must in some lesser or greater way
contribute to the effective functioning of a democratic society and a
vibrant public sphere.

The aspirations of journalists, the expectations of policymakers and
the commercial interests of private news companies have always resulted
in contradictory relationships. Yet commercial ways of gathering and

providing the news and the values of PSB seem to effortlessly mix in the same news ecology, even if styles are different. For example, Sky News, ITV's twenty-four-hour news channel and BBC News 24 use modern news-gathering techniques, take advantage of the latest technology and strive to exhibit high production values. Sky News and the BBC also see the advantage of interactivity which sits behind the linear channel as a way of offering value-added menu-driven options and multi-screen choices. However, despite these similarities the studios are designed differently, the split screen is used by Sky News but not as much by BBC News 24; presenters generally sit when presenting for the BBC and the ITV News Channel and stand for Sky. In spite of differences in style they often (but not always) share the same view of what is newsworthy, and aspire to be seen as reliable by their audiences. As to who follows whom it hardly matters; a consensus is built between the various providers that reflects a shared recognition of what news is and what it should aspire to (Harrison 2000). News journalism standards and the integrity of news have not been lost in recent times; they have evolved. This evolution has occurred largely because the capacity for news and news journalism is so much greater, the reflection of cultural diversity so much more challenging and audiences so much more discerning about which products they prefer to consume. Journalism standards remain, as ever, compromised by excesses (see below).

FUTURE TRENDS IN NEWS

Different types of news journalism

We have seen that many different types of news are available for consumers across a range of different media. This has created a situation in which a plurality of news forms and news interests coexist and are easily accessible within most democratic societies. Authoritarian and totalitarian regimes struggle to keep control of the availability and distribution of news as they attempt (increasingly in vain) to hide their despoliation of human rights from being reported. In the broadcast sector in particular, reduction of spectrum scarcity means a greater availability of bandwidth for more and more channels and subsequently a greater number of news outlets. The introduction of digital services also enables these channels to be increasingly interactive and to carry behind the linear front a greater range of news and more in-depth news services. The opportunity for more news broadcasters and news programmes to coexist within the same medium means that it is increasingly less likely that a single owner or news provider will be able to take control of and dominate the provision of news. Unlike authoritarian and totalitarian regimes, democracies actively enable a diversity of viewpoints to flourish through the development of and tolerance towards an emerging multi-channel broadcasting sector, thereby creating a news space that, for example, simultaneously accommodates both Fox News and Al-Jazeera.[2]

Indeed, it has been argued that the rationale for statutory impartiality restrictions to be placed upon news broadcasters is less justifiable in the multi-channel digital age since news consumers should be free to amass evidence from a variety of different news providers coexisting in a free marketplace of ideas (Gardam 2004). In short, some believe that broadcast news could be accorded the same levels of freedom of expression as the 'views papers' produced by the press, and consequently be relieved of the regulatory restrictions traditionally imposed upon it. Problematically, however, any reduction of impartiality requirements runs the risk of reducing the audience's trust in the medium (broadcast news is still more trusted by its audience than the press). Even post-Hutton, public trust in the BBC remains high. A key consideration for the future regulation of the multi-channel broadcast news environment is whether it is better to allow a plurality of views to exist with their explicit viewpoints and to place the onus on audiences to sort through these various viewpoints and make up their own mind as to what constitutes an accurate representation of contemporary events, or whether a public service broadcaster must remain to ensure that at least 'one panoptic, impartial view' remains (ibid.: 35).

Within the different forms of news currently available today there are many examples of news journalism's excellence: reports which expose injustice, cruelty, human rights abuse, corruption and malaise in public life. Here news journalism operates with an understanding of events grounded in terms of their importance and significance. Or, to put it another way, it is the intrinsic importance of an event that is revealed, even where it falls beyond an audience member's everyday life experiences and/or knowledge. This approach to news reporting tries to reconcile the need to attract and retain audience interests with seeking to understand and accurately account for the importance and significance of an event. The skill to serious news journalism resides in imparting this understanding of events in an intelligible and interesting way that keeps the audience engaged. Many broadsheet newspapers in Britain still follow a largely serious news agenda, as do some documentary programmes and news programmes such as BBC2's *Newsnight, Channel 4 News,* BBC's Radio 4's *Today* programme and BBC's *News at Ten.* Here serious news journalism seeks to serve the public interest. This is not to say that serious news reporters do not also cover more populist items, or use techniques which make the news appear more exciting (Halberstam 1992).

As we have seen, serious news journalism coexists with reporting at the other end of the spectrum where stories are presented as news in such a way as to mobilize prejudice, exacerbate xenophobia or capitalize on fear and loathing of 'the other'. Thankfully, stories falling into this category are frequently deemed unimportant elsewhere in the news agenda. To date, this approach remains largely the domain of the redtop tabloid newspapers, although middle-market tabloids occasionally stray. One outcome of this approach is that it frequently leads to calls for changes in the regulation of news. For example, in April 2004 calls were made for a privacy law to curb the worst excesses of press interest in certain individual's private lives. This followed two weeks of speculation and scrutiny of the Beckhams' relationship in the light of allegations that David Beckham had had an affair with Rebecca Loos. Obviously in between 'serious news and trivial news' dwells a span of news journalism which provides predominantly populist news. The multi-channel digital world shows every sign of continuing to conform to a traditional news span, which consists of high, middle and low news journalism or has what I prefer to call broadsheet values, populist values and tabloid values. The terms *broadsheet* and *tabloid* no longer apply only to paper size but to news values and the types of news journalism that succinctly capture the two ends of the news span. It is likely that in the future we will see more not less of each of these respective types of news journalism. More scientific and cultural news at one end of the news span will be matched by more celebrity and scandal news at the other end.

Good-quality populist journalism seeks to raise issues of public interest which are significant and relevant for most people. It serves the public interest where issues are linked to satisfying real or actual needs (ibid.). Here public interest is regarded not as an abstract Reithian ideal about what people need to know, but what the 'man on the Clapham omnibus' wants to know and indeed would say, if asked, that he both needs and has a right to know. Of course, measuring public interests in this way leads news journalists to compete for 'our man's' attention. As we have seen, this is replete with risks. Populist journalism can hector and shout for attention and drift into the tabloid world, it can dwell within an uninspiring and limited news consensus (while of course maintaining the search for 'exclusives'), it can lead to a predisposition to regard a competitor's story as a news item by running spoiler stories. But by far the greatest risk is that it can turn news which serves the public interest into news which only interests the public. It can render the trivial, the orthodox and blinkered views of its audience into a rehashed news diet. Such a process has been criticized for creating a 'political vacuum' which serves to 'depoliticize and reduce what goes on in the world to the level of the anecdote or scandal' (Bourdieu 1998: 51). This type of news is seen to arouse curiosity and interest for a few minutes, but requires no analysis or engagement on the part of the audience (ibid.). Such news may even lead to a growth in public cynicism, particularly in relation to political communication (Fallows 1996) and a failure to serve the voting public (Dautrich and Hartley 1999). For Keane (1991: 192–193) the effect on democracy is damaging if citizens begin 'to regard politics as a nuisance' and prefer to consume their news passively rather than engage with it as political citizens. At its worst, populist journalism, in a bid for audience interest, can produce a reductive type of journalism. So much so that it becomes a caricature version of tabloid journalism employing deleterious practices which can result in the pursuit of intrusive stories that ultimately are of no public interest. In the very worst cases it may even resort to fabrication[3] of stories and events.

Competition for audiences and readers has, according to some, led to populist journalism concentrating on a narrower range of stories which prioritize human interest, eschew international news, and focus on the politicians in politics rather than their policies (Franklin 1994; Dahlgren 1995; Fallows 1996; Franklin 1997; Bourdieu 1998). As we saw in Chapter 6, evidence which shows the extent to which news content has changed over time is mixed, but criticism of the kind that was levelled at the BBC when its *Six O'Clock News* was accused of being more 'Madonna than Mugabe' (Clarke 2004a: 14) is still prevalent. For example, an independent review of BBC News 24 undertaken for the Department of Culture, Media and Sport in 2002 indicated that 'News-24 did not choose to broadcast very many world news stories which were not also covered in a competitive fashion by Sky' (Lambert 2002: 9) and that 'the result is that its service is not as distinctive as it could be, given the breadth of its resources' (ibid.: 10), a situation that the BBC has since sought to redress.

To conclude, such criticisms will continue to fuel debates over the extent of legislation and regulation, quality, standards and trust. These debates will continue to be grounded in judgements made about the extent of the impact of the private sector on the public worth and value of news and the character of news journalism. As Van Gompel *et al.* (2002) observe, we need to give consideration to the impact of competition and commercialization, both on the content of news media and on the practices of news producers (see also Ursell 2003). For the foreseeable future the 'public responsibility' role of all news media will continue to be evaluated and judged against the worst form of tabloid practices, the pursuit of exclusive and sensational stories which involve the invasion of privacy and the use of exaggeration or fabrication. News journalism will also continue to be evaluated against the tendency to oversimplify complex stories by using a nominalist approach which focuses on isolated events, simplifying complex causes to the extent that context is eliminated (Halberstam 1992). Similarly (although taken to an extreme), the pursuit of particular types of news which breach professional and ethical codes of journalistic conduct and practice will continue to be discussed and debated as providing evidence of declining standards and the devaluation of news. And as we saw in Chapter 4, regulatory controls and codes of practice will be contested at every turn through the conflicting claims of policymakers and private sector news providers. Three types of news and news journalism will remain – broadsheet, populist and tabloid – although only one will probably be judged worthy of the name. Broadsheet values will continue to be admired either in terms of their attachment to the enlightenment ideal of rational debate and their disposition to truthfulness, or (more negatively) because they in part, and with others, resist the mystification of the world and the substitution of prejudice for understanding.

The blurring of boundaries

Changes in presentation styles and news values across a range of broadcast news organizations mean that today and in the future, the news media will not be able to rely upon the use of traditional news formats. The growth of global flows of media products has increased the need for media organizations to be able to export television formats around the world, to experiment with them, to re-version them and to use their characteristics for different audiences. Format now refers as much to the style of presentation of news as it does to the marketing agencies' brief to attract and retain audiences. Because of this, the experimentation with formats both in news and entertainment has led to a blurring of boundaries between what used to be pure news formats and pure entertainment formats. The factual entertainment genre has emerged. The growth in the importance of 'factual' television as entertainment has meant that a high degree of hybridization between formally discrete genre types has occurred (Dovey 2001) leading ultimately to a new type of programme usually referred to as reality TV. This type of programme, which contains characteristics from a variety of previously discrete genre types (such as fly-on-the-wall documentaries, chat shows, quiz shows and other audience participation programmes) has the capacity to develop and mutate to become increasingly excessive in direct response to audience tastes.

In common with news programmes, broadcasters of reality TV believe that the use of 'liveness' as a broadcasting technique makes the programme more exciting and entertaining for viewers. This, combined with the provocative encouragement of viewer participation through voting, using interactive television, mobile phones or the internet, has proved to be a popular means of engaging viewers. Absurdly, some programme-makers at ITV were reported to be interested in using *Pop Idol*-type talent shows to identify and choose MPs who will appeal to the voters (Wells 2004b). More seriously, these types of reality TV programmes and their associated broadcasting and audience involvement techniques have raised problems for television regulators simply because the new genre deals with unconventional content which had not been anticipated when designing the regulatory framework through which broadcasters operate.[4] Broadcasters have been encouraged to exploit the difficulties this new genre causes by opting for more and more extreme content. It is entirely possible that as television news audiences dwindle, the popular appeal of reality TV programmes could be used by news broadcasters in two ways: first, by prioritizing the immediate and the live (even if that means showing reports which are not of conventional broadcast quality or meet requirements of taste and decency), and second, by abandoning traditional formats and experimenting with new formats that conform to the fiat 'engage the audience'. Both are used by reality TV programmes to great effect and secure for them high viewing figures. How far news providers go in this direction is discussed below.

The live coverage of events in the 2003 war in Iraq was criticized for exploiting the power of film, the repeated use of particular visual images and exploiting in a sensational way the impact of the immediate and the 'live'. The old cliché that a picture is worth a thousand words is certainly true when considering the use of film and photographic images both in broadcast news and press news reports respectively. Visual imagery is an important criterion in relation to the effectiveness of certain stories to illustrate or even summarize an event (Tunstall 1971). Sometimes television pictures can produce what Sturken and Cartwright (2002: 36) term 'image icons' where a particular scene or image gains worldwide recognition and acquires a recognizable symbolic value. Sturken and Cartwright identify the image of the lone student standing in front of a tank in Tiananmen Square, Beijing, in 1989 as a profound statement of the struggle for democracy. Similarly, the pictures of the citizens in

Baghdad toppling the statue of Saddam Hussein on 9 April 2003 were broadcast live to millions of homes with one frame captured for the world's press the next day.

More problematic still is the increasing tendency of the press and the broadcast media's use of 'video grabs' (stills taken from video or closed circuit television (CCTV) images). The use of video footage provided by kidnappers or terrorist organizations raises ethical questions. Should journalists have used the distressing pictures of Ken Bigley or Margaret Hassam supplied by their captors? Did the constant news media coverage accorded to Ken Bigley aid the kidnappers' cause? Did the pictures broadcast from within the school in Beslan amount to a form of 'terror-vision' which accorded the hostage-takers unprecedented and unsafe levels of publicity? Here there is a tension between what constitutes news and what constitutes taste, decency and privacy for the victims or, in essence, human dignity. Clearly images such as these, which are increasingly available on the internet, are particularly compelling, and the ability to transmit them live to the television audience, or place an image on the front page of a newspaper, produces dramatic and memo-rable news. Consequently they are unlikely to be ignored by journalists. Indeed, they are often re-shown later when news organizations recall memorable events. As always there are exceptions: the image of the planes hitting the twin towers in New York on 11 September 2001 was regarded as extremely newsworthy for several days, but broadcasters were asked, in respect for those killed, missing or injured, not to continue to use those images when retelling the story. While such a trend of self-censorship may coexist with the use of icons or other disturbing and powerful images to summarize news events, it is interesting to note that it is still those with power who can control the wide-scale distribu-tion and use of these images, no matter how radical or disagreeable they are in content.

A further possible confusion needs to be briefly noted. Here the blur-ring of boundaries is physical, with its implications not yet fully understood. It is a development due to the recent activity of the broad-sheets. The launch of tabloid-size broadsheet newspapers raises several issues. The tabloid-size *Independent* newspaper, launched in the London area on 30 September 2003 and gradually extended to other parts of the country, used the same material (presented slightly differently) as the broadsheet. Peter Preston commenting on the newspaper, says that the *Independent* made a 'decisive choice. No dumbing down, it says. Everything from the broadsheet goes' (Preston 2003: 6). While the *Independent's* redesign is currently that of a 'quality tabloid',[5] its success[6] has motivated other broadsheets to adopt a tabloid size and format, with *The Times* introducing the coyly entitled 'compact' newspaper in November 2003. This replaced the broadsheet in November 2004. Currently the *Guardian* is experimenting with a size (slightly larger than tabloid) called Berliner. The current editor explained recently that this was to accommodate 'big stories', which seems to imply that fuller explanations of significant news stories will remain a feature of the newspaper despite its smaller size.[7] Regional papers have also adopted the tabloid size (e.g. the *Sheffield Star*, the *Western Mail* and the *Scotsman* which have all become tabloid size in recent years). In the absence of content studies it is hard to be systematic about the extent to which fewer words are being used for news stories, whether pictures have increased in frequency and headlines have, or will become more sensational – or more importantly whether broadsheet values are at risk.[8] As Peter Preston (2003: 6) pointed out, we should remain vigilant about the consequences of this redesign, as we might more often see 'a broadsheet playing tabloid and going for broke on its front page . . . to outgun a more modest tabloid'.

Moral tensions within the scope of technological capacity

War reporting is of a different nature from other kinds of news reporting. It is utterly at the beck and call of sporadic but fast changing events occurring against a complex and otherwise dull or uneventful background. Whatever the nature and scope of the war it usually takes a prominent position in news agendas. Obviously there are exceptions – civil wars in Africa will not figure as prominently as American incursions in Kuwait, Afghanistan or Iraq. In addition, where a war involves 'our own' troops, domestic news agendas are altered considerably. Coverage of a war involving British troops will be sliced into dimensions – troops in action, families at home, political support and so on. Even when a war involving one's own nation is a long-running event, it takes an extremely high position on each day's news agendas, as each aspect of the war or new event is reported to an unusually news-hungry audience. Overall, wars generally push almost everything else off the news agenda, and usually news organizations will make high levels of investment to ensure that there are sufficient journalists and technological resources for their coverage to be better than that of their competitors.

One of the most interesting and prominent features of reporting the war in Iraq in 2003 was the use journalists made of a relatively new communication technology (now standard), notably satellite and videophones. These allowed constant live coverage. The capacity for constant live coverage and the journalistic skills associated with their use have already set a trend for contemporary and future war reporting, as well as now making their mark on the coverage of other dramatic or spectacular events. The nature of broadcasting live, from the battlefield, the war zone, the natural disaster area and so on raises issues for news journalism about the extent to which such reporting should be balanced against reflection and considered judgement. Disturbing scenes broadcast instantly deeply affect both the value of the type of news journalism possible in the face of such events and have profound implications for what we mean by human dignity. The communications technology of today is exacerbating an issue that has been with us since radio, namely how to deal with a shocking live event. It is worth considering the following.

During the evening of 6 May, 1937 at the US Naval Air Base, Lakehurst, New Jersey, the German zeppelin Hindenburg was coming in to land. Covering the event was announcer Herbert Morrison and engineer Charles Nehlsen, both of Radio Station WLS, Chicago. They were there to both cover the event and significantly to 'test the practicability of recording a special event live on the scene of action and rushing the transcription back to Chicago by plane for broadcast over WLS a few hours later'.[9] As the Hindenburg approached the mooring mast, Morrison and Nehlsen recorded the following:

> It is practically standing still. Now that (sic) have dropped a rope out of the nose of the ship and it has been taken a hold of down on the field by a couple of men. It is starting to rain again. The back motors of the ship are holding it just enough to keep it from . . . .
> It's burst into flames!
> Get out of the way! GET OUT OF THE WAY!
> Get this, Charlie . . . get this, Charlie!
> It's crashing. [Pause.] It's crashing terrible. Oh! My! Get out of the way, please. It's bursting into flames and it's falling on the mooring mast and all of the folks between. [Gasps.] This is TERRIBLE! This is the worst of the worst catastrophes in the world. Oh! OH! Four or five hundred feet in the sky. It's a terrible crash, ladies and gentleman. The ship is in flames now and it's finally crashing to the ground not quite to the mooring mast. Oh! The humanity! [Gasps.] And all the passengers screaming around here. I told you . . . .. [Sob.] I can't talk to people. . . . [Sob.] Their friends are on there. It's . . . it's . . . oh . . . I can't talk. Ladies and gentleman. Honest, it's just lying there a mass of smoking wreckage and everybody can hardly breath (sic). Lady, I'm sorry. I'm going to step inside where I cannot see it . . .
> Charlie, that's terrible. [Sob.]

I can't . . . I can't. . . . Listen, folks, I'm going to have to stop for a moment because . . ..

Oh, this is the worst thing I have ever witnessed!

Ladies and gentleman, I'm back again. I've sort of recovered from the terrific explosion, and the terrible crash.

This is an utterly human and empathic response to a tragedy, which killed thirty-six people. It is of little informative value, but it is dramatic and moving (to be fair to Morrison and Nehlsen, this extract is taken from three hours' worth of material covering both before and after the event). This extract clearly reveals that the event itself, without reflection, without pause for analysis, is simply drama and on this occasion deeply moving. Death, suffering, or scenes of brutality are not in and of themselves newsworthy. The concerns articulated in Article Seven of *The European Convention on Transfrontier Television* (Council of Europe, 29–30 April 2002) are important in this respect[10] as they address the problems of the use of live footage of events that invade an individual's privacy, especially if they are used, however unwittingly, as something that thrills or even 'entertains' the audience.[11] When reflecting on news coverage of the 2003 war in Iraq, the BBC's Director of News recorded his own concerns, recognizing that 'war coverage has changed forever', saying that, 'we might end up with a death live on TV' (Sambrook 2003: 17). Such an event would have serious implications, not only in terms of the effect it might have on the audience and family members, but also for the dignity and right to privacy of the individual involved. The difficulty for broadcasters is simply one of how far they are willing to go in their judgement of whether an event is newsworthy and how far they are regulated (formally or informally) against excess. In and of themselves graphic images are not news, but with explanation, analysis and comment they are. News stories about famine in all its horror can and has changed things. Extensive coverage of the tsunamis that devastated seven Asian countries on 26 December 2004 elicited a major response from readers, listeners and viewers who were reported to be donating '£1 million an hour' (Preston 2005: 3). News, according to Preston (ibid.), is here 'more than a commodity, a time-filler, an entertainment. News is an arbiter of life and death. News is the difference between aid flowing after 24 hours or 72.' Equally a person who endures torture or systematic injustice and whose voice remains unheard and his or her circumstances unreported amounts to a failure of news. In any event nothing provides a justification for broadcasting live (or possibly at all) mutilated bodies, torture or executions, some of which have been shown on the internet.

With greater technological capacity, associated with increased opportunities for wider viewpoints to achieve greater distribution and reach,
come fresh challenges that will help mark the future of news. News
organizations like Al-Jazeera are both willing and able to push the bounds
of taste and convention to accommodate non-Western news sensibilities
and perspectives. Traditional Western television news broadcasters are
having to re-evaluate their approach and to assess whether cultural limits
that presume a certain geopolitical taste or sensibility should be tested.
The BBC is reconsidering its position on issues of taste and decency
having been accused of being too government-friendly in its reluctance
to show the consequences of the recent Iraq war. Arguably the use of
anodyne film clips of smart bombs hitting non-civilian targets in the
1991 Gulf War did not capture the grim reality of war, rather it served
as an emollient and, it could be argued, had no place in news. In the
future it is possible that news and the different perspectives surrounding the reporting of contemporary events will be increasingly available
as different points of view may well be reflected in the increasing
range of news channels available to us on the same electronic programme
guide (EPG).

Of course, while an increase in the scale of television news coverage
is likely, predictions about its future scope, range, quality and diversity
is less easy. The multi-channel digital television universe is increasingly
more and more difficult to control, but not impossible. As we have noted
above, and as Francis Wheen (2004: 231) writes, Rupert Murdoch in his
commercial dealings with China 'shamelessly kowtowed to tyranny – or
as his defenders might prefer to say, applied the Real-politik techniques
of give and take to international business. Murdoch took BBC World
Service TV off his Star network; the Chinese gave him permission to start
a cable TV station in Guangdong.' As for the BBC, it says much of its
news service that it walks the line between the charges – too friendly to
one government or regime and too critical of another.

With the dominance of digital channels it is possible that news
appointment programmes on mainstream television channels will eventually be replaced by twenty-four-hour news channels, with flagship
programmes shown within them between constant updates. Such a
development exacerbates the need to increase live reporting. Furthermore, as we saw in Chapter 6, journalists themselves acknowledge that
unchecked information is more likely to be transmitted on twenty-four-
hour news programmes than on appointment programmes. Indeed, a
particular problem which emerged during the war in Iraq was that as
different stories and counter-stories unfolded continuously, the main-

stream mass news audience was often left rather confused about events. Evidence for this may be found in the number of online weblogs (blogs) which have attempted to chronicle, comment or make sense of rapidly unfolding events. Some appointment news programmes, in competition with twenty-four-hour news, also increased the number of live links to reporters in the field, apparently for no other reason than to inject the drama of immediacy and excitement into the programme. Thus, showing their understanding of and recognition that this form of broadcasting is an 'attention grabber' even though, as frequently happens in war, there is for lengthy periods of time little or no new information available to be imparted to news journalists (Bennett 2003: 2–3). The growth in the use of news walls or enormous broadcasting screens which dwarf the size of the presenter, 3D maps, mocked-up and dummy battle plans, special effects which show planes apparently flying across the studio, all pander to the drama of excitement and offer a placebo experience through a strongly visual news (Brown 2004). It also indicates, yet again, that the balance between immediacy and judgement will continue to define news, as well as be a source of continued moral confusion which will require regulatory watchfulness.

During a crisis, viewing figures for all news programmes and sources increase (see the '11 September effect' discussed in Hargreaves and Thomas 2002: 37–41; Allan 2002). Appointment programmes, such as those provided by the BBC, remain highly regarded by audiences because of their authority, and are often quoted to be the ones which people turn to in times of crisis. Many news consumers today, however, do not want to wait for specific broadcast times, preferring to look at the immediate news suppliers, such as twenty-four-hour news channels and the internet. After a few days of reporting the 2003 war in Iraq, the technique of constant live news reporting and frequent updates was starting to prove to be a problem. The need to freshen up the news meant that broadcast reports sometimes contradicted military or official statements made later in the day, an issue which has been reported as being of particular concern to the BBC (Byrne 2003b; Burrell 2003: 4; MacArthur 2003: 12). The use of 'embedded journalists' or 'embeds' on official placements with military units allowed news organizations to have greater access to their journalists, expecting them to be able to report events as they unfolded. Journalists were constantly asked for updates by their newsrooms (World Press Freedom Day Seminar, 2 May 2003). This often resulted in exciting footage with journalists talking over gunfire and through sandstorms. It has since emerged that those journalists often felt enclosed within what has been described as a kind of 'bubble', isolated from the other developments which would normally allow for them to establish some wider or deeper context or setting for their reports (ibid.).

This type of embedded reporting led some journalists, editors and media analysts to reflect uneasily on the nature of their own embedded journalists. News reports have been described as nothing but entertainment (Barber 2003), or expressed through a neologism, 'militainment', a new form of reality TV, where 'the viewing public gets a piece of the action via a broadcast media hungry for live pictures' (Sylvester 2003: 8), or of taking on the characteristics of a movie (Donegan 2003: 12; Lawson 2003: 8). Furthermore, these embedded journalists even began to speculate among themselves about their level of detachment and impartiality. The adoption and gusto shown in the use of military acronyms, language and jargon (e.g. MREs – meals ready to eat – and AAVs – amphibious assault vehicles) pointed to the unpalatable truth that some journalists were rather too closely identifying with and becoming locked into perceived military culture. Indeed, some journalists were even warned by the Ministry of Defence to stop wearing military-style clothing (ibid.). All of this (either superficially or symbolically depending on your point of view) seems to militate against the need for constant critical analysis of the political case for war and the subsequent military mission. Over-identification with a particular institution does not foster detachment from it. All of those involved in news must remain careful to assess both the practical and intellectual limitations that emerge as a consequence of being embedded within a certain institution. It seems almost as if 'embedded journalism' is a clever Pentagon response to the media coverage of the Vietnam War, in particular General Westmoreland's (Commander US Military Assistance Command, Vietnam (COMUSMACV) 1964–1968) complaint that free-roving journalists contributed to the loss of domestic and popular support for the war. The tension between embedded journalism and 'free roving' journalism is likely to become more of an issue in the future of war coverage and news coverage of events where access to such events is at the price of being hosted by, or embedded in, a particular group or institution.

TV news: popularist and serious

As we have seen above, there are three distinguishable types of press news journalism. Respectively: news driven by broadsheet values, popularist values and tabloid values. In television the tradition has been the systematic use and deployment of broadsheet values – accuracy, sincerity and impartiality, sometimes presented in a populist style. However, given the forces of competition and the pursuit of audience popularity, the future of television news is increasingly coming under threat to be populist. The extent to which it currently follows the populist path may be related to the different institutional structures that currently exist, which in Britain at least provide a varied approach to news provision. Currently television news agendas in Britain are supported by a combination of regulation, sponsorship (for example, of weather forecasts), advertisements, subsidies, a not-for-profit remit (like Channel 4), and internal cross-company subsidies. The BBC's news services are funded through the licence fee, Sky News' services are subsidized by the rest of the holding organization (the largest shareholder is News International) and ITN is owned by a consortium of shareholders.[12] As such it is apparent that news providers often operate within organizations which have differing goals (Harrison 2000; Kung-Shankleman 2000).

To put it simply and in organizational terms, motives can be utilitarian or normative (Etzioni 1961). Utilitarian motives aim to produce or provide material goods or services for financial ends; normative motives are concerned with the advancement of some value or valued condition such as a public or social purpose. The direction in which a news organization goes is balanced between the pressures placed on both. This pressure will remain. Some news cultures will be predominantly utilitarian, others unashamedly normative. To say that the former is the domain of the private sector and the latter the domain of the public sector, however, is wrong. BSkyB has no obligation to provide news and certainly not to provide news which often pursues a serious news agenda, and yet it does so with Sky News. Similarly, ITV1 and Five were given access to scarce analogue resources in return for commitments to fulfil PSB obligations. In these three cases news provision resides within private sector corporate settings replete with the conventional commercial demands of any other listed company. As we saw in Chapter 3, ITN is in a particularly difficult position with regard to its ability to continue to fulfil a PSB news agenda (Harrison 2005). It has recently lost its contract to supply Five with news to Sky News and, having lost its nominated news supplier status for the ITV, now has a precarious relationship with all its news contractors.

The not-for-profit broadcasters, BBC and Channel 4, may also find that the amount of funding they have to support their PSB requirements falls. For example, the BBC would find that it would have to share its licence fee income with new commercial broadcasters who also wish to offer public services, if the Public Service Publisher model, as suggested by OFCOM in 2004, were to become accepted policy.[13] Equally, if current broadcasting policy came to regard the licence fee as a regressive tax and not as an investment in the intellectual and cultural fabric of the country, that too would raise funding problems for the BBC and affect the scope and scale of its news provision. Meanwhile, Channel 4 with its unique combination of PSB mission and private sector funding base continues to face increasingly serious questions over its revenue streams, dependent as they are on advertising. The funding problems faced by Channel 4 in the recent past have led to reorganization and redundancies, and even talks of mergers. It is now open to question how long this unique broadcasting model will survive and whether its revenue stream will allow it to continue to be a public service broadcaster and to provide news which fulfils a PSB news agenda and attracts low audience ratings.

The continued use of broadsheet values and subsequent differentiation from a populist agenda will in the future continue to come from both public and private sources. And yet, with all of the above news providers, the pressures to go for audiences via a populist route and to define that in terms of a PSB service (or at the very least a public interest remit) is an ever-present option, an option some news providers may wish to pursue more aggressively in the future in order to secure larger audiences. Thus far British television news providers have largely resisted this temptation. Elements of populist news are constantly being identified, particularly with regard to the use of new communication technologies, format designs and an increasing regard for immediacy, but even within the application of these, broadsheet news values still dominate many British television news programmes (Hargreaves and Thomas 2002), and cries of an overall 'dumbing down' of television news may be said to be alarmist and premature.

Internet news

The opportunity for the growth and development of personal news journalism on the internet provides an expanding platform for freedom of expression and at the same time the option to exercise that freedom irresponsibly. Under these circumstances the following choices are available to the personal news journalist: to have or not have a regard for truth, to promote facts or fiction, and either to contribute to the public sphere of rational debate by attending to both moral and materialist arguments and analysis concerning contemporary events, or add to the world's noise and chatter. The requirement to exercise freedom of speech responsibly means, in the context of the internet and personal news journalism, that we are reliant upon how ideologically bigoted or not the personal journalist is: in short, what motivates the personal journalist and his or her critical disposition.

The key to our level of trust in personal news journalism and internet news has, and will remain, the knowledge of its provenance. Not surprisingly, views about the value of personal news journalism on the internet are mixed. Personal journalism which provides eyewitness accounts and opinions about events which have taken place may feed our thirst for information, but may also mislead or distort events. Although a plurality of voices on the internet may in theory offer an alternative and refreshing view of events, and be removed from the so-called constraints of a dominant ideology, or more realistically, particular editorial values, it is highly improbable that their presence will undermine established and trusted news organizations. The presence and popularity of prime and trusted online news sites (e.g. the BBC or the *Guardian*) is evidence of the fact that even on the internet, audiences want the core journalistic disposition to truth-telling and its corollaries, accuracy and sincerity. That is, they want the best practices of established serious news providers replicated online. The element of historical trust in established news sources remains crucial. In this light news journalism and 'blogism' remain capable of being critically distinguishable from each other. News journalism as critique is utterly different from and I believe will remain far more valuable than personal journalism as conviction. Ideally, the former should be accurate and sincere, and the latter partisan and exhortative.

The domination of internet news by established news providers and global media conglomerates has been seen to place a question mark over the extent to which the internet will be able to offer genuinely alternative views to consumers and contribute to knowledge about local and international affairs. On a pessimistic note Hall (2001) argues that while the representation of the local on the internet is likely to continue, concentration of media ownership is likely to result in a monolithic approach to news, which means that it will become more homogenized and lose its particularity. On an optimistic note he also found many examples of flourishing local civic journalism facilitated by the internet, and many instances when local events became global for a day or two, as interest from all over the world was pursued via direct links to local online newspapers (ibid.: 221). Overall, the level and depth of information made available on the internet by mainstream news providers is growing. Hall sees this type of internet news provision as enhancing citizens' knowledge. The availability of greater amounts of information, and background and links to other information sites, provide more opportunities for citizens to have their say and to gain access to reports about their events from different perspectives (increasingly evident during wars and other crises).

For those who want to, there is in principle a much greater opportunity to understand news events in all their complexity than ever before. Consequently, the expansion of these internet news sources is seen as potentially liberating (Youngs and Boyd-Barrett 2002), or creating 'new opportunities for journalists and citizens to be better informed about what happens elsewhere' (Van Gompel et al. 2002: 205). However, the availability of greater sources of news does not guarantee an engaged or enlightened citizenry (any more than anything else does), and earlier claims to this effect about the internet and the digital citizen now seem exaggerated. Norris (2000: 309) suggests a 'virtuous circle' is created whereby the internet reinforces 'the activism of the active' rather than creating new levels of interest. Perhaps the best way to regard some internet news sources is to say that they have a similar function in society to museums and art galleries. They can be repositories of value and education and are generally easily accessed. Serious internet news sources are built on and according to the precepts of good news journalism. Where they are not, they are of no special value as news. Overall, the extent to which the internet can compensate for a person's lack of understanding of a particular contemporary event, or enable people to engage with local and international affairs and politics is still open to question. No doubt the libertarian and spontaneous nature of the internet will continue to surprise us, especially when it enables some to uncover truths missed by others. It will also do this in conjunction with the latest sighting of Elvis, the truth of the Knights Templar and the location of the Holy Grail: but such is the nature of the internet. The internet is not redefining news; even as a potentially revolutionary new medium it is difficult to see how it might effect a wholesale replacement of the core values of news. The news remains what it has always been, namely the pursuit of a truthful account of contemporary events. The fact that this occurs within changing circumstances, or via a high-tech distribution system, does not entail that the character of news has altered, merely that its pursuit is more or less difficult. Does the internet make the pursuit of news easier? Perhaps in some cases it does, but most websites, unless maintained by the devoted or wealthy, go unchanged or are abandoned, and some established internet sites remove items, meaning they can never be found again. Currently, internet users are typically male, middle class and under the age of 35, and the promise of the free digital citizen exposing the truth seems risible, as a visit to many chat rooms might prove.

It is undoubtedly the case that audiences now get some of their 'news' from an array of different sources. These sources of news may not be those provided by the mainstream news organizations, and in this way there is a sense that audiences are defining their own 'news' agenda for themselves. However, the acquisition of news is still by and large a passive affair where people rely on easy forms of news consumption. For them, television news, now and in the future, will remain the most favoured means of acquiring our understanding of contemporary events. As a diverse range of serious television news providers continues to exist and develop, so news consumers will be able either to dip into twenty-four-hour news programmes for their sixty-second bulletins, a 'fast food' (Bourdieu 1998: 29) version of news which is easy to consume and digest; or for a while at least they will be able to visit more specialized appointment programmes. Actively obtaining news will consist of minimal and easy-to-use levels of interactivity. The abundance of choice may seem to create indecision as to where we go to get our news, but evidence proves otherwise: it suggests that once we have found the outlet we trust, we cease to shop around. Public service broadcast news, which has long been targeted at a captive mass audience, may appear old-fashioned in a news environment which provides a variety of tabloid, popular and broadsheet news outlets, but as a way of serving the public sphere(s) it is necessary. To say the same of the internet is like so much else about it: it is still open to question. The internet is a wonderful research tool; it is also a testimony to openness and diversity. Oppressive regimes would ban its use while open societies would not. But the internet does not and cannot define news, nor alter its deep and essential character any more than did the last post, which was so eagerly awaited by printers of the eighteenth century.

News is both a complex concept and product. It has as its ideal an aspiration and disposition to truthfulness. It attempts, through being accurate and sincere, to provide truthful reports and accounts of contemporary events. And yet it is shaped by a multitude of influences. This book has tried to show how the ideal dwells within these influences. News is not immune from attempts to subvert it away from the ideal, nor is the ideal easily achieved, but it is remarkable how truthfulness and its attendant core values remain the unembarrassed and clung-to language of those involved with all aspects of news. Of course, as we have seen, pessimistic accounts and optimistic accounts debate the value of news, but do so only by recognizing (and agreeing) its ultimate purpose.

KEY EVENTS RELATING TO THE HUTTON INQUIRY AND REPORT

April–June 2002
Ministry of Defence (MoD) scientist Dr David Kelly was consulted by the Foreign Office and MoD as a dossier on Iraq's weapons of mass destruction (WMD) was put together to make a case for going to war against Iraq.

5 September 2002
A draft dossier was circulated.

10 September 2002
The forty-five minute claim was inserted for the first time into a new draft of the dossier.

24 September 2002
The dossier was published. It included the statement that Iraq can deploy WMD within forty-five minutes and Prime Minister Tony Blair described the threat as 'serious and current' in the preface to the dossier.

22 May 2003
Dr Kelly met the BBC's defence correspondent Andrew Gilligan in a hotel in London. They discussed the dossier and Gilligan made some notes on his electronic personal organizer.

29 May 2003
Starting at 6.07 a.m. on Radio 4's *Today* programme, Gilligan quoted a source who believed Downing Street wanted the September dossier

'sexed up'. He also reported that the government knowingly inserted the forty-five minute claim into the dossier knowing it to be wrong or questionable. The live two-way between John Humphreys, the presenter, and Andrew Gilligan became the source of a feud between the Blair government and the BBC.

1 June 2003
Andrew Gilligan repeated the allegations made on the *Today* programme in his column in the *Mail on Sunday*. He also named Alistair Campbell as the person who wanted the dossier to be 'sexed up' and provided more details of the information given by his unnamed source (later revealed to be Dr David Kelly).

8 June 2003
Andrew Gilligan used his *Mail on Sunday* column to accuse Downing Street of briefing against him.

25 June 2003
Alastair Campbell appeared before the Foreign Affairs Committee (FAC) and asserted that the BBC's claim 'is completely and totally untrue . . . it is actually a lie'.

26 June 2003
Alistair Campbell wrote to the BBC demanding an apology. Richard Sambrook, the BBC's Director of News, later told the Hutton Inquiry that he felt the BBC was coming under an unprecedented level of pressure from Downing Street.

30 June 2003
Dr David Kelly informed his manager that he had met Gilligan on 22 May 2003.

5 July 2003
The Times newspaper correctly identified Gilligan's source as a scientist working in Iraq.

6 July 2003
The BBC governors gave unconditional backing to Gilligan.

8 July 2003
The MoD released a statement saying an official had admitted speaking to Andrew Gilligan. The BBC issued a statement to say that the MoD official did not sound like Gilligan's source.

9 July 2003
The BBC refused to respond to Geoff Hoon's request to confirm that Dr David Kelly was the source. The MoD press officers were told to reveal Dr Kelly's name if a journalist guessed it correctly.

10 July 2003
The Times, the *Guardian* and *The Financial Times* named Dr Kelly as the source of Gilligan's allegations.

15 July 2003
Dr Kelly was questioned by the FAC. The Committee concluded that it was 'most unlikely' the Kelly was the source of the 'sexed-up' claims.

19 July 2003
Police confirmed that a body found near his home in Oxfordshire was that of Dr Kelly.

20 July 2003
The BBC issued a statement naming Dr Kelly as the source of both Andrew Gilligan's report and that of *Newsnight* reporter Susan Watts.

21 July 2003
Lord Hutton was appointed head of an independent inquiry into the events surrounding Dr Kelly's death.

1 August 2003
The Hutton Inquiry opened.

23 August 2003
The Hutton Inquiry released over 900 documents on its internet site.

15 December 2003
The BBC revealed that it would be introducing new editorial rules. First, BBC's senior journalists would be prevented from writing newspaper columns, following the high-profile criticism of Andrew Gilligan's piece in the *Mail on Sunday* which was published on 1 June 2003, although lower profile correspondents would be allowed to keep writing non-controversial columns which would be vetted prior to publication by a BBC manager. Second, revised editorial guidelines were to be introduced to ensure that controversial stories were told more carefully and made more robust; this included a decision to ensure that stories based on single unnamed sources, such as Andrew Gilligan's dossier story, were scripted prior to being broadcast.

29 December 2003
Caroline Thomson, the BBC's Director of Policy and Legal Affairs, said
the *Today* programme report fell short of the 'truth and accuracy that are
the gold standard of the BBC'. She indicated that resignations may be
imminent.

5 January 2004
In an e-mail to staff, the BBC Director General Greg Dyke said that there
will be 'no scapegoating within the BBC' as a result of the Hutton Report
and emphasized that 'what is important once Hutton is published is that,
if the BBC is criticized, we learn from whatever is written – assuming,
of course, that we agree with what is said'.

20 January 2004
A *Guardian*/ICM poll revealed that 48 per cent of voters thought that
Tony Blair was lying when he said he did not authorize the leaking of Dr
Kelly's name and 63 per cent believed Mr Blair should resign if Lord
Hutton concluded that he had lied.

28 January 2004
Lord Hutton released his Report. Despite careful control of its dissemination, the *Sun*'s Political Editor, Trevor Kavanagh, managed to publish
a leaked summary. The Report exonerated the Blair government and
placed the blame on the BBC, stating that the governors were not acting
in their capacity as regulators, but were primarily defending the BBC
against the government.

   Several elements of Gilligan's report were heavily criticized in
Chapter 12 of the Report. Hutton argued that Andrew Gilligan's report
made a grave allegation which attacked the integrity of the government
and the Joint Intelligence Committee. The Inquiry had revealed that the
forty-five-minute claim which was inserted into the dossier was believed,
at the time, by the government to be accurate. The allegation made by
Gilligan that the reason the claim was not in the original draft of the
dossier was because it was only from one source, and the intelligence
service did not believe it to be true, was incorrect. The government
inserted the source's claim late, because it did not receive the intelligence until September 2002. Lord Hutton stated that:

> 'in the context of the broadcasts in which the "sexing-up" allegation was
> reported and having regard to the other allegations reported in those broad-
> casts, I consider that the allegation was unfounded as it would have been

understood by those who heard the broadcasts to mean that the dossier had been embellished with intelligence known or believed to be false or unreliable, which was not the case.'

In his Report, Lord Hutton also criticized Gilligan's interpretation of David Kelly's views about the reasons for the government's insertion of the forty-five-minute claim:

'I am satisfied that Dr Kelly did not say to Mr Gilligan that the government probably knew or suspected that the forty-five-minute claim was wrong before that claim was inserted in the dossier. I am further satisfied that Dr Kelly did not say to Mr Gilligan that the reason why the forty-five-minutes claim was not included in the original draft of the dossier was because it only came from one source and the intelligence agencies did not really believe it was necessarily true.'

Heavy criticism was also levelled at the editorial system within the BBC. Lord Hutton viewed the system as defective for several reasons. In the first instance it allowed Gilligan's report to go to air without being scripted (the live two-way between John Humphreys and Andrew Gilligan at 6.07 a.m. on 29 May 2003) and was broadcast from Gilligan's home while he was sitting on his bed. Hutton also criticized the BBC's actions after the broadcast had been made and the government had complained, saying that the BBC management failed to appreciate that the notes taken by Andrew Gilligan did not fully support the most serious of the allegations in the 6.07 a.m. broadcast. The governors were at fault for failing to make a detailed investigation into whether the allegation by Gilligan was properly supported by his notes and they also failed to give serious consideration to whether the BBC should have publicly acknowledged that the allegations should not have been broadcast. Lord Hutton concluded that the BBC governors had failed to investigate Gilligan's actions properly and omitted to consider the government's complaints adequately.

The Chairman Gavyn Davis immediately resigned. A member of the Board of Governors, Lord Ryder, took over as acting Chairman and released a contrite statement admitting the BBC's errors. The following statement was later to be viewed as total capitulation to the criticisms made in the Hutton Report:

'On behalf of the BBC I have no hesitation in apologizing unreservedly for our errors and to the individuals whose reputations were affected by them.

We have begun to implement major reforms, including outside journalism, compliance systems, editorial processes and training of new recruits. These changes, and other actions arising from the Hutton Report, will be completed by Mark Byford, the acting Director-General.'

29 January 2004
Director-General Greg Dyke resigned amid tearful scenes as BBC employees left their buildings and protested against his resignation. Press coverage about the report was scathing, labelling it a 'whitewash'. Mark Byford took over as acting Director-General.

PUBLIC OPINION

An opinion poll conducted by the *London Evening Standard* (by NOP) showed widespread public scepticism about the Hutton Report's conclusions, with 56 per cent of people polled saying Lord Hutton had been unfair to heap most of the blame on the corporation, while 49 per cent said it was a whitewash. A separate poll carried out by Sky News reported 67 per cent saying no to the question: Has the Hutton inquiry got to the truth? On 30 January an ICM poll for the *Guardian* which polled 532 adults found that 31 per cent of voters trust the BBC compared with only 10 per cent who trust the government to tell the truth. This figure dropped to 5 per cent among 25- to 34-year-olds, and nearly half of voters, 49 per cent, believed that Andrew Gilligan should resign.

PRESS OPINION

The press led with the Report and continued to cover the developments at the BBC for several days. On 29 January across all the front pages there was almost common agreement that the BBC had been harshly dealt with and the government let off too lightly. the *Independent* had a plain white front page with the word 'Whitewash?' in red in the centre of the page. The *Daily Mail's* front page carried a picture of Sir Max Hastings and Dr Kelly's grave. The newspaper quoted Max Hastings who said, 'we have the wretched spectacle of a BBC chairman resigning while Alastair Campbell crows from the summit of his dunghill'. The *Daily Telegraph's* front page carried a picture of Tony Blair and a picture of Gavyn Davis (BBC Chairman), leading with the words: 'BBC in crisis, Blair in clear.' It listed the main findings of the Report and stated that 'Hutton's clear vindication of ministers leaves MPs stunned'. Its front-page cartoon by Matt read: 'Look, the driven snow is almost as pure as

Tony Blair.' The *Guardian's* front page reported that a 'crisis cuts through the BBC', but Jonathan Freedland echoed the theme reported in many other papers, under the headline 'If it went to the West End they'd call it Whitewash'. *The Times* reported a 'blizzard of blame chills the BBC', but that the 'Judge fails to turn acerbic eye on Downing Street'. *The Financial Times* reported: 'BBC chief quits as Hutton gives boost to Blair'. The *Daily Mirror's* front page carried the words 'UNFOUNDED AND UNFOUND' printed in red. 'UNFOUNDED . . . the charge they "sexed up" dossier' appeared above three circular pictures of Geoff Hoon, Tony Blair and Alastair Campbell. Underneath were the words 'UNFOUND . . . the WMD they took us to war over' and the story was covered extensively in the paper across six more pages. The *Daily Star* and its sister paper the *Daily Express* also followed the whitewash theme on their front pages. The *Sun* adopted a different position from the other papers, choosing to focus on the problems and discomfiture facing the BBC, leading with the words 'BBC in crisis', with its leader column on page 8 asserting that 'The BBC is shamed'.

30 January 2004
Andrew Gilligan resigned from the BBC.

1 February 2004
Mark Byford announced that everyone involved in the Hutton Inquiry would face an internal disciplinary procedure.

3 February 2004
Lord Ryder postponed the publication of the BBC's submission to the Department of Culture, Media and Sport on its Charter renewal as a result of the disruption caused by the Hutton Report. The response was delayed until April 2004.

17 March 2004
The BBC's Director of Editorial Policy, Stephen Whittle, announced plans to overhaul the BBC's complaints procedure.

28 March 2004
The *Observer* newspaper reported that 'top BBC staff' have threatened to walk out because of the 'Politburo-style' nature of the internal Inquiry being conducted at the BBC (Ahmed and Thorpe 2004: 5).

A MAP OF THE MULTI-CHANNEL TV LANDSCAPE

PLATFORM AND VIEWING OPTIONS

1   Analogue television: Aerial; FTA
    BBC1, BBC2, ITV1, C4, Five
    (all five channels also available on all digital platforms below)

2   Digital terrestrial television (DTT) with six multiplexes:
    Aerial; FTA; Pay-TV; STB
    Freeview – Sky, BBC, Crown Castle

3   Digital satellite television: Satellite dish; Pay-TV; OFP; STB
    BSkyB

4   Cable television: Cable; Pay-TV; STB
    Analogue and digital cable
    Telewest and NTL

FTA   =   free-to-air
STB   =   set-top box
D   =   digital
A   =   analogue
Pay-TV   (either via subscription charge or Pay-Per-View for
           individual programmes or by Top Up TV)
OFP   =   one off payment (e.g. Freesat)

There are broadly four types of payment mechanisms for viewers to access digital television services:

- Free-to-view or free-to-air (FTA) services. Services may be viewed by anybody with the appropriate equipment and typically consist of a range of channels with the BBC branded channels and the five terrestrial analogue channels.
- One off payment to receive more channels (e.g. Freesat offered by Sky).
- Subscription services. Viewers pay a fee to be able to access a wider range of channels.
- Pay-per-view is a one-off fee to view a particular broadcast such as a box-office film or sporting event.

APPENDIX 3

CONCENTRATION OF THE ITV SECTOR

Table 1 May 2000

	ITV1 Licensees
The big three ITV1 companies (in order of size)	
Granada Group	Granada Tyne Tees Yorkshire Television ('YTV) London Weekend Television (LWT)
Carlton Communications	Carlton Central Westcountry (Meridian)
United News and Media	Anglia HTV Controlling stake in Meridian
Other ITV companies	
Border Television	Border
Channel Island Communications	Channel Television
Grampian and Scottish Television	Grampian Television Scottish Television
Ulster Television	Ulster Television

Table 2 December 2003

Consolidation of commercial television	The ITV sector: England and Wales
Granada Group	Granada TV
	Border TV
	London Weekend Television
	Tyne Tees TV
	Yorkshire TV
	Meridian TV
	Anglia TV
Carlton Communications	Carlton TV
	Central TV
	Westcountry TV
	HTV
Other ITV1 groups	
Scottish Media Group	Scottish TV
	Grampian TV
Channel Television	Channel Television
Ulster Television	Ulster Television

Table 3 March 2004

Consolidation of commercial television	The ITV sector: England and Wales
ITV plc	Granada TV
	Border TV
	London Weekend Television
	Tyne Tees TV
	Yorkshire TV
	Meridian TV
	Anglia TV
	Carlton TV
	Central TV
	Westcountry TV
	HTV
Other ITV1 groups	
Scottish Media Group	Scottish TV
	Grampian TV
Channel Television	Channel Television
Ulster Television	Ulster Television

APPENDIX 4

CONCENTRATION OF THE NATIONAL PRESS

NATIONAL DAILY NEWSPAPERS

Tabloids	Owner	Executive control	Editor	May 2005 circulation
Sun	News International	Rupert Murdoch	Rebekah Wade	3,230,332
Daily Mail	Daily Mail and General Trust	Lord Rothermere	Paul Dacre	2,359,003
Daily Mirror	Trinity Mirror	Victor Blank	Richard Wallace	1,780,554
Daily Express	Northern and Shell	Richard Desmond	Peter Hill	898, 396
Daily Star	Northern and Shell	Richard Desmond	Dawn Neesom	863,083
Broadsheets				
Daily Telegraph	Telegraph Group Limited owned by Hollyrood Holdings Limited	Sir David and Sir Frederick Barclay	Martin Newland	915,711
Times	News International	Rupert Murdoch	Robert Thomson	684,695
Financial Times	Pearson plc	Pearson board	Andrew Gowers	431,287
Guardian	Guardian Media Group	Scott Trust	Alan Rusbridger	372,562
Independent	Independent News and Media	Tony O'Reilly	Simon Kelner	263,043

Source: Audit Bureau of Circulations (<http://www.abc.org.uk>)

NATIONAL SUNDAY NEWSPAPERS

Tabloids	Owner	Executive control	Editor	May 2005 circulation
News of the World	News International	Rupert Murdoch	Andy Coulson	3,653,168
Sunday Mirror	Trinity Mirror	Victor Blank	Tina Weaver	1,545,789
People	Trinity Mirror	Victor Blank	Mark Thomas	932,200
Sunday Express	Northern and Shell	Richard Desmond	Mark Townsend	919,416
Mail on Sunday	Daily Mail and General Trust	Lord Rothermere	Peter Wright	2,253,176
Daily Star Sunday	Northern and Shell	Richard Desmond	Gareth Morgan	420,739
Broadsheets				
Sunday Times	News International	Rupert Murdoch	John Witherow	1,349,943
Sunday Telegraph	Telegraph Group Limited owned by Hollyrood Holdings Limited	Sir David and Sir Frederick Barclay	Sarah Sands	666,031
Observer	Guardian Media Group	Scott Trust	Roger Alton	441,802
Independent on Sunday	Independent News and Media	Tony O'Reilly	Tristan Davies	206,607

Source: Audit Bureau of Circulations (<http://www.abc.org.uk>)

APPENDIX 5

TIMELINE OF THE COMMUNICATIONS ACT 2003

Communications White Paper	December 2000
Two public consultations held	November 2001 to February 2002
Draft Communications Bill	May 2002
Joint Scrutiny Cttee (Puttnam Cttee)	Summer 2002
Communications Bill to HoC	19 November 2002
Second Reading	3 December 2002
Standing Cttee – 26 sittings	10 Dec 2002 to 6 February 2003
Report Stage, House of Commons	Day one – 25 February 2003
	Day two – 4 March 2003
Third Reading (HoC)	4 March 2003
House of Lords	5 March 2003
Second Reading (HoL)	25 March 2003
Committee Stage	After the Easter break (eight day debate spread over one month, to give peers of different political persuasions a chance to give their views)
Bill back to HoC	Late May/early June 2003
Royal Assent for the Act	7 July 2003

APPENDIX 6

TV NEWS PROGRAMMES

Broadcast news provider	Weekday news appointment programmes	Rolling news programmes
BBC	BBC1	BBC News 24
	Breakfast news	
	Lunchtime news	
	Early evening news	
	Regional news programmes	
	Late evening news	
	BBC2	
	Newsnight	
ITN	ITV1	ITV News Channel
	ITV morning news	
	Lunchtime news	
	Early evening news	
	Late evening news	
	Channel 4	
	Lunchtime news	
	7 p.m. news	
Regional ITV companies	Regional television news programmes such as Calendar News provided by Yorkshire Television	
Sky News (BSkyB)	Five News (from 1 January 2005)	Sky News

Broadcast news provider	Weekday news appointment programmes	Rolling news programmes
Also available in Britain on digital television		
Bloomberg		Bloomberg News Channel
Al-Jazeera		Al-Jazeera (from Qatar)
Fox News		Fox News Channel (from the USA)
CNN		CNN (from the USA)
CCTV-9		CCTV (from China)
CNBC		CNBC (from the USA)

The BBC also provides news bulletins for BBC3 and BBC4, and ITN provides showbiz news programmes for ITV2 and for the ITV London news service launched in March 2004. Regular news bulletins also appear within the GMTV breakfast show shown on ITV1 from 6 a.m. to 9 a.m. on weekdays.

NOTES

1 INTRODUCTION

1   Following the Hutton Inquiry and Report (2003–2004), a panel of inquiry was convened by the acting Director-General Mark Byford. The panel was chaired by Ronald Neil, a former director of BBC News and current affairs. The panel reported on 23 June 2004 (see <http://www.bbc.co.uk/info/policies>), accessed 24 June 2004.

2   In 2003 Eurobarometer reported that only 20 per cent of British people trust newspapers, which is less than half of the EU average, of 46 per cent, whereas 75 per cent of the British public say they tended not to trust the press.

3   When the Peacock Committee was commissioned in 1985 by the Thatcher government to examine the funding of the BBC, it encountered the problems of defining PSB. In 1985 the Broadcasting Research Unit conducted an opinion survey of broadcasters working in both the commercial and public sectors of British broadcasting to attempt to establish a definition of PSB which would help the Peacock Committee. Generally, the principles identified in 1985 by the Broadcasting Research Unit (BRU 1985: 25–32) have been seen to embody PSB. Eight principles were identified and these have been recognized as the main provisions of PSB. These were: (1) universality – geographic (available to the whole population); (2) universality – serving all tastes and interests; (3) catering for minorities (particularly disadvantaged minorities should receive particular provision); (4) recognize their special relationship to the sense of national identity and community; (5) be distanced from all vested interests; (6) one main instrument of broadcasting to be funded by the users (licence fee); (7) structured to encourage competition in good programming

rather than competition for numbers; (8) guidelines for broadcasting, designed to liberate rather than restrict the programme-makers.

4   My own view is that PSB will be transformed by what I call Public Service Communication (PSC). This was first suggested by Harrison (2003) and again by Harrison and Wessels (2005). Currently, my research indicates that PSC will become increasingly important where it has four elements: (1) enduring PSB values (social criticism, disposition to truth and political detachment and cultural asset management; (2) is a trusted knowledge exchange; (3) follows and endorses the editorial principles of human dignity; (4) is interactive and available across all communications platforms. And while I believe that PSC will become increasingly more significant it will not alter the features of news described in this book.

5   A discussion of the problems in providing an operational definition of 'quality' is beyond the remit of this book, but see BRU 1989; Mulgan 1990; Ishikawa 1996.

6   <http://www.ofcom.org.uk/consultations/current/psb/executive_summary/?a=87101> (accessed 21 April 2004).

7   <http://www.ofcom.org.uk/consultations/current/psb2/psb_phase2.pdf?a=87101> (accessed 2 October 2004).

8   <http://www.ofcom.org.uk/consult/condocs/psb3/psb3.pdf> (accessed 10 February 2005).

9   I use the noun 'Britain' and the adjective 'British' throughout to refer to England, Scotland, Wales and Northern Ireland for reasons of style and convention. I leave it to historians to debate how historically accurate and precise these reasons are. See Norman Davies (1999) *The Isles: A History*, London: Macmillan, pp. xxvi–xlii.

10   The implied threats to the BBC by the Hutton Report and BBC Charter Review process, which began in 2003 and will continue until 2006, have been criticized by the Council of Europe Parliamentary Assembly.

11   These refer to the Registrar General's Social Classes (RGSC), renamed in 1990 as Social Class based on Occupation. Class I = Professional, etc. occupations, II = Managerial and Technical occupations, III = Skilled occupations, non-manual (N) and manual (M), IV = Partly skilled occupations, V = Unskilled occupations.

2   VIEWS ABOUT NEWS: COMMON SENSE, PRACTITIONER AND ACADEMIC

1   See e.g., the articles by John Lloyd which are published in *The Financial Times*' FT Magazine on a weekly basis.

2   See <http://www.mori.com/pubinfo/sl/how-do-you-like-your-news.html> (accessed 20 August 2004).

3   Focus groups became established as a marketing research tool used by commercial research agencies from the 1950s. From the 1980s academics studying media audiences from a critical and interpretive perspective began to use focus groups as a qualitative research method. A focus group brings together a group or series of groups of people to discuss an issue or issues in the presence of a moderator. Although the discussion is restricted to particular topics or issues it is also free-ranging and may be used to gather preliminary information about a topic, which may be used in the development of a survey questionnaire. While the focus group method has its disadvantages, not least that the group may be monopolized by one strong voice, or may not be generally representative of the population, its use has been a popular way of finding out more detailed information about consumer attitudes and paving the way for further quantitative or qualitative research using questionnaires, telephone surveys and interviews (Gunter 2000: 42–48).

4   See the BBC's public consultation at <http://www.bbccharterreview.org.uk/pc_index.html> (accessed 14 January 2004).

5   See <http://www.ofcom.org.uk/codes_guidelines/broadcasting/tv/psb_review/> (accessed 16 January 2004).

6   The Frankfurt School was established in Germany in 1917 and comprised a group of Jewish humanist intellectuals who left Nazi Germany and worked in America until the 1950s. One of the most famous second generation scholars to emerge from the school was Jurgen Habermas in the 1970s.

7   They all referred to and believed in Karl Marx's theory of historical materialism.

8   Report of the Broadcasting Committee (chaired by Lord Pilkington), 1961–1962, Cmnd 1753, ix.

9   The meaning of history has roots in the word *historia*, which means inquiry. Herodotus began his work with the words: 'This is the result of the inquiry by Herodotus of Halicarnassus, that time should not blot out the past from mankind nor fame be denied to great and wonderful deeds, accomplished by Greeks and non-Greeks, and in particular the reason why they went to war with one another' (Hammond 1967: 337–338).

10 This quotation is taken from Roshco (1975), reprinted in Tumber (1999: 32–36).

11 Bourdieu (1996: 91) provides a note to explain this observation. He is referring to the controversy which started in France in 1989 when Muslim girls were expelled from school for wearing headscarves, or *hijab* in Arabic (and known as 'le hidjab' in France). This re-emerged as a news story in 2004 when President Chirac banned the wearing of *hijab* and other indications of religious affiliation from schools.

12 Marxist political economy is different from the classical political

economy perspective, with the former offering a critique of the impact of market forces and the latter viewing market forces and the economy as a positive force, providing greater choice for consumers. See Williams (2003) for a more detailed discussion of the distinction between the two.

13 Excerpt from *Autumn of the Moguls* to be published by Flamingo later in 2004 <http://www.mediaguardian.co.uk> (accessed 5 January 2004).

14 'Rupert Murdoch, Conrad Black and Lord Rothermere were bitterly opposed to the Maastricht Treaty negotiated in December 1991' (Greenslade 2003a: 613).

15 Support for political parties may change. For example, the *Sun* supported Margaret Thatcher and her Conservative Party. The newspaper claimed in 1992 that its support for John Major actually helped to win the election for the Conservative Party: 'It was the Sun wot won it' (*Sun* 11 April 1992: 1). Although this has never been adequately proven to be the case, support of the *Sun* in particular is seen to be an important factor in gaining votes. The *Sun* campaigned aggressively against British membership of the European Exchange Rate Mechanism (ERM), blaming the Major government for the subsequent devaluation of the pound following Britain's withdrawal from it in September 1992. The *Sun* followed this up with a series of attacks on the Major government, converting to support the Labour Party in the 1997 election.

16 Large-scale mergers which fall above particular financial thresholds (determined by the European Commission) are dealt with at the European level by the Competition Commission. Smaller mergers fall under the national remit and are therefore subject to national anti-trust and competition law. In Italy, the decision to allow Silvio Berlusconi to own a substantial part of the broadcasting sector is a national decision.

17 From this perspective the news messages are not seen as ideologically neutral, but the audience is able to resist dominant ideological messages through oppositional or negotiated readings of the news (see also Hall *et al.* 1978; Hall 1982).

18 Schudson refers to a political-economic perspective articulated by Herman and Chomsky (1988) which offers a 'propaganda model' of the mass media.

19 Although see Lichter *et al.* (1986).

20 The term has been attributed to the American sociologist and economist Thorstein Veblen (1857–1929).

21 For an American perspective see the article by Todd Gitlin of Columbia University on the Mother Jones website <http://www.mojones.com> (accessed 27 November 2004).

22 <http://www.mediaguardian.co.uk> (accessed 14 October 2003).

3 FROM BALLADS TO BROADCASTING: THE HISTORICAL GROWTH AND DEVELOPMENT OF NEWS

1 Caxton's most well-known printed works are *The Canterbury Tales* and *Troilus and Criseyde* by Geoffrey Chaucer, and *Confessio Amantis* by English poet John Gower.

2 Corantos were digests of foreign news taken and translated from foreign gazettes and letters and the content was mainly about the religious wars in Europe. They contained no domestic news as this was illegal at the time. The Coranto was printed abroad and for purely commercial gain was translated into English (Conboy 2004).

3 Samuel Pepys' (1665) diary entry for 22 November 1665, cited in Cranfield (1962: 2).

4 The first paper is generally recorded as being the *Norwich Post* which may have appeared as early as September 1701 (Allan 1999). This paper was quickly followed by the *Bristol Post-Boy* (1702), the *Exeter Post-Man* (1704) and in 1705, *A Collection of the Most Material Newes in Shrewsbury*, whereas the two university towns of Oxford and Cambridge did not get their own local newspaper until 1746 and 1744 respectively (Cranfield 1962: 16; 24).

5 Each metal letter had to be selected individually and then placed in printers' sticks which produced newspaper reports in columns.

6 The phrase 'tax on knowledge' came from *The Examiner* (1808–1881). The paper was owned by the Hunt brothers, who paid the stamp duty but put on every front page that the reason the paper cost so much was because of the government's 'tax on knowledge'.

7 The telegraph allowed the communication of information using a code which was known as the Morse system. Using a pattern of long and short pulses, each character of the alphabet was converted into an electronic transmission which could be conveyed rapidly over vast distances. See <http://www.babbage.demon.co.uk/morseabc.html> (accessed 10 July 2004).

8 Other daily middle-class newspapers emerged such as the *Morning Chronicle* (1769) and the *Morning Post* (1797) alongside new Sunday papers such as the *Observer* (1791), *Bell's Weekly Messenger* (1796), followed in the nineteenth century by the *Weekly Dispatch* (1801), *The Sunday Times* (1822) and the *News of the World* (1843) (Franklin 1997: 75–6).

9 William Cobbett's *Political Register* in particular had a high distribution rate, selling up to 40,000 copies a week in 1817 (McNair 1996: 136). In contrast, the *Northern Star*, which cost four and a half pence in 1840, estimated (by Curran and Seaton 1997) to be the equivalent of £2 at 1997 prices, sought to educate its readership.

10 In Britain the variety of laws which were introduced in the eighteenth and nineteenth centuries to try to curb free expression and the wide

circulation of ideas met with varying success. Fox's Libel Act of 1792, for example, had proved difficult to enforce in practice, as juries were often unwilling to convict (Curran and Seaton 1997). From 1818 libel laws were used more often, but as Curran and Seaton note, the prosecution of the Editor of the *Republican* in 1819 increased the popularity of the paper and circulation rose by over 50 per cent (ibid.: 11). Financial controls of the press were seen to be a more effective solution to the problem of preventing the lower orders from reading newspapers. The Stamp Act, first introduced in 1712 (which had affected the style and size of the newspapers, but had not managed to fully control them) was extended in 1819 to cover the radical press, imposing taxes upon it. These 'taxes on knowledge' (Allan 1997: 299; Williams 1998: 25) raised the cover price of newspapers in the hope of making them too expensive for the working-class readers they were aimed at. Publishing costs (e.g. the cost of paper) were also increased, aiming to restrict the act of publishing to the wealthy bourgeois class, allowing it to retain power and control in the context of the struggle between capital and labour.

11 Equally though, the provincial press is also credited with slowly educating its readership, particularly in relation to a growing political awareness which was occurring in the regions (Cranfield 1962).

12 Broadly middle-class newspapers such as the *Daily Telegraph* (which was able to become a daily paper once the stamp duty was abolished in 1855) aimed at attracting a wider readership than the wealthy middle classes, as evidenced by its eventual cheap cover price of one penny. Page 3 of the *Daily Telegraph* became illustrative of a particular type of reporting, known as the 'marmalade dropper', a phrase coined because those reading it over breakfast would be so enthralled by the stories of trials, hangings and crime or dramatic events in the British Empire that they would forget to eat their toast and drop their breakfast on to the paper. This is a typical example of the way in which popular news may be seen to be in contrast with radical news: the former was oriented to thrill and entertain rather than incite radicalism.

13 The Anglo-American model of impartial reporting was introduced in the US Zone in Germany following the end of the Second World War in 1945 (Wilke 2002), and the first evidence of the introduction of the so-called 'American paradigm' of impartiality in news reporting into Spain has been attributed to Father Manuel Grana's handbook on journalism, which was published in 1930, wherein the rules for objectivity in writing news appeared for the first time (Sanchez-Aranda and Barrera 2003: 498).

14 The actual technology of radio was developed by an American, R.A. Fissenden, in 1906, and consisted of crystal sets tuned in by their 'cat's whisker'. These sets became increasingly popular in Britain and Europe after the First World War.

15   Following the deliberations of the Sykes Committee (1923) and the Crawford Committee (1926), the British Broadcasting Corporation (BBC) was set up as a public service broadcaster by Royal Charter on 1 January 1927.

16   The special nature of broadcasting and its importance in society helped to ensure that the BBC held a monopoly of television news broadcasting until 1954, when the Television Act introduced the independent television system. The BBC held a monopoly of radio news broadcasting, until the Sound Broadcasting Act legalized commercial radio in Britain in 1972.

17   Initially this regulatory body was the Independent Television Authority (ITA) which was also given wide-ranging powers (with similar PSB concerns about content as the BBC) to ensure matters of taste, decency and impartiality as well as a range of good quality news and other programming. The ITA also had the power to preview programming and, as it owned the transmission system, could control what was broadcast. The ITA was replaced by the Independent Broadcasting Authority (IBA) via the Sound Broadcasting Act 1972. The IBA was later replaced by the Independent Television Commission (ITC), and the Radio Authority (RA) via the Broadcasting Act 1990, and the ITC and RA were replaced by the Office of Communications (OFCOM) in 2003.

18   The BBC launched new radio stations Radio 1 and Radio 4 (an all-talk formula which resulted in a big expansion of news comment programmes and drama on radio), and its first local radio station. Local radio was a problem for the BBC; it cost the company more money, but didn't bring in extra revenue. The majority of the radio audience was already listening to national BBC channels and, in effect, it was taking its own audience.

19   See <http://www.irn.co.uk/> (accessed 12 December 2003).

4   THE MODERN NEWS ECOLOGY: TECHNOLOGY, REGULATION, CONCENTRATION AND COMPETITION

1   Again it is worth repeating what I have argued elsewhere that Public Service Communication (PSC) will transform PSB where PSC has four elements: (1) enduring PSB values (social criticism, disposition to truth and political detachment and cultural asset management; (2) is a trusted knowledge exchange; (3) follows and endorses the editorial principles of human dignity; (4) is interactive and available across all communications platforms (see Introduction, n. 4 above).

2   This chapter does not intend to take a technological determinist view of news technology (see Chapter 1) but recognizes the significance of other social, economic and political considerations such as

the migration of workers to urban centres and the growth in literacy
and other changes (for example, media concentration occurring in the
news media environment).

3   The National Graphical Association (NGA) – a single skilled craft
union for print workers; The Society of Graphical and Allied Trades
'82 (SOGAT) – the non-craft manual workers' union; The National
Union of Journalists (NUJ) – the journalists' union; The Electrical,
Electronic, Telecommunications and Plumbing Union (EETPU) –
electrical and other technical workers' union.

4   In March 1984 a strike in London lost Murdoch 23.5 million copies
of the *Sun* and three million copies of the *News of the World* (McNair
1996: 145–146).

5   In 1987, the ITV company TV-am was faced with industrial action
when the technical union, the ACTT, had declared it would undertake a twenty-four-hour strike over plans to introduce remote-control
studios. Those who would strike were locked out and the head of TV-
am, Bruce Gyngell and his loyal staff, ran the company on a skeleton
staff for four months, using programming sent from America by old
contacts. At the end of the four months all 229 strikers were sacked
(Davidson 1991).

6   See <http://www.ft.com> (accessed 14 January 2004).

7   Although in principle, cable is the cheapest and best technical vehicle
to provide a very large range of programmes, as well as the best means
by which to provide interactive services such as home banking and
shopping, its development has been hampered by policy measures.
Although the arrival of cable in Britain preceded satellite delivery, the
Thatcher government argued that it should be entertainment-led and
privately funded. Without public subsidy, cable operators struggled
to meet the costs of establishing a cable infrastructure. In 1982 eleven
regional franchises were awarded to cable, but these have gradually
been taken over in a series of mergers. Today there are only two cable
companies, NTL and Telewest, and their merger is imminent.

8   Although the BBC's World Service radio had been broadcasting to an
international audience, using shortband signals since December 1932,
WSTV used satellite technology to expand its international broadcasting beyond radio into television.

9   Sky News' rolling format, modelled on the style of CNN and the
twenty-four-hour news format, was eventually adopted by the BBC
in 1997 and ITN in 2000. ITN offered a similar format to Sky News
and BBC News 24, with a round-up of news every fifteen minutes.
The ITN News Channel was launched as a joint venture with cable-
broadband company NTL, but remained a loss-making company. ITV
bought out the majority share of ITN's News Channel in June 2002
and relaunched it as the ITV News Channel. This has led to greater
integration of news-gathering and news production between ITV's

main terrestrial news programmes (shown on ITV 1, Channel 4 and Channel Five) and the twenty-four-hour channel shown only on digital television.

10   In 2002 BBC News 24 had a budget of approximately £40 million, Sky News approximately £30 million and ITN a budget of £10 million (Hodgson 2002).

11   Broadcasters throughout Europe are also in the process of introducing digital newsrooms. In Finland the public service broadcaster YLE introduced a digital system in 1996. In Spain the commercial sector was the first to introduce digital newsrooms, with Telecinco launching in August 1998, followed by Antena 3 in September 1999. The BBC introduced its digital twenty-four-hour news channel in November 1997, followed by Sky News in 1998 and ITN in 2000. Italy's Mediaset and its public service broadcaster (RAI) France's TF1, also went digital throughout 2000. In the USA, a number of local stations, as well as the main twenty-four-hour news channels (CNN, MSNBC and Fox News) have implemented digital newsrooms since 2001. However, none of the main networks (NBC, ABC and CBS) have yet converted to digital (see Garcia Aviles *et al.* 2004).

12   See, for example text alerts which may be acquired via the Media Guardian website (<http://www.mediaguardian.co.uk>).

13   Take-up rates were reported by Bell and Alden (2005) to be Satellite (Sky Digital) 6.96 million homes (March 2004); Cable (NTL and Telewest) 3.3 million homes of which 2.1 million are digital (March 2004); DTT (Freeview) 3.47 million homes; total digital homes 12.53 million.

14   The determination of Britain's ITV Digital company to acquire the rights to the English Football League's games in order to increase audiences and digital TV take-up sales led to a massive overspend. This, coupled with a set-top box giveaway in competition with BSkyB in 1999, led to ITV Digital's collapse in June 2002.

15   Digital satellite television is owned by BSkyB and was launched in October 1998, rendering analogue satellite broadcasting obsolete. BSkyB is a vertically integrated company which both broadcasts and controls the satellite platform, which allows it to set the price that rival channels pay to access it.

16   Cable technology is very significant in the digital era. The use of cable rather than aerials or satellite dishes means that cable television is usually offered along with a telephone or internet service. It has much greater flexibility than satellite technology and greater capacity than terrestrial technology to provide interactive services.

17   Initially cable companies used broadband to introduce one-way television and telephony services.

18   See <http://www.mediaguardian.co.uk> (accessed 1 February 2004). In April 2004 13 million homes had internet access, of which 3.99 million were broadband connections (Alden 2005: 211).

19   The British Prestel service offered home banking, flight bookings and
      news bulletins. It had very low subscription levels (Gunter 2003).
20   Personal communication with the Head of BBC News Interactive
      (2 April 2004).
21   See <http://www.express.co.uk/> (accessed 19 December 2004).
22   In May 2005 Nokia, O₂ and NTL launched their Digital Video
      Broadcast Handheld DVB-H trial in Oxford, where 500 test users
      were able to watch high quality broadcasts of television channels on
      a mobile screen.
23   See <http://www.ananova.com> (accessed 22 March 2004).
24   See <http://www.drudgereport.com> (accessed 10 September
      2003).
25   See <http://dear_raed.blogspot.com/2003_03_01_dear_raed_archive.
      html> (accessed 22 March 2004).
26   There were 5,400 news sources available online in 2000; see
      <http://www.newslink.org> (accessed 15 November 2003).
27   Policy changes are not only occurring in the British context. A period
      of deregulation of ownership rules has occurred in many Western
      democracies over the past two decades. In December 2003 the Italian
      Parliament gave approval to a bill which allows for the privatisation
      of the state broadcaster RAI and which overturns a ruling by the
      constitutional court that would have forced Berlusconi (Italian Prime
      Minister and media entrepreneur) to transfer one of his three free-to-
      air TV channels to satellite by the end of the month (see
      <http://www/mediaguardian.co.uk> (accessed 3 December 2003).
28   See the Peacock Report 1986.
29   In 1988 the licence fee was linked directly to the retail price index
      (RPI), which had the effect of reducing the BBC's real income to 0.8
      per cent below inflation. In 2000 an above-inflation formula of
      1.5 per cent was agreed, and to date is still maintained, to give the
      BBC extra funding to launch its digital channels. In April 2004
      the BBC licence fee rose to £121 from £116 for colour television and
      the black and white licence rose from £38.50 to £40.50. The BBC
      claims that the colour television licence fee is relatively cheap when
      compared with subscription television at under £10 per month or 32
      pence per day. Those over the age of 75 do not pay the licence fee
      and it is half-price for those who are registered blind.
30   See <http://www.cpbf.org.uk/> (accessed 14 September 2003).
31   See < http://www.journalism.org/> (accessed 19 August 2004).
32   Collins and Murroni (1996) have suggested that there are benefits for
      the quality of journalism when organizations belong to larger com-
      mercial groups, although of course this is disputed by the critical view
      of media concentration.
33   See <http://www.cjr.org/issues/2003/6/comment.asp> (accessed
      19 August 2004); see also <http://www.gradethenews.org>, a

media watchdog attached to Stanford's graduate journalism programme (accessed 20 August 2004).

34 See <http://www.cjr.org/issues/2003/6/comment.asp> (accessed 19 August 2004).

35 See the USA Project for Excellence in Journalism reported at <http://www.stateofthenewsmedia.org/index.asp> (accessed 19 August 2004).

36 See e.g. <http://www.vlv.org.uk/> (accessed 10 August 2003).

37 The Act has relaxed the 20:20 rule preventing owners of national newspapers with a national market share of 20 per cent or more, from controlling a licence or owning more than 20 per cent of a regional or national television broadcaster, and a local or national radio service; to allow a newspaper owner with more than 20 per cent of the market to purchase Five (formerly Channel 5) and/or a national radio licence, although the 20:20 rule is to be retained for ITV's Channel 3 (ITV1). No one controlling more than 20 per cent of the national newspaper market may hold any licence for ITV1 or more than a 20 per cent stake in an ITV1 service. A regional requirement also states that no one owning a regional ITV1 licence may own more than 20 per cent of the local or regional newspaper market in the same region.

38 In March 2004, OFCOM offered thirty-five FM licences. Emap, GWR, GMG, Chrysalis, Capital and Scottish Media Group (SMG) have all 'pledged to apply for at least the majority of the larger [metropolitan] licences' (Rosser 2004: 10), with Emap reported to be applying for all thirty-five licences (ibid.) with IRN providing most of the news.

39 Two rules were repealed. First, the limit on ITV licence holders being allowed to own no more than 15 per cent of the television audience was overturned, and second, the rule which prevented the same company from holding two London licences (then both held by Carlton and London Weekend Television LWT) was removed.

40 ITN is currently owned by the following consortium: ITV plc, 40 per cent, Daily Mail and General Trust, 20 per cent; Reuters, 20 per cent and United Business Media, 20 per cent. This consortium will invite bids from potential news contractors to ITV1 in 2008. ITN is contracted to supply news to Channel 4 until December 2006, but lost the contract to provide news for Five to Sky in 2004. Sky News took over the ITN contract for Five news in January 2005.

41 The coverage of the different regions of Britain by ITN news was already skewed towards news from London and other big metropolitan areas (Harrison 1997).

42 See The Broadcasting Policy Group's Report on the future of the BBC published in February 2004.

43 ITV1 is constrained by its PSB obligations; according to Revoir (2004c 13), 33 per cent of its schedule is taken up with PSB requirements

which is estimated to cost it about £250 million on top of the £200 million licence payment it also makes.

44   Newspaper mergers and acquisitions still fall under the Fair Trading Act 1973 which states that all acquisitions by newspaper proprietors whose titles, including those to be bought, have an average paid-for circulation of 500,000 or more, must seek the consent of the Secretary of State for Trade and Industry (the DTI).

45   A similar strategy was used in the digital television market. In 1999 BSkyB began to give digital decoders away for free, costing the company around £1 billion. The strategy initiated a price war with BSkyB's rivals, digital cable and DTT. The free distribution of set-top boxes hastened the arrival of the digital television mass market, but contributed to the eventual collapse of ITV Digital which was unable to compete with BSkyB.

46   *Metro* was launched in London in 1999 and is now available in Leeds, Sheffield, Manchester, Newcastle, Birmingham, Glasgow and Edinburgh.

47   In March 2003 Newsquest bought forty-five London newspapers from Independent News and Media (Bell and Alden 2003).

48   For details of circulation figures and the owners of national, regional, local and free newspapers see the Audit Bureau of Circulations website <http://www.newscorp.com/investor/index.html> (accessed 15 June 2005).

49   In June 2003 it had total assets of approximately US$45 billion and total annual revenues of approximately US$17 billion. News Corporation has a diverse range of interests in eight main areas: filmed entertainment; television; cable network programming; direct broadcast satellite television; magazines and inserts; newspapers; book publishing; and 'other' media, and operates in America, Europe, Britain, Australia, Asia and the Pacific Basin. See <http://www. newscorp. com/investor/index.html> (accessed 15 June 2005).

50   APTV and Reuters Television are part of the enormously influential print news agencies, Reuters and AP.

51   Interview with Reuter's editor in October 2001.

52   A series of conferences were held on the theme of a New World Information and Communication Order (NWICO) in the 1970s and 1980s (Thompson 1995: 156). The outcome was greater cooperation between Third World countries and the expansion of alternative news agencies and new methods of information exchange (see Boyd-Barrett and Thussu 1992).

53   The EBU was formed in 1950 and is the biggest union of broadcasters in the world, with seventy-one active members in fifty-two countries in Europe, North Africa and the Middle East, and forty-six associate members in twenty-nine other countries.

54   The EBU website reports that its permanent network has fifty digital channels on a Eutelsat satellite, which relay up to 25,000 news items

and 8,000 hours of sport and cultural television programmes via radio, while two satellite channels relay 120 major news events each year; see <http://www.ebu.ch> (accessed 8 November 2003).

55 See also Cohen *et al.* (1995) for an insight into the workings of the EVN information exchange system and its role in setting the editorial agenda.

56 On 1 January 1993, the EuroNews channel began broadcasting on five terrestrial circuits and twelve satellite circuits in English, French, German, Italian and Spanish. In 2001 an agreement was reached with the Russian state broadcaster, RTR, and EuroNews now broadcasts to the country in Russian for twenty-four hours a day via satellite, and twelve hours a day via terrestrial television. It also has an online news site. Since 1997 Independent Television News (ITN) has had operating control of EuroNews.

57 EuroNews is a post-production channel, with none of its own reporters in the field, and it generally accesses Eurovision material and news agencies for its content; see <http://www.itn.co.uk/history/> (accessed 14 November 2003).

58 See <http://www.euronews.net/create_html.php?page=accueil_info> (accessed 10 December 2003).

59 Al-Jazeera was established in 1996 and was funded by the Emir of Qatar.

60 Clausen (2003) identifies the big three news agencies as being AFP (France), AP and APTV (America) and Reuters Television.

61 Hypothetically, if only two competitors dominate the market, company A and company B, a fair distribution would be for each to have 50 per cent of the market. This type of division may occur when each company supplies only one product (or in this case, one channel). However, if company A decides to introduce a new channel, then company B's market share will be reduced, possibly to 33.3 per cent, with company A now holding two-thirds of the market. It is likely that company B will then introduce another channel to regain market share. Provided both companies have the financial means, the fragmentation of the market can continue until many channels exist. However, because there are only two companies supplying the material, the channels may not be as different as they appear, since each company fights to retain its original market share.

5 NEWS AND SOCIETY

1 Although the Alien and Sedition Acts of 1798 and the Sedition Act of 1819 allowed the American government to apply restrictions to the press, subsequent opinions of the Supreme Court in a number of First Amendment cases have generally sought to continue to protect press freedom; see <http://www.firstamendmentcenter.org> (accessed 10 November 2003).

2   The ICCPR came into force on 23 March 1976.

3   Article 19 of the ICCPR states: 'Everyone shall have the right to hold opinions without interference. Everyone shall have the right to freedom of expression; this right shall include freedom to seek, receive and impart information and ideas of all kinds, regardless of frontiers, either orally, in writing or in print, in the form of art, or through any other media of his choice'.

4   Article 10, section 2 of the ECHR states that:

> The exercise of these freedoms, since it carries with it duties and responsibilities, may be subject to such formalities, conditions, restrictions or penalties as are prescribed by law and are necessary in a democratic society, in the interests of national security, territorial integrity or public safety, for the prevention of disorder or crime, for the protection of health or morals, for the protection of the reputation or rights of others, for preventing the disclosure of information received in confidence, or for maintaining the authority and impartiality of the judiciary.

5   Article 19 section 3 of the ICCPR states that:

> The exercise of the rights provided for in paragraph 2 of this article carries with it special duties and responsibilities. It may therefore be subject to certain restrictions, but these shall only be such as are provided by law and are necessary:
>
> (a) For respect of the rights or reputations of others;
>
> (b) For the protection of national security or of public order (ordre public), or of public health or morals.

6   In December 2003, at an international criminal tribunal held in Tanzania, two Rwandan journalists, Ferdinand Nahimana of Radio Television Libres des Mille Collines, and Hassan Ngeze, the owner and Editor of the Hutu extremist newspaper *Kangura*, were both sentenced to life in prison for using their journalism to incite the Hutu majority to commit genocide on Tutsis and politically moderate Hutus. The court argued that by 'soaking their journalism in ethnic hatred, the three men turned their media into weapons of war'. Whereas the American lawyer who defended Ngeze argued that freedom of expression is a right, the international court disagreed, arguing that freedom came with responsibility; see <http://www.mediaguardian.co.uk> (accessed 5 December 2003).

7   See the list of legislation that restricts journalistic practice in England and Wales, in Harcup (2004: 22). These laws affect how journalists are able to gather information, their access to information and restrictions on how it is published. See also Welsh and Greenwood (2003); and <http://www.societyofeditors.co.uk> (accessed 10 February 2004).

8   Qualified privilege is sometimes referred to as the Reynolds defence
     and is named after the case in which it was first developed, involving
     former Irish premier Albert Reynolds (*Reynolds vs Times Newspapers Ltd*
     [2001 2 AC 127]).

9   On 15 May 2004 the *Daily Mirror* printed a front-page apology,
     claiming 'We were hoaxed: we've admitted our mistake now what
     about yours?' The Editor was sacked immediately and the Board of
     Trinity Mirror attempted to make amends, apologizing unreservedly
     to the Queen's Lancashire Regiment.

10   Conversation with the Editor of ITN's 5.40 p. m. *News* during field-
     work visits in June and July 1994.

11   For example, the BBC interprets its own news role as: serving the
     public interest; being impartial, reflecting a diversity of opinion; and
     being independent and accountable (see the Neil Report 2004: 6).
     These standards (even more rigorously articulated and applied since
     the Hutton Report) are reflected in a comprehensive set of *Pro-
     ducers' Guidelines*, produced in hard copy and online which each BBC
     journalist must follow; see <http://www.bbc.co.uk/info/policies/
     producer_guides/> (accessed 10 November 2004).

12   The development of PSB led Habermas to consider a more optimistic
     interpretation of some of the media (see Calhoun 1992).

13   Recommendation 7 of *New News, Old News*, by Hargreaves and Thomas
     (2002: 7) states that 'the news media should redouble their efforts to
     engage with Britain's ethnic minorities . . . [t]his will require new
     initiatives in digital radio and television from public service broad-
     casters'.

14   Keane (1995) argues that three typologies may be distinguished:
     micro-public spheres, meso-public spheres and macro-public spheres.
     At the subnational level, Keane finds hundreds of micro-public
     spheres which arise through local disputes found in discussion groups,
     the church, town-level meetings, and drinks and a chat in a bar. News
     and information reflecting local interests and discussions may be medi-
     ated to citizens in the local news media. These micro-public spheres
     for Keane are the twentieth- (and twenty-first-) century manifestation
     of the bourgeois coffee houses and literary groups identified by
     Habermas (1989). Keane links meso-public spheres with the bound-
     aries of nation-states, although they may extend beyond if there are
     common interests such as language or cultural connections between
     members of different states. Information in the meso-public spheres
     is generally provided by neutral news media organizations to millions
     of people. Macro-public spheres occur at the global or world regional
     level (for example, the European Union).

15   See Royal Commission on the Press 1947–1949; 1961–1962; 1974–
     1977.

16   Report of the Committee on Privacy and Related Matters (1990) Cmnd. 1102.

17   The use of unsubstantiated website material as a source of news by the mainstream news media is proving to be very problematic for the character of news. For example, an allegation of infidelity which appeared on the Drudge Report, a gossip internet site, against Senator John Kerry on 12 February 2004, while he was campaigning to be the Democrat Party candidate for the next presidential elections, was picked up as news by some news organizations, which reported the nature of the unsubstantiated allegations (but did not go so far as to claim them to be factually accurate) and set in train gossip and speculation which could have damaged the Senator's campaign.

18   Accuracy, privacy and discrimination (Clause 16, amended 1991); use of listening devices to obtain information (Clause 5, amended 1993); the definition of the nature of private property which was extended to include parts of the hospital or nursing home where patients are treated (Clause 4, amended 1993); while the way in which information is obtained was reviewed in 1993, and Clause 8 on harassment was amended to include new rules in regard to taking long-lens photographs.

19   See <http://www.pcc.co.uk/> (accessed 19 January 2004).

20   Three photographers who took pictures of the car crash that killed Diana, Princess of Wales, went on trial in Paris in October 2003. The case was reported as important as it would focus on the debate between privacy and press freedom. The three French photographers: Jacques Langevin, Christian Martinez and Fabrice Chassery, were charged with taking photographs of the inside of the wreckage of the car. In France, which has stricter privacy laws than Britain, the inside of a car is regarded as being as private as the inside of a house. Consequently the photographers are deemed to have invaded the privacy of the Princess. The photographs were confiscated at the site of the crash and have never been published.

21   A further important development at this time was the introduction of the ECHR by member states into their legal systems. In the British context the Human Rights Act 1998 which incorporated the ECHR is particularly important. Article 8 of the ECHR states that 'everyone has the right to respect for private and family life and there should be no interference by a public authority, except in specific cases'. The PCC Code of Practice was amended, and its new Clause 3 included provisions largely drawn from the ECHR.

22   There may be exceptions to the clauses marked * [Clause 3, privacy; Clause 4, harassment; Clause 6, children; Clause 7, children in sex cases; Clause 8, use of listening devices; Clause 9, hospitals; Clause 10, reporting of crime; Clause 11, misrepresentation, where

journalists must not generally try to obtain information or pictures through subterfuge]. These exceptions occur where they may be demonstrated to be in the public interest.

23   See e.g. the BBC's *Producer's Guidelines*, Section 2: *Values, Standards and Principles*, sub-section 4, *Privacy*; <http://www.bbc.co.uk/info/policies/producer_guides/text/section3.shtml> (accessed 12 October 2003).

24   Several recent cases illustrate this point. In June 2003 DJ Sara Cox was awarded a record settlement for a privacy complaint. Her complaint and victory were against the *People*, which had published nude pictures of her on honeymoon on a private Pacific island. In October 2003 Diana Rigg won £30,000 in libel damages, plus an £8,000 payment for an invasion into her privacy, from the *Daily Mail* and the *London Evening Standard* over reports that wrongly portrayed her as an embittered woman who held British men in low regard. In October 2003 the *Sun* newspaper apologized to Nicole Kidman and agreed to pay her libel damages and legal costs (the amount was undisclosed). The allegations, which appeared in the *Sun* on 5 March 2003, implied that she had had an adulterous affair with Jude Law, leading to the breakdown of his marriage with Sadie Frost. The *Sunday Telegraph* also repeated the allegations, but issued an apology to the star, an example of the broadsheet press straying into tabloid territory. In October 2003 The *Daily Mirror* was forced to apologize when it wrongly alleged that the actress Amanda Holden had complained about her accommodation arrangements during the filming of BBC1 hairdressing drama *Cutting It*.

25   See <http://www.mori.com/polls/2000/bma2000.shtml> (accessed 10 September 2003).

26   See Sanders (2003: 4–5) for a detailed breakdown of the different circulation figures in Britain, France, Germany and Spain for 2000 and 2001.

27   The Communications Act identifies particular requirements, classing the BBC and S4C, every Channel 3 service, Channels 4, 5 and the public teletext service as having public service obligations (The Communications Act (2004), Chapter 4, Section 264(11)).

28   See the survey conducted for *The Times*. MORI Telephone Surveys interviewed a representative quota sample of 969 British adults aged 18+ on 28–31 March 2003; see <http://www.mori.com/pubinfo/> (accessed 23 October 2003).

29   For example, broadcasting material which incites racial hatred.

30   For example, providing a certain amount of news, current affairs or religious programming.

31   The relationship between regulators and the broadcasting sector has changed over time. The Independent Television Authority (ITA, 1955–1972) and the Independent Broadcasting Authority (IBA,

1972–1990) were sympathetic to the principles of PSB, and as such used their powers and influence to uphold those values (Gibbons 1998).

32   ITN has ultimately been the loser in this scheduling battle and its audience has shrunk from an average of 6 million in 1992 to about 3.5 million in 2003, but rising to 4.34 million in 2004, whereas BBC1's *News at Ten* regularly gets audiences of between 5 and 6 million (*Broadcast* 16 January 2004: 42; *Broadcast* 2 July 2004: 34).

33   Today ITN produce all the news bulletins for ITV1 and for the twenty-four-hour ITV News channel as well as Channel 4 News and ITV.com/news, although it has lost the contract with Five to Sky News.

34   See ITN website at <http://www.itn.co.uk/> (accessed 15 July 2004).

35   See ITN website at <http://www.itn.co.uk/> (accessed 15 July 2004).

36   See ITN website at <http://www.itn.co.uk/> (accessed 15 July 2004).

37   Section 2.2 provides special provision for news programmes, which states that: 'The Agreement specifies that news should be presented with due accuracy and impartiality. Reporting should be dispassionate, wide-ranging and well-informed. In reporting matters of industrial or political controversy the main differing views should be given due weight in the period during which the controversy is active. News judgements will take account of events as well as arguments, and editorial discretion must determine whether it is appropriate for a range of views to be included within a single programme or item.' See http://www.bbc.co.uk/info/policies/producer_guides/> (accessed 12 January 2004).

38   Evidence given by Andrew Gilligan at the Hutton Inquiry on 17 September 2003 under cross-examination by James Dingemans QC – Senior Counsel to the Inquiry.

6   NEWS PRACTICE

1   See for examples, films such as *Broadcast News* (1987); *All The President's Men* (1976); *The Front Page* (1931); *The Paper* (1994); *The Philadelphia Story* (1940) and so on. There have been more than 2,000 films made that feature reporters as a central character (Lloyd 2004: 10). More recently, reporting the events has been undertaken by journalists in what Lloyd refers to as 'polementaries' in a behind-the-scenes look at Al-Jazeera (*Al-Jazeera Control Room* (2004) by Hassan Ibrahim, and in *Fahrenheit 9/11* (2004) by Michael Moore (ibid.)), again exhibiting a mission to uncover 'The Truth'.

2   The Labour Party, under the leadership of Tony Blair, entered into dialogue with the newspaper's owner; according to Greenslade (2003a: 620), 'they found themselves knocking at an open door with Rupert Murdoch'. In 1995 Blair was invited to Australia as a guest at the News Corporation conference. His speech raised speculation in Britain that he had indicated that ownership restrictions might be lifted in return for more positive coverage of the party in the *Sun* newspaper (ibid.). In short, it would seem that deals relating to the tenor of news reports may be struck with the partisan press who are free to change sides at will.

3   See <http://news.bbc.co.uk/1/hi/uk_politics/3892809.stm> (accessed 20 August 2004).

4   Andrew Gilligan was giving evidence to Ms Rogers on 17 September 2004.

5   Alistair Campbell claimed that this was a key reason for his intervention (BBC 2's *Newsnight*, 28 January 2004), although since then the BBC has said that at that stage the story did not achieve global prominence.

6   Here the iconic American journalist Hildy Johnson springs to mind (see note 1 above). Hildy Johnson, a character in the Hollywood film *The Front Page*, symbolizes a hard news reporter, a tenacious and investigative journalist, who places gathering and telling the news above everything else. In his quest to expose a corrupt city administration and to save the life of a murderer, he is prepared to lose the chance to marry his fiancée. Although Hildy Johnson worked for a newspaper in the USA, he elicits an attractive journalistic image of the investigative and tenacious journalist. The role of Hildy may be seen as a metaphor for press and broadcasting freedom, and as Colin Sparks (1991: 72) remarks, the modern Hildy Johnson 'no longer dreams of bringing down the mayor or the government in the wake of a great scandal. That only happens in the movies.'

7   Although Walter Lippmann had already taken a few initial steps in this area in 1922.

8   The first eight factors were based on reasoning about what facilitates and what impedes perception, regardless of the culture or origin of the selector, and briefly relate to the following: how well an event fits into a newsday (frequency); the bigger and the more violent the event, the more likely it is to be reported (threshold); the more clear and unambiguous the event, the more likely it is to be reported (unambiguity); the more relevant the story, the more likely it is to be reported (meaningfulness); the more consonant the signal is with the mental image of what one expects to find, the more probable it is that it will be recorded as worth listening to (consonance); the more unexpected the event, the more likely it is to be included in the news (unexpectedness); once an event has hit the headlines and been

defined as news, the more likely it is that it will continue to be defined as news (continuity); because the journalists have to ensure that the whole 'news picture' is balanced and not repetitive and boring, very different kinds of events may be reported in order to ensure that a different news programme is produced each time (composition). Galtung and Ruge's other four factors were deemed to be related to Western culture: the more an event concerns elite nations and elite people (elites); the more an event may be seen in personal terms (personalisation), and the more negative an event is in its consequences, the more likely it will become news (negativity).

9   The power elite (stories about powerful individuals and organizations); celebrity (stories about famous people); entertainment (stories about showbusiness, sex, human interest, animals, drama, humour); surprise; bad news (conflict or tragedy or negative news); good news (positive news); magnitude (high impact or large numbers of people involved); relevance (stories perceived to be relevant to the audience); follow-ups (stories about subjects already in the news); media agenda (stories that set or fit the news organization's own agenda).

10 This problem relates not only to the BBC. The Canadian public service broadcaster, CBC, has had difficulty trying to balance its commercial and non-commercial activities (*Broadcast* 25 January 2002: 15). In Germany the public service broadcaster ARD is currently undergoing scrutiny about whether it should be allowed to spend its profits on additional web services that are not essential to support its core programming (Europemedia.net, February 2002).

11 A bureaucratic 'phase structure' refers to the typical way a story unfolds and develops within in a bureaucratic institution.

12 Section 10 of the Contempt of Court Act 1981 recognizes that disclosure is necessary in the interests of justice, national security or for the prevention of crime and disorder.

13 The National Council for the Training of Journalists (NCTJ) requires that copy is free of innuendo and ambiguity, is balanced, free of personal comment, reflects the brief given to the journalist, and that quotes are accurate and given in context (NCTJ 2002: 12–14). Print and broadcast journalists are expected to be able routinely to write in a manner which is precise and succinct, produce an introduction which interests the reader, write in an active rather than a passive style and avoid jargon or complicated language. The requirement to be able to interview successfully (although as Harcup (2004: 96) observes, acquiring the technique is often a matter of 'trial and error') and then to report a story, using the inverted pyramid style and the five 'W's and 'how' in a simple, unambiguous and balanced manner, are at the heart of journalistic practice.

14 See <http://www.indymedia.org/peace> (accessed 10 January 2004) for links to news and comment.

15   Digitalization of newsrooms is also occurring across Europe; the
      Finnish public service broadcasting, YLE, introduced a digital, autom-
      atized system in 1996. In Spain, the commercial network Telecinco
      launched a fully digital news operation in August 1998, followed by
      Antena on 3 September 1999. The BBC introduced its digital twenty-
      four-hour news channel in November 1997, and Sky's services were
      all converted to digital satellite in 1998. Throughout 2000 ITN, Italy's
      Mediaset and RAI and France's TF1, also went digital. Since 2001,
      CNN, MSNBC and Fox News in America have implemented digital
      newsrooms, although none of the main networks NBC, ABC and CBS
      has yet converted (see Garcia Aviles *et al.* 2004).
16   Although Garcia Aviles *et al.* (2004) also found that journalists over
      40 years old were likely to show more scepticism about the benefits
      of new technology, and more often voiced concerns about the quality
      of the news produced using new technology, and that journalists at
      Telemadrid in Spain were unhappy about the digitization of their
      newsroom.

7   NEWS: CHARACTER AND AUDIENCE

1   Consultation published: 21 April 2004; Consultation closed: 15 June
      2004. See <http://www.ofcom.org.uk/consultations/past/psb/
      ?a=87101> (accessed 10 July 2004). See also <http://www.ofcom.
      org.uk/consultations/past/psb/psb/volume2/social_values/
      informed democracy/news?a=87101> (accessed 12 July 2004).
2   For example the realism of violent news images, which are more
      disturbing to audiences than fictional depictions of violence, has meant
      that restrictions on showing the graphic nature of events have been
      imposed in the interests of protecting audiences and children in
      particular (Gunter, *et al.* 2003).
3   See, for example, the work by Kitzinger (1999) which recognizes that
      while audiences are active, the media may also have effects.
4   MORI conducted the research using a sample of 1,355 people who
      self-completed a questionnaire in their own homes in the presence of
      an interviewer. The survey took place between 6 and 12 March 2003
      using 192 sampling points throughout Britain.
5   The age group 25 to 34 years showed the largest decline, with a 14.6
      per cent reduction in viewing since 1994.
6   These refer to the Registrar General's Social Classes (RGSC), re-
      named in 1990 as Social Class based on Occupation. Class I =
      Professional, etc. occupations; II = Managerial and Technical occu-
      pations; III = Skilled occupations; non-manual (N) and manual (M);
      IV = Partly skilled occupations; V = Unskilled occupations.
7   The desire to make the BBC's news provision distinctive from its com-
      petitors in the run-up to a Charter renewal is not new. In the run-up

to the 1996 Charter renewal, Director General John Birt's priority was to reclaim the 'high ground' in news and current affairs. This was important and affected BBC news throughout the 1990s. This vision had begun in the mid-1970s when John Birt and Peter Jay wrote a series of articles bemoaning the state of news reporting on British television. Their important contribution to the news values of the BBC revolved around what became known as the Birt–Jay thesis which subsequently became the blueprint for wholesale changes in BBC journalism (see *The Times,* 30 September 1975; 1 October 1975; 2 September 1976; 3 September 1976, discussed further in Harrison 2000).

8   For the entire study of seven polls the total sample was 9,611 respondents, and for the in-depth analysis for the polls conducted from June to September 2003 the sample was 3,334 respondents. See <http://www.pipa.org/OnlineReports/Iraq/Media_10_02_03Report.pdf> (accessed 10 August 2004).

9   See <http://www.barb.co.uk> (accessed 13 November 2003). In 1981 BARB replaced the Joint Industry Committee for Television Audience Research (JICTAR). BARB is a private organization which is jointly funded by broadcasters and advertising agencies, and produces monthly audience measurement and audience reaction data for the television industry.

10   See <http://www.rajar.co.uk> (accessed 10 January 2004).

11   See <http:www.itc.co.uk>, <http:www.bbc.co.uk>.

12   Reprinted with the permission of the Head of BBC News Online.

13   In December 2004 the *Daily Mail* and General Trust (owner of the *Daily Mail* and the *London Evening Standard*) completed a £90 million upgrade of its presses to allow it to print bigger papers with more colour. In Autumn 2004 The *Daily Mail* relaunched its Femail pages, providing a new pull-out colour section entitled 'Lifestyle' and also expanded its sports section to increase appeal to male readers.

14   The Saturday version of the *Daily Telegraph* was relaunched in March 2003 to include new sections: fresh food and home sections in the magazine and a twenty-page tabloid of arts and books, producing an eleven section paper.

15   ITN's *News at Ten* was removed from the 10 p.m. slot in March 1999. At the time some people believed this effectively signalled the end of ITV as a public service network. When the ITC decided that ITV's Channel 3 could run films without being interrupted by *News at Ten,* an agreement was made that ITV produce two new news programmes at 6.30 p.m. and 11 p.m. and a weekly current affairs show. Since 1999 ITN has lost its brand, with the programmes now being known as ITV News programmes.

16   Six new BBC Directorates were formed with BBC News responsible for a combined television and radio news operation across the range of BBC news and current affairs services.

17   When BBC1's viewing figures fell to below 30 per cent for the first time in 1998, many believed that the BBC had fallen below an important psychological barrier. This drop in ratings finally opened up the question about the BBC's long-term role.

18   See http://www/bbc.co.uk/info/news/newsfutures/res_page6.shtml> (accessed 9 October 1998).

19   See <http://www.bbc.co.uk> (accessed 10 December 2002).

20   For example, the BBC covered the Madrid bombs in 2004, the Hutton Report and the Conservative Party leadership election result within the terrestrial channel schedule.

21   The paper was originally known as the *Daily Mirror* but changed its name to the *Mirror* when it was last relaunched in 1997.

22   See <http://www.mediaguardian.co.uk> (accessed 3 April 2003).

23   See <http://www.journalism.org/> (accessed 19 August 2004).

24   There was some disquiet at the BBC about the amount of coverage devoted to the Soham murders, as this was not felt to be a 'BBC story', particularly when coverage intensified and involved the location of a large number of journalists in the village itself (BBC Correspondent, April 2004).

25   See <http://www.bbc.co.uk/info/statements2003/docs/text_nations_regions.shtml> (accessed 19 December 2004). In December 2004 the BBC was reported to be planning to launch an ultra-local network of television services, which would include short news bulletins (Holmwood 2004: 21).

26   Serif and sans-serif are the name of two types of typefaces. These generic types have given rise to many different type faces available today.

8   POSSIBILITIES AND PROBLEMS: TRENDS IN THE FUTURE OF NEWS

1   The BBC (Britain); DR (Denmark); VRT (Belgium); YLE (Finland) and SVT (Sweden) use the licence fee. ZDF and ARD (Germany); RTE (Ireland); NOS (Netherlands); ORF (Austria) and TV2 (Denmark) use the licence fee and advertising. France TV (France); RAI (Italy); RTBF (Belgium) use public funding, the licence fee and advertising. RTP (Portugal) uses advertising and public funding; RTVE (Spain) uses advertising and public debt, and ERT (Greece) uses advertising and a levy on electricity bills to fund PSB (see http://europa.eu.int/comm/).

2   It is beyond the scope of this book to assess the character of 'Arab News' carried by satellite channels such as Al-Arabiya and Al-Jazeera. Increasingly though, such assessments will become more and more significant in direct relationship to the impact these channels are

having both in the West and more intriguingly and importantly on Arab societies where journalistic openness is officially oppressed. For one such analysis, albeit critical, see *The Making of Arab News* by Noha Mellor (2005).

3 Fabrication has also occurred in 'serious' newspapers and magazine journalism in America. In these cases the decision seems to have been made entirely by one individual journalist acting in an aberrant manner. For example, Stephen Glass worked for the *New Republic* magazine and made up stories. A film about Stephen Glass starring Tom Cruise was released in 2004. It is aptly named *Shattered Glass*. Jayson Blair of the *New York Times* was caught when an old colleague accused him of plagiarizing a story she had written for her local newspaper in Texas, rather than going to the scene and researching the story for himself. Revelations about Jayson Blair caused shock waves at the *New York Times*, and the editor Howell Raines resigned.

4 For example, regulatory structures have normally protected the viewer rather than the participants. Despite the plethora of reality-style programmes which have emerged, participants still appear to be naive about the consequences of negative publicity. The owner of a West Yorkshire restaurant whose business collapsed after an appearance on Channel 4's *Ramsay's Kitchen Nightmares* claimed that she was planning to sue Gordon Ramsay, Channel 4 and the programme-makers Optomen, all of whom she blames for the closure (Worth and Banton 2004) <http://www.mediaguardian.co.uk> (accessed 27 July 2004).

5 The 'mini-indy', launched in the Southeast of England on 30 September 2003, was reported as boosting sales in the London region by 35 per cent which meant an overall increase for *Independent* sales of up to 15 per cent in November.

6 To date the *Independent* is reporting increased sales and the tabloid size broadsheet is currently seen as an important strategy in fighting the long-term circulation decline that has been occurring in the newspaper market.

7 Alan Rusbridger, interviewed on *The Culture Programme* on 4 December 2004.

8 It is still unclear what the lasting effect on existing newspapers will be. The increase in sales of the 'mini-indy' has not reduced sales of existing newspapers by the same amount. It seems that there might be a new readership for a tabloid-sized newspaper, possibly those commuting who would not necessarily buy a paper. The free *Metro* paper has also successfully tapped into this market.

9 This transcript is taken and adapted from the website entitled *The Hindenburg Disaster*. <http://www.otr-shop.com/The%20 Hindenburg%20Disaster.htm> (accessed 8 December 2004).

10 The Council of Europe (2002) has recently raised concerns about the quality and dignity of the content used within reality TV programmes.

11 See, for example, the complaints made by viewers to the ITC of a video clip of a man falling to his death, which was dealt with as an infringement of taste and decency that might affect the audience's sensibilities, rather than as an invasion of the man's privacy or an infringement of his human dignity ('Death Defying Thrills', *ITC Complaints*, August 2002).

12 In 2004 ITN was owned by the following shareholders: ITV plc (40 per cent); *Daily Mail* and General Trust (20 per cent); Reuters (20 per cent) and United Business Media (20 per cent).

13 See <http:www.ofcom.org.uk> (accessed 1 December 2005).

BIBLIOGRAPHY

BOOKS AND ARTICLES

Abbate, J. (2000) *Inventing the Internet*, Cambridge, MA: MIT Press.

Adorno, T. and Horkheimer, M. (1973) *Dialectics of Enlightenment*, London: Allen Lane.

Ahmed, K. and Thorpe, V. (2004) 'Top BBC staff threaten Hutton probe walk-out', *Observer*, 28 March, p. 5.

Alden, C. (2005) *Media Directory 2005*, London: Guardian Newspapers.

Allan, S. (1997) 'News and the public sphere: towards a history of objectivity and impartiality', in M. Bromley and T. O'Malley (eds) *A Journalism Reader*, London: Routledge, pp. 296–329.

Allan, S. (1999) *News Culture*, Buckingham: Open University Press.

Allan, S. (2002) 'Reweaving the internet: online news of September 11', in B. Zelizer and S. Allan (eds) *Journalism after September 11*, London: Routledge, pp. 119–140.

Altheide, D. L. (1976) *Creating Reality: how the news distorts events*, Thousand Oaks, CA: Sage.

Altheide, D. (1984) 'Media hegemony: a failure of perspective', *Public Opinion Quarterly*, 48: 476–490.

Altick, D. (1957) *The English Common Reader*, Chicago, IL: University of Chicago Press.

Altschull, J. (1984) *Agents of Power: the role of the news media in human affairs*, New York: Longman.

Anderson, B. (1983) *Imagined Communities*, London: Verso.

Anderson, P.J. and Weymouth, A. (1999) *Insulting the Public? The British press and the European Union*, London: Longman.

Ang, I. (ed.) (1996) *Living Room Wars*, London: Routledge.

Asquith, A. (1978) 'The structure, ownership and control of the press 1855–1914', in G. Boyce, J. Curran and P. Wingate (eds) *Newspaper History: from the 17th century to the present day*, London: Constable, pp. 98–117.

Atherton, I. (1999) 'The itch grown a disease: manuscript transmission of news in the seventeenth century' in J. Raymond (ed.) *News, Newspapers and Society in Early Modern Britain*, London: Frank Cass.

Atton, C. (2002) *Alternative Media*, London: Sage.

Bagdikian, B. (1990) *The Media Monopoly*, Boston, MA: Beacon.

Bantz, C. (1985) 'News organisations: conflict as a crafted cultural norm', *Communication*, 8: 225–244.

Baran, S. and Davies, D. (1995) *Mass Communications Theory*, Belmont, CA: Wadsworth.

Barber, L. (2003) 'The media get conscripted to the fight', *FT Reports, Creative Business*, 24 March 2003. Available online at <http://www.ft.com> (accessed 24 March 2003).

Barendt, E. and Hitchens, L. (2000) *Media Law: cases and materials*, London: Longman.

Barnett, S. (1997) 'New media, old problems: new technology and the political process', *European Journal of Communication*, 12(2): 193–218.

Barnett, S. (1998) 'Dumbing down or reaching out', in Jean Seaton (ed.) *Politics and the Media*, Oxford: Blackwell.

Barnett, S. and Gaber, I. (1993) *Changing Patterns in Broadcast News*, London: Voice of the Listener and Viewer.

Barnett, S., Seymour, E. and Gaber, I. (2000) *From Callaghan to Kosovo: changing trends in British television news 1975–1999*, London: University of Westminster.

Barrett, O. and Newbold, C. (eds) (1995) *Approaches to Media,* London: Arnold.

BBC (1996) *Producers' Guidelines*, London: BBC.

BBC (2002) *A Review of BBC News*, London: BBC.

BBC (2003) *Annual Report*, London: BBC.

BBC (2004) *BBC Diary*, London: BBC.

Bell, A. (1991) *The Language of News Media*, Oxford: Blackwell.

Bell, A. and Garrett, P. (eds) (1998) *Approaches to Media Discourse*, Oxford: Blackwell.

Bell, D. (1973) *The Coming of Post-Industrial Society,* Harmondsworth: Penguin.

Bell, E. and Alden, C. (2003) *Media Directory 2004*, London: Guardian Newspapers Limited.

Bell, M. (2002) 'Glamour is not good news', *Independent*, 19 February 2002.

Benjamin, W. (1970) *Illuminations*, London: Jonathan Cape.

Bennett, C. (2003) 'And now over to Fairford where there is nothing to see', *The Guardian,* 27 March, pp. 2–3.

Berkowitz, D. (1997) *Social Meanings of News*, Thousand Oaks, CA: Sage.

Berlin, I. (1969) *Four Essays on Liberty*, Oxford: Oxford University Press.

Birt, J. (1995) 'Why our interviewers should stop sneering and start to listen', *The Times*, 4 February.

Birt, J. and Jay, P. (1975a) 'Television journalism: the child of an unhappy marriage between newspapers and film', *The Times*, 30 September.

Birt, J. and Jay, P. (1975b) 'The radical changes needed to remedy TV's bias against understanding', *The Times*, 1 October.

Birt, J. and Jay, P. (1976a) 'How television news can hold the mass audience', *The Times*, 2 September.

Birt, J. and Jay, P. (1976b) 'Why television news is in danger of becoming an anti-social force', *The Times*, 3 September.

Blumler, J.G. (1999) 'Political communication systems: all change', *European Journal of Communication*, 14(2): 241–249.

Boorstin, D. (1964) *The Image: a guide to pseudo events in America,* New York: Harper & Row.

Bourdieu, P. (1996) *On Television and Journalism*, London: Pluto Press (translated into English in 1998).

Boyce, G., Curran, J. and Wingate, P. (eds) (1978) *Newspaper History: from the 17th century to the present day*, London: Constable, pp. 98–117.

Boyd, A. (1994) *Broadcast Journalism: techniques of radio and TV news*, Oxford: Focal Press.

Boyd, A. (2001) *Broadcast Journalism: techniques of radio and TV news*, 2nd edn, Oxford: Focal Press.

Boyd-Barrett, O. and Rantanen, T. (1998) *The Globalization of News*, London: Sage.

Boyd-Barrett, O. and Thussu, D.K. (1992) *Contra-Flow in Global News: international and regional news exchange mechanisms*, London: John Libbey.

Boyer, J. H. (1981) 'How editors view objectivity', *Journalism Quarterly,* 58: 24–28.

Brants, K. (1998) 'Who's afraid of infotainment?', *Journal of Communication*, 13(3): 323.

Breed, W. (1955) 'Social control in the newsroom: a functional analysis', *Social Forces*, 33: 326–335.

Briggs, A. (1961) *The Birth of Broadcasting: the history of broadcasting in the United Kingdom*, Oxford: Oxford University Press.

Briggs, A. (1995) *The History of Broadcasting in the United Kingdom: competition 1955–1974*, Oxford: Oxford University Press.

Briggs, A. and Cobley, P. (1998) *The Media: an introduction*, Harlow: Longman.

Broadcasting Act (1990) London: HMSO.

Broadcasting Act (1996) London: HMSO.

Broadcasting Policy Group (2004) *Beyond the Charter: the BBC after 2006*, London: Broadcasting Policy Group.

Broadcasting Research Unit (BRU) (1985) *The Public Service Idea in British Broadcasting: main principles*, Luton: John Libbey.

BRU (1989) *Quality in Television*, London: John Libbey.

Bromley, M. (1997) 'The end of journalism? Changes in workplace practices in the press and broadcasting in the 1990s', in M. Bromley and T. O'Malley (eds) *A Journalism Reader*, London: Routledge, pp. 330–350.

Bromley, M. and O'Malley, T. (eds) (1995) *A Journalism Reader*, London: Routledge.

Brown, M. (2004) 'War of the news walls', *Guardian*, 26 January. Available online at <http://www.mediaguardian.co.uk> (accessed 26 January 2004).

Buchman, J. (2000) 'Television newscast promotion and marketing', in S. Eastman (ed.) *Research in Media Promotion*, Mahwah, NJ: Lawrence Erlbaum Associates.

Burns, T. (1969) 'Public service and private world', in P. Halmos (ed.) *The Sociological Review Monograph*, 13: 53–73.

Burrell, I. (2003) 'BBC news chief admits problems of accuracy', *Independent*, 27 March, p. 4.

Byrne, C. (2002) 'Readers flee "serious" Mirror', *Guardian*, 11 November. Available online at <http://www.mediaguardian.co.uk> (accessed 11 November 2002).

Byrne, C. (2003a) 'Has the Mirror lost the plot?', *Guardian*, 3 April 2003. Available online at <http://www.mediaguardian.co.uk> (accessed 3 April 2003).

Byrne, C. (2003b) 'BBC chiefs stress need to attribute war sources', *Guardian*, 28 March 2003. Available online at <http://www.mediaguardian.co.uk> (accessed 28 March 2003).

Calcutt, D. (1990) *The Report of the Committee on Privacy and Related Matters*, London: HMSO, Cmnd 1102.

Calcutt, D. (1993) *Review of Press Self-regulation*, London: HMSO, Cmnd 2135.

Calhoun, C. (ed.) (1992) *Habermas and the Public Sphere*, London: MIT Press.

Cameron, D. (1996) 'Style policy and style politics: a neglected aspect of the language of the news', *Media Culture and Society*, 18(3): 315–333.

Carlyle, T. (1901) *On Heroes and Hero Worship*, London: Chapman and Hall.

Carpenter, R. (1946) *Folk Tale, Fiction and Saga in the Homeric Epics*, Berkeley and Los Angeles: University of California Press.

Carr, P. (2003) 'How to get the yoof interested in politics', *Guardian*, 24 November. Available online at <http://www.mediaguardian.co.uk> (accessed 25 November 2003).

Castells, M. (1997) *The Power of Identity*, Oxford: Blackwell.

Castells, M. (2001) 'The information city, the new economy, and the network society', in F. Webster (ed.) (2004) *The Information Society Reader*, London: Routledge, pp. 150–164.

Chalaby, J.K. (1996) 'Journalism as an Anglo-American invention: a comparison of the development of French and Anglo-American journalism, 1830s–1920s', *European Journal of Communication*, 11(3): 303–326.

Chalaby, J.K. (2000) 'Journalism studies in an era of transition in public communication', *Journalism*, 1(1): 33–39.

Chippendale, P. and Horrie, C. (1992) *Stick it up your Punter*, London: Heinemann.

Chisholm, A. and Davie, M. (1993) *Beaverbrook: a life*, London: Pimlico.

Clarke, S. (2004a) 'News faces the spotlight', *Broadcast*, 9 January, p. 14.

Clarke, S. (2004b) 'An impossible jigsaw', *Broadcast*, 12 March, p. 13.

Clausen, L. (2001) *The 'Domestication' of International News: a study of Japanese television production*, Copenhagen: Copenhagen Business School Press.

Clausen, L. (2003) *Global News Production*, Copenhagen: Copenhagen Business School Press.

Clegg, S., Hudson, A. and Steel, J. (2003) 'The Emperor's New Clothes: globalisation and e-learning in higher education', *British Journal of Sociology of Education*, 24(1): 39–53.

Cohen, A.A., Levy, M.R., Roeh, I. and Gurevitch, M. (1995) *Global Newsrooms: local audiences*, London: John Libbey.

Cohen, B.C. (1963) *The Press and Foreign Policy*, Princeton, NJ: Princeton University Press.

Cohen, E.D. (ed.) (1992) *Philosophical Issues in Journalism*, Oxford: Oxford University Press.

Cohen, J. and Young, S. (eds) (1973) *The Manufacture of the News*, London: Constable.

Cohen, J. and Young, S. (eds) (1981) *The Manufacture of the News*, 2nd edn, London: Constable.

Collini, S. (ed.) (1989) *On Liberty and Other Writings*, Cambridge: Cambridge University Press.

Collins, R. (1990) *Television: policy and culture*, London: Unwin Hyman.

Collins, R. and Muroni, C. (1996) *New Media, New Policies*, London: Polity Press.

Communications Act (2003) London: HMSO.

Conboy, M. (2004) *Journalism: a critical history*, London: Sage.

Cottle, S. (1993) *TV News, Urban Conflict and the Inner City*, Leicester: Leicester University Press.

Cottle, S. (1999) 'From BBC newsroom to BBC news centre: on changing technology and journalist practices', *Convergence: Journal of New Information and Communication Technologies*, 5(3): 22–43.

Cottle, S. (ed.) (2003) *Media Organization and Production*, London: Sage.

Council of Europe (2002) *European Convention on Transfrontier Television*, Standing Committee on Transfrontier Television, T-TT (2002) 9, 29–30 April 2002.

Cox, G. (1995) *Pioneering Television News*, London: John Libbey.

Cranfield, G.A. (1962) *The Development of the Provincial Newspaper 1700–1760*, London: Oxford University Press at the Clarendon Press.

Crisell, A. (1986) *Understanding Radio*, London: Methuen.

Crisell, A. (1997) *An Introductory History of British Broadcasting*, London: Routledge.

Crowley, D. and Mitchell, D. (eds) (1994) *Communication Theory Today*, Cambridge: Polity Press.

Curran, J. (1991) 'Rethinking the media as a public sphere', in P. Dahlgren and C. Sparks (eds) *Communication and Citizenship: journalism and the public sphere in the new media age*, London: Routledge, pp. 27–57.

Curran, J. and Seaton, J. (1997) *Power without Responsibility*, 5th edn, London: Routledge.

Curran, J. and Seaton, J. (2003) *Power without Responsibility*, 6th edn, London: Routledge.

Dahlgren, P. (1995) *Television and the Public Sphere*, London: Sage.

Dautrich, K. and Hartley, T. (1999) *How the News Media Fail American Voters: causes consequences, remedies*, New York: Columbia University Press.

Davidson, A. (1991) *Under the Hammer*, London: Mandarin Paperbacks.

Dayan, D. and Katz, E. (1992) *Media Events*, Cambridge, MA: Harvard University Press.

Deacon, D., Pickering, M., Golding, P. and Murdock, G. (1999) *Researching Communications*, London: Arnold.

Deans, J. (2004a) 'ITV news goes upmarket', *Guardian*, 26 January. Available online at: <http://www.mediaguardian.co.uk> (accessed 26 January 2004).

Deans, J. (2004b) 'Jermey to head ITV regional news', *The Guardian*, 14 April. .Available online at <http://www.mediaguardian.co.uk> (accessed 14 April 2004).

Delano, A. (2000) 'No sign of a better job: 100 years of British journalism', *Journalism Studies*, 1(2): 261–272.

Department of National Heritage (DNH) (1995) *White Paper, Media Ownership: the government's proposals*, London: HMSO, Cmnd 2872.

Deverell, R. (2004) Head of BBC News Interactive, interview with the author, 2 April 2004.

Djerf-Pierre, M. (2000) 'Squaring the circle: public service and commercial news on Swedish television 1956–99', *Journalism Studies*, 1(2): 239–260.

Donegan, L. (2003) 'How Private Jessica became America's icon', *Observer*, 6 April, p. 12.

Dovey, J. (2001) *Freakshow: first person media and factual television*, London: Pluto.

Dow, G. and Parker, R. (eds) (2001) *Business, Work and Community: into the new millennium*, South Melbourne: Oxford University Press.

Dutton, W.H. (ed.) (1996) *Information and Communication Technologies*, Oxford: Oxford University Press.

Dyke, G. (2000) 'BBC programming and the digital television marketplace', *MacTaggart Memorial Lecture*, Edinburgh International Film Festival.

Dyke, G. (2004) GMTV, 30 January.

Eldridge, J. (ed.) (1993) *Getting the Message*, London: Routledge.

Eliasoph, N. (1988) 'Routines and the making of oppositional news', *Critical Studies in Mass Communication*, 5: 313–334.

El-Nawawy, M. and Iskandar, A. (2002) *Al-Jazeera: how the free Arab news network scooped the world and changed the Middle East*, Cambridge, MA: Westview Press.

Entman, R.M. (1989) *Democracy without Citizens*, New York: Oxford University Press.

Epstein, E.J. (1973) *News from Nowhere*, New York: Random House.

Epworth, J. and Hanna, M. (1998) 'Media payments to witnesses – the press faces the first breach of its post-Calcutt defences', paper presented to the first annual conference of the Association for Journalism Education, London, 15 May.

Ericson, R.V., Baranek, P.M. and Chan, K.B.L. (1991) *Representing Order: crime, law and justice in the news media*, Milton Keynes: Open University Press.

Etzioni, A. (1961) *Complex Organizations*, Glenco, IL: Free Press.

Fairclough, N. (1995) *Media Discourse*, London: Edward Arnold.

Fallows, J. (1996) *Breaking the News: how the media undermine American democracy*, New York: Pantheon Books.

Feintuck, M. (1999) *Media Regulation, Public Interest and the Law*, Edinburgh: Edinburgh University Press.

Ferguson, M. and Golding, P. (1997) *Cultural Studies in Question*, London: Sage.

Fishman, M. (1980) *Manufacturing the News*, Austin: University of Texas Press.

Fishman, M. (1982) 'News and nonevents: making the visible invisible', reprinted in D. Berkowitz (ed.) (1997) *Social Meanings of News*, Thousand Oaks, CA: Sage, pp. 210–229.

Fiske, J. (1992) 'Popularity and the politics of information', in P. Dahlgren and C. Sparks *Journalism in Popular Culture*, London: Sage.

Fowler, R. (1991) *Language in the News*, London: Routledge.

Frank, J. (1961) *The Beginnings of the English Newspaper 1620–1660*, Cambridge, MA: Harvard University Press.

Franklin, B. (1994) *Packaging Politics: political communications in Britain's media democracy*, London: Edward Arnold.

Franklin, B. (1997) *Newszak and News Media*, London: Arnold.

Franklin, B. (ed.) (2001) *British Television Policy: a reader*, London: Routledge.

Franklin, B. (2003) ' "McJournalism": the McDonaldization thesis and junk journalism'. Available online at <http://www.psa.ac.uk/cps/2003%5CBob%20Franklin.pdf> (accessed 1 February 2003).

Franklin, B. and Murphy, D. (1991) *What News? The market, politics and the local press*, London: Routledge.

Fraser, N. (1989) 'What's critical about critical theory? The case of Habermas and gender', in N. Fraser (ed.) *Unruly Practices: power, discourse and gender in contemporary social theory*, Minneapolis: University of Minnesota Press.

Frost, C. (2002) *Reporting for Journalists*, London: Routledge.

Galtung, J. and Ruge, M. (1965) 'The structure of foreign news', *Journal of Peace Research*, 2: 64–91.

Gans, H. (1979) *Deciding What's News: a study of CBS evening news, NBC nightly news, Newsweek and Time*, New York: Pantheon.

Garcia Aviles, J.A.G., León, B., Sanders, K. and Harrison, J. (2004) 'Journalists at digital television newsrooms in Britain and Spain: workflow and multi-skilling in a competitive environment', *Journalism Studies*, 5(1): 87–100.

Gardam. T. (2004) 'Airing differences', *FT Magazine*, 24 April, pp. 32–35.

Garnham, N. (1990) *Capitalism and Communication*, London: Sage.

Garnham, N. (1998) 'Information society theory as ideology', *Loisir et Societé*, 21(1): 97–120.

Gaunt, P. (1990) *Choosing the News: the profit factor in news selection*, New York: Greenwood Press.

Gibbons, T. (1998) *Regulating the Media*, London: Sweet & Maxwell.

Gibson, O. (2004) 'Charter review "will take Hutton into account"', *Guardian*, 30 January. Available online at <http://www.mediaguardian.co.uk> (accessed 30 January 2004).

Giddens, A. (1984) *The Constitution of Society*, Berkley: University of California Press.

Giddens, A. (1990) *The Consquences of Modernity*, Stanford, CA: Stanford University Press.

Giddens, A. (1999) *Runaway World: the Reith Lectures revisited*. Available online at <http://www.lse.ac.uk/Giddens/reith_99/week1/week1.htm>.

Gitlin, T. (1998) 'Public sphere or public sphericules?', in T. Liebes and J. Curran (eds) *Media, Ritual and Identity*, London: Routledge, pp. 168–174.

Glasgow University Media Group (1976) *Bad News*, London: Routledge.

Glasgow University Media Group (1980) *More Bad News*, London: Routledge.

Glasgow University Media Group (1982) *Really Bad News*, London: Writers and Readers.

Glasser, T. (1984) 'Competition and diversity among radio formats: legal and structural issues', *Journal of Broadcasting*, 28(2): 127–142.

Goffman, E. (1963) *Stigma: notes on the management of spoiled identity*, Englewood Cliffs, NJ: Prentice-Hall.

Golding, P. (1994) 'The communication paradox: inequality at the national and international levels', *Media Development*, 4: 7–11.

Golding, P. and Elliott, P. (1979) *Making the News*, Harlow: Longman.

Golding, P. and Murdock, G. (1978) 'Theories of communication and theories of society', *Communication Research* 5(3), pp. 339–56.

Golding, P. and Murdock, G. (2000) 'Culture, communications and political economy', in J. Curran and M. Gurevitch (eds) *Mass Media and Society*, London: Edward Arnold, pp. 70–92.

Goodwin, A. and Whannel, G. (eds) (1990) *Understanding Television*, London: Routledge.

Graham, A., Kobaldt, C., Hogg, S., Robinson, B., Currie, D., Siner, M., Mather, G., Le Grand, J., New, B. and Corfield, I. (1999) *Public Purposes in Broadcasting*, Luton: University of Luton Press.

Greenslade, R. (2003a) *Press Gang*, London: Macmillan.

Greenslade, R. (2003b) *Guardian*, 12 November. Available online at <http://www.mediaguardian.co.uk> (accessed 12 November 2003).

Greenslade, R. (2004) 'Cracks in the Code', *Guardian*, 23 August. Available online at <http://www.mediaguardian.co.uk> (accessed 24 August 2004).

Greenwood, W. and Welsh, T. (2001) *McNae's Essential Law for Journalists*, London: Butterworth.

Grice, A. (2004) 'Why media and politicians must share blame', *Independent*, 31 January, p. 10.

Gunter, B. (2000) *Media Research Methods: measuring audiences, reactions and impact*, London: Sage.

Gunter, B. (2003) *News and the Net*, Mahwah, NJ: Lawrence Erlbaum.

Gunter, B. and Winstone, P. (1992) *TV: the public's view*, London: John Libbey.

Gunter, B., Harrison, J. and Wykes, M. (2003) *Violence on Television: distribution, form, context and themes*, Englewood Cliffs, NJ: Lawrence Erlbaum Association Inc.

Gurevitch, M., Levy, M. and Roeh, I. (1991) 'The global newsroom: convergences and diversities in the globalisation of television news', in P. Dahlgren and C. Sparks (eds) *Communications and Citizenship: journalism and the public sphere in the New Media Age*, London: Routledge.

Habermas, J. (1984) *The Theory of Communicative Action*, Cambridge: Polity Press.

Habermas, J. (1989) 'The structural transformation of the public sphere', in O. Boyd-Barrett and C. Newbold (eds) (1995) *Approaches to Media*, London: Arnold, pp. 235–244.

Haddon, L. (2000) 'Social exclusion and information and communication technologies', *New Media and Society*, 2(4): 387–406.

Halberstam, J. (1992) 'A prolegomenon for a theory of news', in E.D. Cohen (ed.) *Philosophical Issues in Journalism*, Oxford: Oxford University Press, pp. 11–21.

Hall, J. (2001) *Online Journalism: a critical primer*, London: Pluto Press.

Hall, S. (1980) 'Encoding/decoding', in S. During (ed.) (1993) *The Cultural Studies Reader*, London: Routledge, pp. 90–103.

Hall, S. (1982) 'The rediscovery of ideology: return of the repressed in media studies', in M. Gurevitch, T. Bennett, J. Curran and J. Woollacott (eds) *Culture, Society, Media*, London: Methuen, pp. 56–90.

Hall, S., Critcher, C., Jefferson, T., Clarke, J. and Roberts, B. (1978) *Policing the Crisis: mugging, the state and law and order*, London: Macmillan.

Halloran, J. (1969) *The Effects of Television*, London: Panther.

Hammond, A. (1967) *History of Greece*, Oxford: Oxford University Press.

Harcup, T. (2004) *Journalism: principles and practice*, London: Sage.

Harcup, T. and O'Neill, D. (2001) 'What is news? Galtung and Ruge revisited', *Journalism Studies*, 2(2): 261–280.

Hardt, H. (1990) 'Newsmakers, technology and journalism history', *Critical Studies in Mass Communication*, 7: 346–365.

Hargreaves, I. (2003) *Journalism: truth or dare*, Oxford: Oxford University Press.

Hargreaves, I. and Thomas, J. (2002) *New News, Old News*, London: ITC and BSC.

Harris, M. (1977) 'The structure, ownership and control of the press, 1620–1780', in D.G. Boyce, J. Curran and P. Wingate (eds) *British Newspaper History*, London: Constable.

Harrison, J. (1997) 'Rescheduling the news: an analysis of ITN's *News at Ten*', *Political Economy Research Centre (PERC) Policy Paper*, No.10, November, p. 28.

Harrison, J. (2000) *Terrestrial Television News in Britain: the culture of production*, Manchester: Manchester University Press.

Harrison, J. (2002a) 'The diversification of the British TV news genre: a cause for comfort or concern?', paper presented at the *What's News Symposium*, University of Syracuse, USA, April.

Harrison, J. (2002b) 'e-public services and interactive television: re-evaluating the remit and scope of public service broadcasting (PSB) in the digital age', *Communications Law*, 7(5): 145–151.

Harrison, J. (2003) 'Interactive Digital Television (iDTV) and the expansion of the public service tradition: a new public service communications template for the digital age', *Communications Law*, 8(6):4 40–412.

Harrison, J. (2005) 'From newsreels to a theatre of news: the growth and development of independent television news', in C. Johnson and R. Turnock (eds) *ITV Cultures: independent television over 50 years*, Buckingham: Open University Press.

Harrison, J. and Wessels, B. (2005) 'A new public service communications environment? Public service broadcasting values in the reconfiguring media', *New Media and Society* (forthcoming).

Harrison, J. and Woods, L.M. (2001) 'Defining European public service broadcasting', *European Journal of Communications*, 16(4): 477–504.

Hartley, J. (1988) *Understanding News*, London: Routledge.

Hartley, J. and Montgomery, M. (1985) 'Representations and relations: ideology and power in press and TV news', in T.A. Van Dijk (ed.) *Discourse and Communication*, Berlin: Walter de Gruyter, pp. 233–269.

Herman, E. and Chomsky, N. (1988) *The Political Economy of the Mass Media*, New York: Pantheon Books.

Herman, E. and McChesney, R. (1997) *The Global Media*, Washington: Cassell.

Hess, S. (1984) *The Government/Press Connection*, Washington, DC: Brookings Institute.

Hewitt, G. (2004) Personal interview with the author, 2 April.

Hicks, W. (1999) *Writing for Journalists*, London: Routledge.

Hodgson, F. (1989) *Modern Newspaper Practice: a primer on the press*, Oxford: Heinemann Professional Publishing.

Hodgson, J. (2002) 'ITN news channel losing £3/4m a month', *Guardian*, 12 July. Available online at <http://www.mediaguardian.co.uk> (accessed 12 July 2003).

Hodgson, P. (2002) 'Introduction', in I. Hargreaves and J. Thomas *New News, Old News*, London: ITC & BSC, p. 4.

Hoggart, R. (1958) *The Uses of Literacy*, London: Pelican.

Hoggart, R. (1995) *The Way we Live Now*, London: Chatto & Windus.

Hoggart, R. (2004) *Mass Media in a Mass Society*, London: Continuum.

Holland, P. (1997) *The TV Handbook*, London: Routledge.

Holmwood, L. (2004) 'BBC's big regional idea', *Broadcast*, 3 December, p. 21.

Hood, S. (1975) *On Television*, London: Pluto Press (reprinted in 1997).

Hoyer, S. (2003) 'Newspapers without journalists', *Journalism Studies*, 4(4): 451–463.

Hume, E. (1996) 'The new paradigm for news', in K. Jamieson (ed.) *The Annals of the American Academy of Political and Social Science: the media and politics*, Thousand Oaks, CA: Sage, pp. 141–153.

Humphreys, P. (1997) 'Power and control in the new media', paper presented at the ECPR Workshop, *New Media and Political Communication*, Berne, 27 February to 4 March.

Inglis, F. (2002) *People's Witness*, New Haven, CT, and London: Yale University Press.

Innes, M. (1999) 'The media as an investigative resource in murder enquiries', *British Journal of Criminology*, 39(2): 269–286.

Ishikawa, S. (1996) *Quality Assessment of Television*, Luton: University of Luton Press.

ITC (2001) *Annual Report*, London: ITC.

ITC (2003) *Annual Report*, London: ITC.

Jenkins, S. (2001) 'Vulgar, crude – and absolutely vital', *The Times*, 11 April.

Jenks, C. (ed.) (1995) *Visual Culture*, London: Routledge.

Jones, C. (2004) 'Back on form', *Television: Journal of the RTS*, London: RTS, pp. 18–19.

Jones, N. (1996) *Soundbites and Spin Doctors*, London: Cassell.

Keane, F. (2004) 'These have been depressing days. But this is why I stand so proudly by the BBC', *Independent*, 31 January, p. 43.

Keane, J. (1991) *The Media and Democracy*, Cambridge: Polity Press.

Keane, J. (1995) 'Structural transformations of the public sphere', in F. Webster (ed.) (2004) *The Information Society Reader*, London: Routledge.

Keighron, Peter (2003) 'Frontline kit', *Broadcast*, 9 May, p. 31.

Kelley, D. and Donway, R. (1995) 'Liberalism and free press', in J. Lichtenberg (ed.) *Democracy and the Mass Media*, Cambridge: Cambridge University Press, pp. 66–101.

Kemp, A. (1982) *Pick of the Herald*, Glasgow: Richard Drew Publishing.

Kent, R. (1994) *Measuring Media Audiences*, London: Routledge.

Kevill, S. (2002a) *Beyond the Soundbite: BBC research into public disillusion with politics*, London: BBC.

Kevill, S. (2002b) 'Talking 'bout my generation', *Television*, March, pp. 24–25.

Key, V.O. (1961) *Public Opinion and American Democracy*, New York: Knopf.

Kitzinger, J. (1999) 'A sociology of media power; key issues in audience reception research', in G. Philo (ed.) *Message Received*, London: Longman.

Kung-Shankleman, L. (2000) *Inside the BBC and CNN Managing Media Organisations*, London: Routledge.

Lambert, R. (2002) *Independent Review of BBC News-24*, London: DCMS (The Lambert Report).

Langer, J. (1998) *Tabloid Television: popular journalism and the 'other news'*, London: Routledge.

Lawson, M. (2003) 'Come the movie, it's a role for Will Smith', *Guardian*, 28 March, p. 8.

Leadbeater, C. (1999) 'Living on thin air: the new economy', in F. Webster (ed.) (2004) *The Information Society Reader*, London: Routledge, pp. 21–30.

Lee, A. (1976) *Origins of the Popular Press in England 1855–1914*, London: Croom Helm.

Lichtenberg, J. (1991) 'In defence of objectivity revisited', in J. Curran and M. Gurevitch (eds) *Mass Media and Society*, London: Edward Arnold, pp. 238–254.

Lichtenberg, J. (1995) 'Foundations and limits of freedom of the press', in J. Lichtenberg (ed.) *Democracy and the Mass Media*, Cambridge: Cambridge University Press, pp. 102–135.

Lichter, S.R., Rothman, S. and Lichter, L.S. (1986) *The Media Elite: America's new powerbrokers*, Bethesda, MD: Adler & Adler.

Lippmann, W. (1922) *Public Opinion*, New York: Harcourt.

Livingstone, S. (1998) *Making Sense of Television*, 2nd edn, London: Routledge.

Livingstone, S. and Lunt, P. (1994) *Talk on Television*, London: Routledge.

Lloyd, J. (2004) 'Who shot Liberty Valence?', *FT Magazine*, 28 August, p. 10.

Lorimer, R. (1994) *Mass Communications*, Manchester: Manchester University Press.

Lough, J. (2002) 'The analysis of popular culture', in C. Newbold, O. Boyd-Barrett and H. Van Den Bulck (eds) *The Media Book*, London: Arnold, pp. 212–258.

Luckhurst, T. (2004) 'Vultures scent blood as *Today* counts cost of the story that stole its reputation', *Independent*, 31 January, pp. 6–7.

MacArthur, B. (2003) 'Joining up to report: is war reporting by "embeds" a better way?', *The Times*, 28 March, p. 20.

McChesney, R. (2000) *Rich Media, Poor Democracy: communication politics in dubious times*, New York: New Press.

MacGregor, B. (1997) *Live, Direct and Biased? Making television news in the satellite age*, London: Arnold.

McKean, M.L. and Stone, V.A. (1992) 'Deregulation and competition: explaining the absence of local broadcast news operations', *Journalism Quarterly*, 69: 713–723.

McLuhan, M. (1962) *Gutenberg Galaxy*, London: Routledge & Kegan Paul.

McLuhan, M. (1964) *Understanding Media*, London: Routledge and Kegan Paul.

McManus, J.H. (1994) *Market-driven Journalism: let the citizen beware?*, Thousand Oaks, CA: Sage.

McNair, B. (1996) *News and Journalism in the UK*, 2nd edn, London: Routledge.

McNair, B. (2003) 'What a difference a decade makes', *British Journalism Review*, 14(1): pp. 42–48.

McQuail, D. (1992) *Media Performance: mass communication and the public interest*, London: Sage.

McQuail, D. (2000) *McQuail's Mass Communication Theory*, London: Sage.

McQuail, D. (2002) *McQuail's Reader in Mass Communication Theory*, London: Sage.

Mannheim, K. (1936) *Ideology and Utopia*, London: Routledge & Kegan Paul.

Marcuse, H. (1972) *One-dimensional Man: studies in the ideology of advanced industrial society*, London: Abacus.

Marjoribanks, T. (2000) *News Corporation, Technology and the Workplace: global strategies, local change*, Cambridge: Cambridge University Press.

Marjoribanks, T. (2003) 'Strategizing technological innovation', in S. Cottle (ed.) *Media Organization and Production*, London: Sage, pp. 59–76.

Martindale, D. (1961) *The Nature and Types of Sociological Theory*, London: Routledge & Kegan Paul.

Marx, K. and Engels, F. (1976) *The German Ideology*, London: Lawrence & Wishart (first published in 1867).

Masuda, Y. (1990) 'Image of the future information society', in F. Webster (ed.) (2004) *Information Society Reader*, London: Routledge, pp. 15–20.

Matthews, J. (2003) 'Cultures of production: the making of children's news', in S. Cottle (ed.) *Media Organization and Production*, London: Sage, pp. 131–145.

Meier, W.A. and Trappel, J. (1998) 'Media concentration and the public interest', in M. McLuhan (1987) *Understanding Media*, London: Routledge, pp. 80–95.

Mellor, N. (2005) *The Making of Arab News*, Maryland: Rowman and Littlefield.

Miliband, R. (1969) *The State in Capitalist Society: the analysis of the Western system of power*, London: Quartet.

Mill, J.S. (1989) 'On Liberty', in S. Collini (ed.) *On Liberty and Other Writings*, Cambridge: Cambridge University Press, pp. 1–116.

Minogue, K. (1997) *The Silencing of Society: the true cost of the lust for news*, London: The Social Affairs Unit.

Molotch, H. and Lester, M. (1974) 'News as purposive behaviour: on the strategic use of routine events, accidents and scandals', *American Sociological Review*, 39: 101–112.

Morgan, P. (2003) *World Press Freedom Day Seminar*, London, 2 May.

Mott, F.L. (1949) *American Journalism*, London and New York: Macmillan.

Mulgan, G. (1990) 'Television's Holy Grail: seven types of quality', in G. Mulgan (ed.) *The Question of Quality*, London: BFI, pp. 4–32.

Murdock, G. (1980) 'Class, power and the press: problems of conceptualisation and evidence', in H. Christian (ed.) *The Sociology of Journalism and the Press*, Keele: Keele University Press, pp. 48–61.

Murdock, G. and Golding, P. (1974) 'For a political economy of communications', in R. Miliband and J. Saville (eds) *The Socialist Register*, London: Merlin Press, pp. 205–234.

Murdock, G. and Golding, P. (1999) 'Common markets: corporate ambitions and communications trends in the UK and Europe', *Journal of Media Economics*, 12(2): 117–132.

NCTJ (2002) *Syllabus in Newspaper Journalism: writing*, Harlow: National Council for the Training of Journalists.

Negrine, R. (1989) *Politics and the Mass Media in Britain*, London: Sage.

Negrine, R. (1996) *The Communication of Politics*, London: Sage.

Negroponte, N. (1996) *Being Digital*, London: Hodder & Stoughton.

Neuman, W. R. (1991) *The Future of the Mass Audience*, Cambridge: Cambridge University Press.

Newbold C., Boyd-Barrett, O. and Van Den Bulck, H. (eds) (2002) *The Media Book*, London: Arnold.

Noelle-Neumann, E., Schultz, W. and Wilke, J. (1989) *Publizistik Massenkommunikation*, Das Fischer Lexikon, Frankfurt: Fisher.

Norris, P. (ed.) (1999) *Critical Citizens: global support for democratic governance*, Oxford: Oxford University Press.

Norris, P. (2000) *A Virtuous Circle: political communications in post-industrial societies*, Cambridge: Cambridge University Press.

Nylund, M. (2003) 'Asking questions, making sound-bites: research reports, interviews and television news stories', *Discourse Studies*, 5(4): 517–533.

OFCOM (2004) 'Public consultation on PSB'. Available online at http://www.ofcom.org.uk/consultations/past/psb/psb/volume2/social_values/informed_democracy/news?a=87101 (accessed 10 August 2004).

O'Neill, O. (2002) 'A question of trust', in *The BBC Lectures 2002*, Cambridge: Cambridge University Press.

Ong, W. (1982) *Orality and Literacy: the technologizing of the world*, London: Methuen.

Ostgaard, E. (1965) 'Factors influencing the flow of news', *Journal of Peace Research*, 2: 39–63.

Page, B. (2003) *The Murdoch Archipelago*, London: Simon & Schuster UK.

Papacharissi, Z. (2002) 'The virtual sphere: the internet as a public sphere', in F. Webster (ed.) (2004) *The Information Society Reader*, London: Routledge.

Park, R.E. (1940) 'News as a form of knowledge: a chapter in the sociology of knowledge', *American Journal of Sociology*, 45: 669–686.

Paulu, B. (1981) *Television and Radio in the United Kingdom*, London: Macmillan.

Pavlik, J. (1999) 'New media and news: implications for the future of journalism', *New Media and Society*, 1(3): 54–59.

Pavlik, J. (2000) 'The impact of technology on journalism', *Journalism Studies*, 1(2): 229–237.

Pavlik, J. (2001) *Journalism and New Media*, New York: Columbia University Press.

Peak, S. and Fisher, P. (1997) *The Media Guide*, London: Fourth Estate.

Phillis, B. (2004) *An Independent Review of Government Communications*, London: Cabinet Office.

Philo, G. and Berry, M. (2004) *Bad News From Israel*, London: Pluto Press.

Poster, M. (1995) *The Second Media Age*, Cambridge: Polity Press.

Pottker, H. (2003) 'News and its communicative quality: the inverted pyramid – when and why did it appear?', *Journalism Studies*, 4(4): 501–512.

Press Complaints Commission (1997) Code of Practice. Available online at <http://www.pcc.org.uk/> (accessed 16 December 2003).

Preston, P. (2003) *The Observer Business Section*, 6 November, p. 6.

Preston, P. (2004) 'Now here's a real killer of a story for you', *Observer*, 28 March, p. 7.

Preston, P. (2005) 'Tide of news that carried all before it . . . eventually', *Observer*, 2 January, p. 3.

Private Eye (2004) 'Going Live', p. 9.

Programme on International Policy Attitudes (PIPA) (2003) 'Misconceptions, the media and the Iraq war'. Available online at <http://www.pipa.org/OnlineReports/Iraq/Media_10_02_03Report.pdf> (accessed 10 August 2004).

Randall, D. (2000) *The Universal Journalist*, 2nd edn, London: Pluto Press.

Ray, V. (2003) *The Televison News Handbook: an insider's guide to being a great broadcast journalist*, London: Macmillan.

Raymond, J. (ed.) (1999) *News, Newspapers and Society in Early Modern Britain*, London: Frank Cass.

Read, D. (1992) *The Power of News: the history of Reuters*, Oxford: Oxford University Press.

Report of the Broadcasting Committee (Crawford Report) (1926) London: HMSO, Cmnd 2599.

Report of the Broadcasting Committee (Ullswater Report) (1936) London: HMSO, Cmnd 5091.

Report of the Broadcasting Committee (Pilkington Report) (1961–1962) London: HMSO, Cmnd 1753.

Report of the Committee on the Future of Broadcasting (Annan Report) (1977) London: HMSO, Cmnd 6753.

Report of the Committee on Financing the BBC (Peacock Report) (1986) London: HMSO, Cmnd 9824.

Report of the Independent Review Panel, Department of Culture Media and Sport (Davies Report) (1999) *The Future Funding of the BBC*, 28 July.

Report of the Inquiry into the Circumstances Surrounding the Death of Dr David Kelly C.M.G. (Hutton Report) (2004) London: House of Commons, HC247, 28 January.

Report of the Secretary of State for National Heritage (1992) *The Future of the BBC: a consultation document*, Green Paper, London: HMSO, Cmnd 2098.

Report of the Secretary of State for National Heritage (1994) *The Future of the BBC: serving the nation competing world-wide*, London: HMSO, Cmnd 2621.

Reporters without Borders (2003) *Freedom of the Press Throughout the World: 2003 report*, Paris: Reporters Without Borders.

Revoir, P. (2003) 'ITV's £100m savings plans', *Broadcast*, 5 December, p. 9.

Revoir, P. (2004a) 'SMG fears news agenda change', *Broadcast*, 23 January, p. 3.

Revoir, P. (2004b) 'ITV creates news chief for regions', *Broadcast*, 16 April, p. 5.

Revoir, P. (2004c) 'Welcome to ITV's world', *Broadcast*, 2 July, p. 13.

Richardson, J.E. (2004) *(Mis)Representing Islam: the racism and rhetoric of British broadsheet newspapers*, Amsterdam: John Benjamins.

Robertson, G. and Nichol, G.L. (1990) *Media Law: the rights of journalists and broadcasters*, 2nd edn, London: Longman.

Roche, M. (2002) 'Mega-events, time and modernity: on time-structures in global society', *Time and Society*, 12(1): 99–126.

Rock, P. (1973) 'News as eternal recurrence', in J. Curran and S. Young (eds) *The Manufacture of News*, London: Constable, pp. 64–70.

Rosenberg, J. (2000) *The Follies of Globalisation Theory*, London: Verso.

Rosengren, K. E. (1977) 'Four types of tables', *Journal of Communication*, 27(1): 67–75.

Roshco, B. (1975) 'Newsmaking', reprinted in H. Tumber (1999) *News: a reader*, Oxford: Oxford University Press, pp. 32–36.

Rosser, M. (2004) 'Ofcom opens FM licence bidding', *Broadcast*, 19 March, p. 10.

Royal Commission on the Press, 1947–1949 Report (1949) London: HMSO, Cmnd 7700.

Royal Commission on the Press, 1961–1962 Report (1962) London: HMSO, Cmnd 1811.

Royal Commission on the Press, 1974–1977 Final Report (1977) London: HMSO, Cmnd 6810.

Rudin, R. and Ibbotson, T. (2002) *An Introduction to Journalism: essential techniques and background knowledge*, Oxford: Focal Press.

Sambrook, R. (2003) 'War coverage has changed for ever. We might end up with a death live on TV', *Independent*, 31 March, p. 17.

Sanchez-Aranda, J.J. and Barrera, C. (2003) 'The birth of modern newsrooms in the Spanish press', *Journalism Studies*, 4(4): 489–500.

Sanchez-Tabernero, A. (1993) *Media Concentration in Europe: commercial enterprise and the public interest*, Dusseldorf: European Institute for the Media.

Sancho, J. and Glover, J. (2003) *Conflict around the Clock*, London: ITC.

Sande, O. (1971) 'The perception of foreign news', *Journal of Peace Research*, 8: 221–237.

Sanders, K. (2003) *Ethics and Journalism*, London: Sage.

Scannell, P. (ed.) (1991) *Broadcast Talk*, London: Sage.

Scannell, P. (2003) 'The Brains Trust: a historical study of the management of liveness on radio', in S. Cottle (ed.) *Media Organization and Production*, London: Sage, pp. 99–112.

Scannell, P. and Cardiff, D. (1991) *A Social History of British Broadcasting: 1922–1939*, London: Blackwell.

Schiller, D. (1981) *Objectivity and the News*, Philadelphia, PA: University of Philadelphia Press.

Schiller, H.I. (1989) *Culture Inc: the corporate takeover of public expression*, Oxford: Oxford University Press.

Schiller, H.I. (1996) *Information Inequality*, New York: Routledge.

Schlesinger, P. (1978) *Putting Reality Together*, London: Methuen.

Schlesinger, P. (1987) *Putting Reality Together*, 2nd edn, London: Methuen.

Schlesinger, P. and Tumber, H. (1994) *Reporting Crime*, Oxford: Oxford University Press.

Schudson, M. (1978) *Discovering the News: a social history of American newspapers*, New York: Basic Books.

Schudson, M. (1989) 'The sociology of news production', *Media Culture and Society*, 11: 263–282, reprinted in D. Berkowitz (ed.) (1997) *Social Meanings of News*, Thousand Oaks, CA: Sage, pp. 7–22

Schudson, M. (2000) 'The sociology of news production revisited (again)', in J. Curran and M. Gurevitch (eds) *Mass Media and Society*, 3rd edn, London: Arnold, pp. 175–200.

Schudson, M. (2002) 'News, public, nation', *American History Review*, 107(2): 481–495.

Scollon, R. (1998) *Mediated Discourse as Social Interaction: a study of news discourse*, London: Longman.

Seymour-Ure, C. (1991) *The British Press and Broadcasting since 1945*, London: Blackwell.

Sherrin, N. (2003) *The Oxford Dictionary of Humorous Quotations*, 2nd edn, Oxford: Oxford University Press.

Sherwin, A. (2004) 'Mutinous employees acquire the taste for rebellion', *The Times*, 31 January, p. 16.

Shoemaker, P. J. (1991) *Gatekeeping*, London: Sage.

Shoemaker, P. J. and Reese, S. (1996) *Mediating the Message: theories of influences on mass media content,* USA: Longman.

Siebert, F. (1965) *Freedom of the Press in England 1476–1976: the rise and decline of government control*, Urbana-Illinois: University of Illinois Press, pp. 69–70.

Sigal, L.V. (1973) *Reporters and Officials*, Lexington, MA: Lexington Books.

Sigalman, L. (1973) 'Reporting the news: an organizational analysis', *American Journal of Sociology*, 79(1): 132–151.

Silverstone, R. (1999) *Why Study the Media?*, London: Sage.

Smith, A. (1979) *The Newspaper: an international history*, London: Thames & Hudson.

Smith, A. (1980) *The Geopolitics of Information: how western culture dominates the world*, Oxford: Oxford University Press.

Soloski, J. (1989) 'News reporting and professionalism: some constraints on the reporting of the news', *Media, Culture and Society*, 11: 207–228.

Sparks, C. (1991) 'Goodbye Hildy Johnson: the vanishing serious press', in P. Dahlgren and C. Sparks (eds) *Communication and Citizenship*, London: Routledge.

Sparkes, V.M. and Winter, J.P. (1980) 'Public interest in foreign news', *Gazette*, 20: 149–170.

Sreberney-Mohammadi, A. (1995) 'Forms of media as ways of knowing', in J. Downing, A. Mohammadi and A. Sreberny-Mohammadi (eds) *Questioning the Media*, 2nd edn, London: Sage, pp. 42–54.

Sreberney-Mohammadi, A. (2000) 'The global and the local in international communications', in J. Curran and M. Gurevitch (eds) *Mass Media and Society*, London: Arnold, pp. 93–119.

Stephens, M. (1988) *A History of News*, New York: Viking Press.

Stephenson, H. and Bromley, M. (1998) *Sex, Lies and Democracy: the press and the public*, London: Longman.

Stevenson, N. (2002) *Understanding Media Cultures*, 2nd edn, London: Sage.

Storey, J. (1993) *An Introduction to Cultural Theory and Popular Culture*, 2nd edn, Hemel Hempstead: Harvester Wheatsheaf.

Sturken, M. and Cartwright, L. (2002) *Practices of Looking*, Oxford: Oxford University Press.

Swingewood, A. (1977) *The Myth of Mass Culture*, London: Macmillan.

Sylvester, R. (2003) 'The UK media has lost the plot . . . it's the equivalent of reality TV', *Daily Telegraph*, 7 April, p. 8.

Tait, R. (2004a) 'Why can't the market decide? Should competition law regulate television and radio?', *Oxford Media Convention*, 13 January.

Tait, R. (2004b) 'Really objective news outguns the liberals', *Television: Journal of the RTS*, London: RTS, pp. 12–13.

Taylor, P. (1992) *War and the Media: propaganda and persuasion in the Gulf War*, Manchester: Manchester University Press.

The Third World and Environment Broadcasting Project (3WE) (2000) *Losing Perspective: global affairs on British terrestrial television*, London: Stanhope Press.

Thompson, J.B. (1992) *Ideology and Modern Culture: critical social theory in the era of mass communication*, Cambridge: Cambridge University Press.

Thompson, J.B. (1994) 'Social theory and the media', in D. Crowley and D. Mitchell (eds) *Communication Theory Today*, Cambridge: Polity Press, pp. 27–49.

Thompson, J.B. (1995) *The Media and Modernity: a social theory of the media*, Cambridge: Polity Press.

Thussu, D. (ed.) (1998) *Electronic Empires: global media and local resistance*, London: Arnold.

Toffler, A. (1970) *Future Shock*, New York: Pan-Collins.

Toffler, A. (1980) *The Third Wave*, New York: Pan-Collins.

Tuchman, G. (1972) 'Objectivity as strategic ritual: an examination of newsmen's notions of objectivity', *American Journal of Sociology*, 77(4): 660–679.

Tuchman, G. (1973) 'Making news by doing work: routinizing the un-expected', *American Journal of Sociology*, 79(1): 110–131.

Tuchman, G. (1978) *Making News: a study in the construction of reality*, New York: Free Press.

Tuggle, C.A. and Huffman, S. (2001) 'Live reporting in television news: breaking news or black holes?', *Journal of Broadcasting and Electronic Media*, 45(2): 335–344.

Tumber, H. (1999) *News: a reader*, Oxford: Oxford University Press.

Tumber, H. and Palmer, J. (2004) *Media at War: the Iraq crisis*, London: Sage.

Tunstall, J. (1971) *Journalists at Work*, London: Constable.

Tunstall, J. (1977) *The Media are American: Anglo-American media in the world*, London: Constable.

Tunstall, J. (1993) *Television Producers*, London: Routledge.

Turrow, J. (1984) *Media Industries: the production of news and entertainment*, New York: Longman.

Tusa, J. (1994) *Programme or Products: The management ethos and creative values*, James Cameron Memorial Lecture, London: City University, 14 June.

Ungerer, F. (ed.) (2000) *English Media Texts Past and Present: language and textual structure*, Amsterdam: John Benjamins.

Ursell, G. (2001) 'Dumbing down or shaping up? New technologies, new media, new journalism', *Journalism: Theory, Practice and Criticism*, 2(2): 175–196.

Ursell, G. (2003) 'Creating value and valuing creation in contemporary UK television: or "dumbing down" the workforce', *Journalism Studies*, 4(4): 31–46.

Van Dijk, T.A. (1988) *News as Discourse*, Hillsdale, NJ: Lawrence Erlbaum.

Van Gompel, R., Van den Bulck, H. and Biltereyst, D. (2002) 'Media indus-tries', in C. Newbold, O. Boyd-Barrett and H. Van Den Bulck (eds) *The Media Book*, London: Arnold, pp. 162–211.

Walker, D. (2002) 'Low visibility on the inside track', *Journalism: Theory, Practice and Criticism*, 3(1): 101–110.

Wallis, R. and Baran, S. (1990) *The Known World of Broadcast News*, London: Routledge.

Ward, I. (1995) *Politics of the Media*, Sydney: Macmillan.

Ware, J. (2004) 'Don't run for cover', *Television*, London: Royal Television Society.

Waugh, E. (1938) *Scoop*, Harmondsworth: Penguin.

Weaver, D.H. (1998) *The Global Journalist: news people around the world*, Cresskill, NJ: Hampton Press.

Webster, F. (1995) *Theories of The Information Society*, London: Routledge.

Webster, F. (ed.) (2004) *Information Society Reader*, London: Routledge.

Webster, R. (1990) *A Brief History of Blasphemy*, Suffolk: Orwell Press.

Wells, M. (2001) 'BBC's "brighter" news to beat rising rival', *Guardian*, 22 November. Available online at <http://www.mediaguardian.co.uk> (accessed 22 November 2001).

Wells, M. (2004a) 'BBC to be reined in, says Jowell's adviser', *Guardian*, 27 January. Available online at <http://www.mediaguardian.co.uk> (accessed 27 January 2004).

Wells, M. (2004b) 'Pop Idol-style show will select potential MPs: ITV launches Vote for Me to tackle political apathy', *Guardian*, 16 April. Available online at <http://www.mediaguardian.co.uk> (accessed 22 December 2004).

Welsh, T. and Greenwood, W. (2003) *McNae's Essential Law for Journalists* (17th edn), London: Butterworth.

Whale, J. (1980) *Politics and the Mass Media*, London: Fontana.

Wheen, F. (2004) *How Mumbo-Jumbo Conquered the World*, London: Harper Perennial.

Whitaker, B. (2004) 'Al-Jazeera has made news in Arabic . . . now it hopes to make its mark in English', *Guardian*, 2 September, p. 23.

White, D.M. (1950) 'The gatekeeper: a case study in the selection of news', *Journalism Quarterly,* 27: 383–390.

White, T. (1996) *Broadcast News Writing, Reporting and Producing*, Boston, MA: Focal Press.

Whittle, S. (2004) BBC Controller of Editorial Policy, interview with the author, 2 April.

Wilke, J. (2002) 'News values in transformation? About Anglo-American influence on post-war journalism', in Austria Presse Agentur (ed.) *The Various Faces of Reality: values in news (agency) journalism*, Innsbruck: Studienverlag, pp. 65–72.

Williams, B. (2002) *Truth and Truthfulness*, Princeton, NJ: Princeton University Press.

Williams, F. (1957) *Dangerous Estate: the anatomy of newspapers*, London: Longmans, Green & Co.

Williams, K. (1998) *Get Me A Murder A Day! A history of mass communication in Britain*, London: Arnold.

Williams, K. (2003) *Understanding Media Theory*, London: Arnold.

Williams, R. (1974) *Television: technology and cultural form*, New York: Schocken Books.

Williams, R. (1976) *Keywords: a vocabulary of culture and society*, New York: Oxford University Press.

Williams, R. (1977) *Marxism and Literature*, Oxford: Oxford University Press.

Williams, R. (1980) *Problems in Materialism and Culture*, London: Verso.

Wilson, J. (1996) *Understanding Journalism*, London: Routledge.

Winseck, J. (1999) 'Back to the future: telecommunications, online information services and convergence from 1840–1910', *Media History*, 5(2): 137–157.

Winston, B. (1998) *Media Technology and Society. A history: from the telegraph to the internet*, London: Routledge.

Winston, B. (2002) 'Towards tabloidization? Glasgow revisited, 1975–2001', *Journalism Studies*, 1: 18–29.

Wolff, M. (2004) *Autumn of the Moguls*, New York: HarperCollins.

Worth, P. and Banton, L. (2004) 'Ramsay's legal nightmare?' Available online at <http:www.mediaguardian.co.uk> (accessed 26 July 2004).

Yorke, I. (1997) *Television News*, Oxford: Focal Press.

Youngs, G. and Boyd-Barrett, O. (2002) 'Interactive electronic media', in C. Newbold, O. Boyd-Barrett and H. Van Den Bulck (eds) *The Media Book*, London: Arnold, pp. 372–419.

Zelizer, B. and Allan, S. (eds) (2002) *Journalism after September 11*, London: Routledge.

WEBSITES

www.aoltimewarner.com
www.bertelsmann.com
www.clearchannel.com
www.comcast.com
www.gannett.com
www.ge.com/en
www.newscorp.com
www.sony.com
www.viacom.com
www.vivendiuniversal.com
http://disney.go.com

The BBC

http://www.bbc.co.uk/info/statements/
http://www.bbc.co.uk/info/bbc/archive.shtml
http://www.itv.com/about/

Review of BBC News 1999–2000

http://www.bbc.co.uk/info/news/newsfuture/
http://www.bbc.co.uk/info/report2002/review/news.shtml

Statements of the BBC's editorial policy

http://www.bbc.co.uk/info/editorial/prodgl/

Government and Regulators

http://europa.eu.int/comm/avpolicy
http://www.culture.gov.uk/
http://www.dti.gov.uk

http://www.bbc.co.uk/info/revolution
http://www.itc.org
http://www.itv.co.uk
http://www.ofcom.org

Reports

Graf Report

http://news.bbc.co.uk/no1/shared/bsp/hi/pdf5/05_07_04_graf.pdf

Hutton Report

http://news.bbc.co.uk/1/hi/in_depth/uk/2003/david_kelly_inquiry/
    inquiry_documents/default.stm

Butler Report

http://news.bbc.co.uk/1/hi/uk_politics/3892809.stm

Neil Report

http://www.bbc.co.uk/info/policies/pdf/neil_report.pdf

Cases

Handyside *vs* United Kingdom [1976].
European Court in the Sunday Times *vs* United Kingdom [1979].
Reynolds *vs* Times Newspapers [1998].

INDEX

news formats *see* formats, news
news genre: expansion of 148–52
News International 87, 88
news journalism: deep characteristics of 3; development of professional practices in 57–61; different types of 81, 190–4
'news net', trawling the 57
news organizations 127; and audiences 18–19, 34, 164–71; conflict between journalists and 32, 138; influence of 134–41
news selection 60, 108, 115, 134–5, 147, 163; factors contributing to 136–7, *245–6*; matters of interest and importance 163; and news values 136–7
news standards 186, 190; concerns over 171–81
news values 128, 136; accepting of by journalists and socialization 137–8; and news selection 136–7
News of the World 88, 135, 231–2
'Newshounds' 159
newsletters 48, 48–9
newspapers 10, 48; and advertising 51–2; changes in as response to readers 166; and circulation 88, 157; emergence of diversity of accounts 49; emergence of first provincial 50, *231*; expansion of 53–5; format changes 179–80; free 89–90; increase in number 49; internationalization of 93–4; and mergers 87, *238*; online 77–8; origins and history 46–53; price war 87; providing different types of news for different readers 61; and public trust issue 117, *227*; *see also* individual titles; press
NewsProNet 84
Newsquest 90, *238*
newsreaders 66

newsrooms: computerization of 150; conflict in 138; demographics of 33, 73, 139; digital 74, 76, 149, *235*, *247*; fictitious accounts of 127
Newsround 34
Ngeze, Hassan *240*
NGOs (non-governmental organizations) 112
Nicholls, Lord 106
'Night owls' 160
Nine O'Clock News 175
Norris, P. 39, 175, 187, 206
Northcliffe, Lord (Alfred Harmsworth) 26, 56
Northern Star 231
Norwich Post 231
NTL *234*

objectivity 11, 144, 145, 146–8
Observer 231
OFCOM (Office of Communications) 19, 82, 118, 125, 165, *233*; review of PSB 8, 160, 161–2
Oklahoma bomb (1995) 149
O'Neill, Onora 7
Ong, W. 43
online news *see* internet news
ORACLE 67, 76
oral cultures 9, 42, 43–4, 49, 64
organizational approaches 31–4
owners: exertion of influence 27–8, 139
ownership 26–7, 97; [concentration of 28, 61, 68, 82–3, 85–91, 176; and Communications Act (2003) 85; deregulatory policies 82, 85, 96; and local press 88–91; and national press 87–8; and regional television 85–7; restrictions on 81–2]; cross-media 70, 85; liberal pluralist view of 71–2; policies aimed atensuring diversity of 28, 82